ST. CHARLES COUNTY COMMUNITY C

0835 00061910 0

RÍO AZUL

Modeled stucco glyphs on Río Azul Str. A-2 roof comb. The upper right-hand glyph has been identified by David Stuart as the Río Azul emblem glyph. (See Figure 3–19 for a drawing of the hieroglyphic text.) (Photo by R. E. W. Adams)

RÍO AZUL

AN ANCIENT MAYA CITY

Richard E. W. Adams

University of Oklahoma Press : Norman

WITHDRAWN

SCCCC - LIBRARY
4601 Mid Rivers Mall
St. Peters, MO 63376

Also by Richard E. W. Adams

The Ceramics of Altar de Sacrificios (Cambridge, 1971)
Prehistoric Mesoamerica (Boston, 1977)
(ed.) *The Origins of Maya Civilization* (Albuquerque, 1977)
Prehistoric Mesoamerica, rev. ed. (Norman, 1991)
Ancient Civilizations of the New World (Boulder, 1997)

Library of Congress Cataloging-in-Publication Data

Adams, Richard E. W., 1931–
    Río Azul : an ancient Maya city / Richard E. W. Adams.
        p.   cm.
    Includes bibliographical references and index.
    ISBN 0–8061–3076–8 (cloth : alk. paper)
    1. Río Azul Site (Guatemala) 2. Mayas—Antiquities. 3. Mayas—
Warfare. 4. Excavations (Archaeology—Guatemala—Péten (Dept.)
5. Péten (Guatemala)—Antiquities. I. Title.
F1435.1.R56A33   1999
972.81′2—DC21   98-45078
                                                            CIP

The paper in this book meets the guidelines for permanence and durability of the Committee on Production Guidelines for Book Longevity of the Council on Library Resources, Inc. ∞

Copyright © 1999 by the University of Oklahoma Press, Norman, Publishing Division of the University. All rights reserved. Manufactured in the U.S.A.

1   2   3   4   5   6   7   8   9   10

To the memories of

John L. Gatling
Carolina Foncea de Ponciano
Enrique Ordoñez
Barbara Robichaux
Patricia Solís
Carl Stapleton

CONTENTS

ILLUSTRATIONS

Plates

Figures

Tables

Charts

PREFACE

SIXTEEN YEARS AGO we were preparing for our first short season at the site of Río Azul. In 1981 my friend Ian Graham, a Harvard archaeologist, called me to say that in the course of his epigraphic search and record expedition to the Petén that year he had heard rumors of looting at Río Azul, where many rich tombs had reportedly been found and opened. Graham had traveled to the site and had found the stories to be true and, indeed, understated. He arranged for the expulsion of the looters and took pictures of the looted tombs. Because I had been involved in the initial discovery and exploration of the site in 1962, he sent me the photos, which were revelatory. The walls of these illegally excavated tombs were painted with bright red hieroglyphs and graceful artistic renditions of dates, names, and other intriguing matters. We had never seen such wall paintings before. So in the spring of 1981, we began the search for funds to salvage the painted tombs and to explore the city that housed them. At first, all our requests were denied. Finally, in 1982, Douglas and Barbara Cannell of Winnipeg, Canada, suggested that a friend of theirs might put up some seed money. With this we could spend two or three weeks at the site, record the data available, and prepare a proposal with which to convince the skeptical funding agencies. The Cannells were successful in their approach, and in May 1983 Graham and I found ourselves back in the Guatemalan jungle, leading a group bound for Río Azul. The team was made up of Douglas and Barbara Cannell, Fred Valdez, Jr., Grant D. Hall, Stephen Black, and Daniel Potter. Graham not only furnished us with valuable guide services and supplies, he also put his two landrovers at our disposal, thereby vastly elevating his standing as a project benefactor.

We set off early one morning and over a long day made our way through the dry and almost silent forests of the northern Petén. The road was not much more than a track through the jungle with a distressing number of *desvíos* (detours). Darkness came and I began to think that we had made a wrong turn and were in either Belize or Mexico, when suddenly my lights went off the road and into space. We crashed to a halt on the edge of a very steep descent, which turned out to be the crossing for the Río Azul. We had arrived at the camp at Ixcanrio.

This trip began the most exciting, exhausting, exasperating, exhilarating project that I have ever undertaken. Using Graham's revised map as a guide, we found tombs, paintings, palaces, and giant temples. As we explored we realized that the place was larger than we had thought in 1962 and even larger than Graham had found in 1981. Our Guatemalan workers were continually coming in with news of new structures—a new group, a new stela, or another tomb. Clearly, we had a tiger (or a jaguar) by the tail. Fortunately, the National Geographic Society agreed, and this began our long association with that estimable institution.

The four years of intense work that followed (1984–1987) were full of discovery, intensely interesting analysis, frustration, disappointment, and even adventure. We did not do as much as we had hoped and planned for, but in spite of everything, the archaeological work got done and done well. This book is a tribute to the persistence, professionalism, and extraordinary efforts of our staff and workers. I hope to write another book about the human side of the project and what it took to produce the data that this book presents.

The information and interpretations presented here are an attempt to recreate the life of a Maya city. As I will explain, this city was not an innovative place, not a seedbed of Maya civilization. It seems to have spent most of its career as a subordinate administrative center and a fortified guardian of the frontier. However, our work at Río Azul did offer new insights that we have gained from no other site. I hope that this book will provide readers with some sense of the city's history, its functioning, and its disasters and triumphs. I have also tried, within the limits of our data, to give some impression of life in the city during the Early Classic period for members of various social classes that lived in and around it. Of course, as always, we know more about the people at the top of the social structure because they were able to memorialize themselves in writing, art, and tombs. However, we dug into commoner housing as well, and have some ideas about how that group lived.

It is currently the fashion to present the Maya as intoxicated with and driven by their religious beliefs. This view is mainly another form of the old philosopher-king theories of another generation and seems the result of an undue emphasis on the written texts. Joyce Marcus (1992) has convincingly demonstrated that many of these texts were written for purposes of propaganda and legitimization, and thus are full of myth as well as a special form of history. The Río Azul project tried to integrate the findings of field archaeology with those of epigraphy and art history analysis, using each as a corrective for the other. In my view, the reconstruction of Río Azul and the theories derived from the data are the stronger for their reliance on diverse data. However, here we are getting into professional debates and those arguments should be saved for the following pages.

I have attempted in this preface to communicate some of the interest, the intellectual stimulation, the sheer hard work, and the fun of field archaeology. Few other fields reward its practitioners with such profound and fascinating problems of human history. We worked hard in the project, many times at full strain, and we were sometimes alarmed, often perplexed and amused, but we were never bored. I hope that the reader catches some of that excitement in the following pages.

For general readers who may become impatient with the presentation of the data and arguments in chapters 2, 3, and 4, it is recommended that they proceed directly from chapter 1 to chapters 5 and 6. These give both specific and larger scale interpretations of Río Azul and Southern Lowland Maya civilization and may better prepare the nonprofessional to grapple with the discussions of architecture, site layouts, stone tools, pottery, ancient demography, and other details that underpin the interpretations. The outline of culture history found in appendix 1 also provides helpful background. The other appendices bring together technical information that has been presented in various publications but summarized nowhere else between two covers. The appendices also relieve the text of much of the documentation that is required to back up arguments and interpretations but that may be of minimal interest to nonprofessionals.

I hope the text will interest some readers in subjects that they were unaware of before setting out on this vicarious voyage of discovery. Bon voyage!

RICHARD E. W. ADAMS
San Antonio, Texas

ACKNOWLEDGMENTS

OUR DEBTS ARE SO NUMEROUS and so heavy that it is difficult to give adequate credit to our benefactors, supporters, staff, workers, and a multitude of friends. Two individuals stand out in the history of the project: Wilbur E. Garrett, Jr., and David Wise. The former was the editor of *National Geographic Magazine* during the life of the project, and the latter was the long-suffering program manager for the project at the National Endowment for the Humanities. In the summer of 1990 a month-long stay in paradise, otherwise known as the Rockefeller Study Center at Bellagio, gave me an unrivaled opportunity to begin this book. I am very grateful to the Rockefeller Foundation for its support and to the manager of the program, Susan Garfield, the late manager of the Center, Roberto Celli, and his wife Gianna for making the stay extraordinarily productive. In thirty days I managed to write 130 pages.

Ian Graham has both the credit and the responsibility for having shown us the matchless opportunities that Río Azul presented. Douglas and Barbara Cannell made the first season possible and enabled us to obtain further aid from Canadian sources in 1984 and 1985. We are deeply grateful to them and to Ross MacDonald, Academic Vice President of the University of Winnipeg, for this aid. The Canadian philanthropist who provided the funds, and who insists on maintaining her anonymity, of course has our deepest gratitude. We also very much appreciate the yearly donation of plastic shower bags and water bags by Sheldon Burney of Winnipeg.

The Lende Foundation of San Antonio aided us in our initial work, and we are most appreciative to W. E. Lende and Robert Lende. They provided constant aid later in the project and interested other donors on our behalf. We are indebted to them for this and much other substantive aid.

Of all our supporters, Floy Fontaine Jordan is among the most faithful and one to whom we owe an immense debt for her unfailing support and for what she calls "giving us our luck." For this we are most grateful. Robert Washington interested Emily Alexander of the Kleberg Foundation in our agronomy work, and they furnished us with crucial aid.

We formed a group of individual supporters, some of whom continued with us into the next phase of the Río Azul work, the Río Azul Regional Project (1990–1994). Sadly, one of the most engaged of this group, Maj. General (ret.) Carl Stapleton, USAF, is no longer with us and is listed on the dedication page; Mrs. Stapleton has continued to support us. The entire donor group helped immensely, but many of its members requested anonymity. We mention those we can with pleasure, and thereby thank Diane Jewell Hayden, Mr. and Mrs. Robert Rosow, Mr. and Mrs. Richard Goldsmith, Ing. Luis Greñas, Edward Westphal, James Farrior, Robert Persellin, Etelka McCluer, John Keshishian, Francis Robicsek, Jorge Garcia, Mr. and Mrs. George Judson, and A. C. Grona of Zachry Construction Company.

Our contingent of volunteer physicians paid their own way to the site and worked double duty as field archaeologists and medical specialists, dealing with many exotic and ordinary illnesses and injuries. Heading the list is our project physician for 1985, 1986, and 1987, Dr. Edward Westphal, who also worked as a carpenter when not patching us together or digging in the trenches. Among other miracles performed, he saved one of our workmen from the effects of a stroke. He has my unbounded admiration and thanks. Dr. Bruce Wood had the leading role in what was probably the most traumatic of our experiences, as he literally saved the life of one of our workmen from the secondary effects of a severe snakebite. We are also very grateful to Drs. Robert Persellin, Nancy Fishback, Timothy Flynn, and John Faggard for their professional care. These physicians also provided valuable medicines.

James Farrior is an old and valued friend who has developed a second vocation in archaeology after a distinguished career in space engineering. A longtime "ham radio" operator, he set up and operated a morse code set in camp through which we were able to communicate with the United States and, thereby, Guatemala. Mrs. Marty Morrison was outstanding in her faithfulness and helpfulness.

My wife, Jane Jackson Adams, displayed unusual endurance and patience, provided good advice, and answered mysterious collect phone calls in the middle of the night from total strangers on our radio network. She also worked as Laboratory Director for the project in 1985.

Richardson Gill of San Antonio went to extraordinary lengths to provide us with a backhoe/front-end loader, which he refurbished and shipped to Guatemala for us. It was of great service to us in exploring the drained field zones around Río Azul.

Many Guatemalan officials helped us in the work. The most consistently helpful and encouraging were the former Director of the Institute of Anthropology and History of Guatemala, Licda. Edna Nuñez de Rodas, and the now retired Director of Prehispanic Monuments, Lic. Rafael Morales. We worked under permits negotiated annually through the Ministry of Culture and Sports.

Others in Guatemala who aided us greatly at various times were Bertoldo Nathusius, James Hazard, J. D. Nottebohm, Ing. Luis Greñas, Dr. Rudolfo Herrera, Eugenio Schwendener, Juan Schwendener, Lucia Hempstead, Lic. Jose Sanchez, Olga Hazard, and William Carter of Texaco, Guatemala. Mr. Nottebohm went far out of his way to help us when one of our workers was bitten by a snake during the 1990 season. We must also express our admiration for the Director of Hospital Privada Herrera, Dr. Rudolfo Herrera, and the excellent team he assembled to care for the stricken worker.

Vivian Broman Morales helped us in so many ways that it is not possible to enumerate the extent of our debt to her. She acted as our agent in Guatemala City, forwarded mail, calmed anxious families, gave sage advice—all with good humor and professional competence.

Our long-suffering agent in the Petén was G. Edmundo Solís, who, with his wife Patricia, solved nearly every problem imaginable and some that were truly unimaginable. Sad to say, Patty is no longer with us, having died in an accident in 1996. We miss her greatly.

Frank Ambuhl, a longtime friend, cheerfully undertook the task of reading the manuscript for punctuation, grammar, logic, and redundancies, at great cost in time and tedium.

Our contacts with the National Geographic Society were cordial, professional, and highly productive. We are especially grateful to Edwin Snider, George Stuart, Douglas Paynter, and W. E. Garrett, Jr. Robert Hernandez acted as our liaison at NGS headquarters in

Washington, and we thank him. Our admiration and affection for NGS photographer George Mobley is unbounded. Mobley was assigned to the project for several weeks in 1984 and 1985. Melvin M. Payne and the late Joseph Judge, Paul Sampson, Mercer Cross, and Robert P. Jordan all have our thanks for many services rendered.

Work was performed under grants from the National Geographic Society given in 1984, 1985, 1986, and 1987 as well as in 1993 and 1994. The National Endowment for the Humanities also partially funded our work in 1986, 1987, 1990, 1991, 1992, 1993, and 1994.

The University of Texas at San Antonio aided us in ways too numerous to list. We are especially grateful to former President James W. Wagener, former Financial Vice-President Daniel Williams, Dean Dwight Henderson, Carol Hollingsworth, Jane Bonham, Ernest DeWinne, Betty Murray, Raymond Baird, and Thomas R. Hester.

Finally, to the staff and workers go my admiration, thanks, and affection for the extraordinary efforts and the highly professional conduct generally displayed throughout the project. A few people bent under the stresses of the work and eventually eliminated themselves from the project. On the whole, however, both local personnel and professional staff surpassed themselves in carrying out difficult, sometimes dangerous, and always significant work.

To Clemency Coggins, Peter Dunham, and Norman Hammond go heartfelt thanks for their highly professional performance of the thankless task of reviewing this book in its various manuscript stages. David Stuart also reviewed the manuscript to my benefit. Hubert R. Robichaux has endured several harrowing seasons with the project, first as student and later as colleague. He has contributed to and improved the book in several ways, as will be noted in the text. As always, however, failings, flaws, and sins of omission and commission in this book fall to me as the author.

Finally, thanks is due, as always, to my wife, Jane Jackson Adams, for the support and love given through the whole of the project.

RÍO AZUL

CHAPTER 1

INTRODUCTION

History of Discovery, Looting, and
Archaeological Investigation

THE ANCIENT CITY THAT WE know as Río Azul was reported in 1962, partially explored the same year, published in 1964, looted from 1976 to 1981, and investigated by a five-year project between 1983 and 1987. A five-year regional project between 1990 and 1994 accomplished work at the fortress site of Kinal, at six small sites in the Río Azul region, and at more than sixty small sites 40 km to the east in Belize around the major site of La Milpa. The examination of the countryside to date has produced evidence of eighty small sites within an area of about 2,000 sq km.

This book summarizes the findings of the scientific work, the supporting evidence for these findings, and their interpretations. It also presents the artistic treasures, the historical and functional reconstructions of the city, and some implications of the data for important questions of Maya prehistory. The research problems include the vexing puzzles of the origins of Maya civilization, its complex political, economic, and social forms, and the nature of its eventual and catastrophic collapse. Detailed data are presented in the main body and appendices of this book and in the separately published Río Azul Reports 1–5 (Adams 1984, 1986a, 1987a, 1989, and 1998).

Most archaeological sites are not discovered by archaeologists but by people who live and work in the area. Río Azul was discovered and reported in 1962 by Trinidad Pech, a native of the northern department of Guatemala, the Petén. Pech was probably not the first modern visitor to the site; it apparently had long been known as "Las Gardemias" (The Gardenias) after a local flower that grows there in profusion. At the time he reported the site, Pech was employed by

Sun Oil Company, which then held the oil exploration concession for that part of the Petén. In the late 1950s and early 1960s the Petén was still an area of vast, trackless forests littered with the undisturbed remains of ancient Maya cities, towns, villages, and farmsteads. Most contemporary population was concentrated around a set of lakes in the central zone. To some degree this is still true, although pioneer farmers have colonized and cut down vast tracts of tropical forest in the central and southern zones. The northern zones, although exploited for valuable timber, remain largely unmodified and have been set aside as national reserves or are otherwise protected from overdevelopment.

However, exploitation of the Petén is taking place as farmers and loggers from Mexico and Belize intrude upon the area. As they have for the past eighty years, residents of the region take periodic expeditions into these forests to log and to gather *chicle* for the chewing gum industry and *chate* (a fern) for the North American floral industry. During the brief period of oil exploration (ca. 1956–1963), they also systematically surveyed the concessions granted to oil companies. All of these activities have yielded great amounts of archaeological information on new sites and on various features of ancient Maya civilization. However, recent activities have also led to some rather reprehensible practices that are degrading and destroying large amounts of information about the ancient Maya. I refer, of course, to looting and associated depredations, much of which is stimulated by a voracious world art market. First, Maya sculpture from the area was prized and promoted by art dealers, and when those pieces became too hot to handle legally and practically, they turned to ceramics. This development has been particularly disastrous. Most intact ceramics are to be found in tombs, and Maya tombs are often under or in large buildings. Therefore, the shift of demand in the art market to ceramics has resulted in the destruction of buildings during the search for tombs, where ceramics as well as other items are to be found: jades, carved shell items, bone items, and even carved wooden boxes and bowls. Huge trenches and networks of tunnels, nearly worthy of subway systems, now undermine many major buildings at Maya sites. As will be seen in the case of Río Azul, the loss of cultural heritage has been enormous. It is especially distressing in the case of Río Azul because we had seen it nearly intact in 1962 when only minor depredations had taken place.

In 1962 John L. Gatling was the resident geologist in Guatemala for Sun Oil Company and had become interested in Maya ruins in the concession where he was directing the exploration for oil. He instructed his geological and gravity survey crews to record each site and grade it according to size. In 1959, he had reported the major site of Kinal to Ian Graham, who explored and later published it (1967).

In 1962 Gatling informed me about Pech's discovery of Río Azul and offered to set up a trip of exploration. With permission from the Guatemalan government, we set off to make a sketch map and to dig a few test pits to determine the main period of occupation. With the help of one of Gatling's colleagues, we managed to finish in two days. As Pech had reported, the site included standing stone walls, one of which had remains of modeled stucco on it. This wall was actually the intact roof comb of Str. A-2, and the modeled hiero-glyphic text included the Río Azul name glyph, although we did not recognize it at the time. Our sketch map turned out to be lamentably incomplete, showing only about 40 of the 729 buildings that were in the city. The test pits indicated a strong Early Classic (A.D. 250–550) occupation. Only two instances of illegal excavation were noted. Gatling and I published our findings in short papers in Spanish (Adams and Gatling 1964, 1965). The site was so isolated and diffi-cult to reach (and my status at the time was so junior) that there was little hope of mounting a project to explore it more thoroughly. Sun Oil Company and the rest of the North American oil companies were pulling out of Guatemala by 1963, and zones that had been temporarily accessible were left either abandoned or isolated for lack of logistical support. Camps, roads, water filtration systems, power systems, workshops, airfields—all disappeared under the encroaching jungle even faster than had been the case with the ancient Maya cities during their collapse.

I went to the University of Minnesota in 1963 and scarcely thought of Río Azul until 1981. Gatling was transferred to Australia, where he spent the rest of his career. Lamentably, he died in 1983 just as we were reentering the site to begin the project.

In 1976 the site was selected for illegal excavation by a wealthy collector in Guatemala. For about two years small groups of workers were employed in a search for tombs and their contents, earning only a pittance for their work. Illegal digging on a truly devastating scale began around 1978 and employed up to eighty workers. This enterprise was under the leadership of another Guatemalan. Again, the actual diggers worked under very poor conditions and were furnished bad food and paid low wages. The later effort evidently created most of the large trenches and tunnels. Field bosses and some of the workers were experienced in archaeological work through prior training on legitimate archaeological projects. According to reports, small planes landed regularly on the old Sun Oil Company airstrip at Dos Lagunas, twenty-five miles distant, to carry off the major finds from the tombs. The efforts were richly rewarding to the organizers of the illicit project and to the art dealers in the United States who accepted these contraband objects. The dealers reportedly sold individual ceramic pieces for as much as twenty-five or thirty thousand dollars apiece. Against all ethics of the profession, at least two U.S. archaeologists reportedly evaluated, authenticated, and interpreted the stolen materials for the dealers.

Unfortunately, dealers found a ready market for the Río Azul artifacts among private collectors and institutions, mainly museums, even though the buyers were advised of the illicit and unethical excavation of these items. Indeed, the name Río Azul came to have a cachet among dealers, museums, and collectors alike, and many more items that probably came from elsewhere were attributed to the site. Río Azul materials have been traced to private collections from Scottsdale, Arizona to Brussels, and to public collections in Denver and Detroit. Río Azul material is reportedly in Japan and the United Kingdom. While some artifacts apparently remain in private hands in Guatemala, none of the items sold outside the country have been returned. All items have lost about 90 percent of their scientific value in terms of culture history. The dozens of artifacts looted from at least twenty-eight tombs at Río Azul represent a great loss to the cultural patrimony of Guatemala and humanity in general, as well as a considerable setback in the efforts to reconstruct a picture of Classic Maya civilization. In 1981 the looting was forcibly stopped through the efforts of two dedicated scholars, Ian Graham of the Peabody Museum of Harvard University and Rafael Morales, then Director of Prehispanic Monuments of Guatemala.

As it began in 1983, the work of the Río Azul Archaeological Project was oriented by an overall research design with two major aims. First, we intended to salvage information left from the depredations of the looting activities and to record and, if necessary, conserve the murals in the tombs. We accomplished this objective. All open tombs were carefully recorded, and the few artifacts left in them were salvaged. We examined all of the 125 or more open trenches and tunnels and recorded stratigraphic and construction sequence data. We excavated in search of untouched tombs, hoping to produce data on elite burials complementary to that lost to the vandals.

Our second aim was to reconstruct the function of each part of the city through its entire history. To put it into scientific jargon, we wanted to establish a functionally integrated picture of the site as well as deal with specific theoretical and culture-historical problems. The latter included testing of the Maya origins and collapse models (Adams 1977; Culbert 1973), which meant, among other things, grappling with the problem of lowland Maya relationships to the central Mexican city of Teotihuacan during the Early Classic and dealing with emerging patterns of military intrusion in the period of the collapse. Many more specific but important details were to be considered within these overall contexts. To these ends, planimetric and contour mapping was given priority and final maps of Río Azul and its suburb site of BA-20 were produced in 1985 (Orrego 1987; Orrego and Ponciano 1998; Black 1987). Mapping also helped to orient excavations designed to sample functionally distinct parts of the site. As the project developed, we extended excavations to the northern suburb, BA-20, which was found to be associated with intensive gardening and high-volume stone tool production (Black 1987).

Some unexpected findings were also exploited, as in the case of a huge and previously unknown structure that turned out to be a Preclassic temple, Str. G-103 sub 1.

By 1987 we had pretty well accomplished our second aim and had a good idea what most of the city zones were used for. Of course, as in all research projects, circumstances sometimes prevented us from carrying out planned digging; a malaria epidemic in camp cut short the 1987 season, for instance. Some developments in our work led us to a new, interesting, and more detailed level of understanding of various problems. This is the familiar phenomenon of solving the initial research problem but raising a host of new and interesting questions. Our work on covered space calculations, for example, led us to an unexpected implication. We concluded that construction crews had to have been imported to erect the major structures at Río Azul because the resident population was so small and so much of it was of the elite class. For lack of time and funds we were unable to check the surrounding countryside as thoroughly as we wanted in order to confirm this idea. As in all archaeological work, we left a significant residue of problems and tasks for the next project or the next generation.

In the end, we probably could have continued digging at Río Azul for the next twenty years while maintaining a steady flow of interesting and new information. By 1987, however, it was time to pause and attempt to synthesize and publish the information.

The present account is aimed at the audiences of general interested readers, archaeologists not specialized in the Maya, and students. For my colleagues who want all the available detail and technical facts there are the Río Azul Reports, various papers already published or in press and preparation, as well as unpublished masters and doctoral theses listed in the bibliography.

Classic Maya Civilization in Outline

The following is not intended to be a complete introduction to the complexities of the majestic and varied structure that was Maya civilization. For that the reader may turn to two excellent introductory books (Hammond 1988; Sharer 1994) and for a broader picture of all Mesoamerican civilizations to a book of my own (Adams 1991).

Lowland Maya civilization developed in part of a vast area known as Mesoamerica, which encompassed a set of related civilizations including the Zapotec, Aztec, Totonac, and many other groups (Fig. 1–1). The total area occupied by civilized peoples was about 1,015,280 sq km (392,000 sq mi), roughly the space occupied today by the modern nation-states of Guatemala and Belize, plus about half of Mexico and the western parts of Honduras and El Salvador. The first complex societies in Mesoamerica, known as the Olmec, appeared in the limited zone now known as Veracruz about 1200 B.C. Within a few hundred years Olmec culture was joined by other civilized societies. Some of these cultures developed independently as early as the Olmec. The stage was set for the characteristic Mesoamerican pattern of interaction among diverse cultural variations on a few basic themes. These themes included a technology that was essentially based on a Stone Age set of techniques and tools. Urban growth and community types evolved within a basic pattern of centrally located elite-class residences and public buildings for administration, surrounded by homes of the lesser elite and interspersed with the residences of retainer families.

Some Mesoamerican cities were always "ceremonial centers," where nearly the entire population and almost all construction directly or indirectly supported the small class of elite residents. Many other cities developed into urban centers similar to those familiar to us from the ancient Middle East, early China, or the Classical Mediterranean world. That is, they became centers of large-scale artisan manufacturing and commerce. They also grew to hold thousands of people of various social classes, organized into artisan guilds and occupational specialties of other kinds. Huge public works were planned and directed by the elite class and carried out by well-organized labor teams. Networks of irrigation or drainage canals, causeways, and road systems supplemented the large urban construction of huge palaces, temples, and acres of pavement. Taxes in the form of labor, manufactured goods, and commodities supported the superstructure of elite leadership and bureaucracy and financed public works and state activities. The latter included warfare, diplomacy, and long-distance trade. The concepts of ancestor veneration, divine kingship, and the direct intervention of supernatural powers in human affairs gave secular as well as religious leadership a tinge of the sacred. Social relationships among the occupational groups and social classes were governed by generalized feudal principles, in which individual land ownership often was reserved for the elite. Mutual obligations characterized interaction between classes, while kinship ties governed the relationships on horizontal levels.

Political structures had origins in the innumerable villages and hamlets that had appeared as early as 5000 B.C. and had grouped themselves into regional clusters by 1500 B.C. Some of these had grown to be regal-administrative centers dominating their regions by 900 B.C. A number of these early regional centers later became cities, having already politically organized the surrounding villages and countryside. Political structures similar to those of the ancient Mediterranean city-states appeared by 250 B.C. Larger administrative and commercial networks were developed by about 100 B.C. These large regional states became the dominant and most

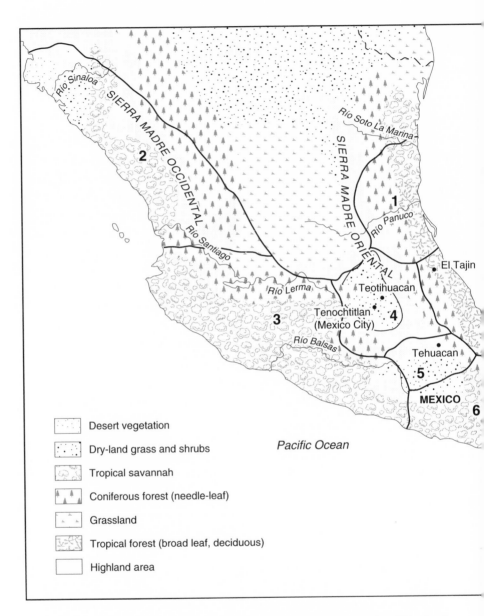

Fig. 1–1. The Maya Lowlands and Río Azul within Mesoamerica. Río Azul is on the border between the Central and Southern Maya Lowlands, although culturally it belongs to the latter. (From Richard E. W. Adams, Prehistoric Mesoamerica, *Revised Edition,* © 1991 by the University of Oklahoma Press)

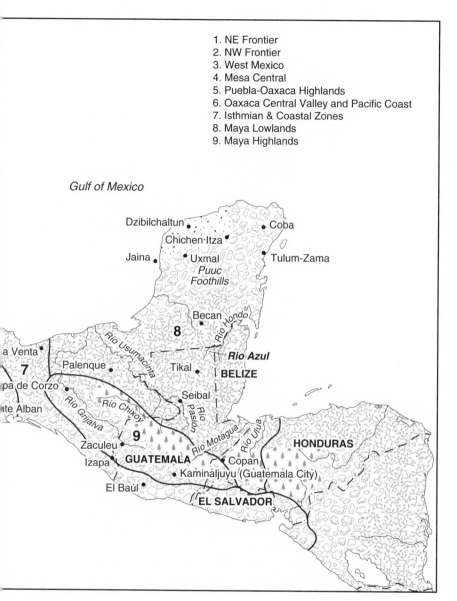

1. NE Frontier
2. NW Frontier
3. West Mexico
4. Mesa Central
5. Puebla-Oaxaca Highlands
6. Oaxaca Central Valley and Pacific Coast
7. Isthmian & Coastal Zones
8. Maya Lowlands
9. Maya Highlands

Gulf of Mexico

Dzibilchaltun

Coba

Chichen·Itza

Jaina · Uxmal

Tulum-Zama

Puuc Foothills

Becan

Rio Hondo

8

a Venta

Rio Usumacinta

Rio Azul

7

Palenque

Tikal

BELIZE

pa de Corzo

Río Chixoy

Seibal

te Alban

Río Grijalva

Río Pasión

Río Motagua

Río Ulúa

HONDURAS

9

Zaculeu

GUATEMALA

Copan

Izapa

Kaminaljuyu (Guatemala City)

El Baúl

EL SALVADOR

stable political forms of the period up to the time of the Spanish conquest in 1521 (Fig. 1–2). However, as early as A.D. 100 a few centers developed into what may be fairly termed empires. These were inherently fragile and usually lasted only a few generations and then broke down into their constituent parts of regional states and city-states. The historic Aztec empire was one such phenomenon, as was the earlier imperial structure centered on the huge city of Teotihuacan.

Art was patronized by the elite leadership for purposes of self-glorification and legitimization as well as for aesthetic reasons. Textiles, stone sculpture, modeled stucco reliefs, ceramics, jade and other lapidary work, as well as mosaic concoctions and, in later periods, metallurgical productions were among the various art media used. Mural painting provided a lively and freer expression than that of the stiffer, more monumental forms. Writing was used as a way to disseminate legitimizing information about rulers, priests, and military leaders. Names and titles of kings, their distinguished genealogies, and lists of their conquests and other accomplishments make up the formal texts. More utilitarian documents were created in the form of priestly almanacs, filled with guides to ceremonies, auguries for the future, histories of states, agricultural guides, beekeepers' almanacs, and other data set down in regular and organized formats. Most new ideas, technologies, and commodities ultimately spread throughout the vast Mesoamerican zone by means of diplomacy, conquest, long-distance trade, elite intermarriage, and religious pilgrimages.

The Maya groups of the highlands and lowlands were an integral part of Mesoamerica. United by related languages and cultural patterns, but never unified politically, the Maya formed a large block of cultures in eastern Mesoamerica. Of the Highland Maya, we will only note that they followed a somewhat different trajectory of development than did their neighbors and colleagues in the lowlands and spoke many more diverse and mutually unintelligible languages.

The Lowland Maya occupied a large area of about 250,000 sq km (ca. 97,000 sq mi). The area is divided ecologically and culturally into three major zones: northern, central, and southern.

Earlier scholars divided Maya history into various periods, designed to reflect major developmental events. These periods with their current dating are as follows:

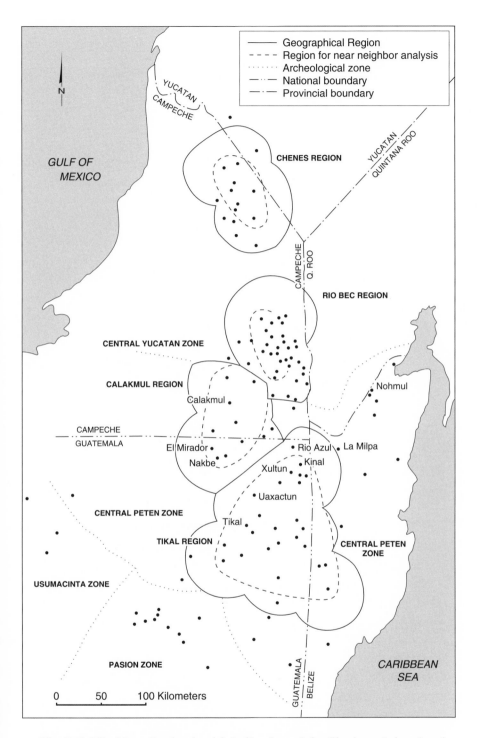

Fig. 1–2. The Maya Lowlands with indications of the Classic period regional states. These states are defined by geographical analyses, material culture patterns, and Maya political texts. (From Richard E. W. Adams, Prehistoric Mesoamerica, Revised Edition, © 1991 by the University of Oklahoma Press)

Early Preclassic: ? 2500 B.C. to 1000 B.C.
Middle Preclassic: 1000 B.C. to 250 B.C.
Late Preclassic: 250 B.C. to A.D. 250
Early Classic: A.D. 250 to A.D. 550
Late Classic: A.D. 550 to A.D. 900
Early Postclassic: A.D. 900 to A.D. 1250
Late Postclassic: A.D. 1250 to A.D. 1540

These periods are now used mainly as convenient chronological blocks of time rather than as the segments of evolution that they were originally intended to be.

The lowlands were probably first colonized extensively by pioneer farmers about 2000 B.C. Small villages widely scattered through the forests were the way of life for generations. Population growth was apparently the main impetus for the spread of these villages. By about 1000 B.C., small regional centers developed. These were large villages in which there were small platforms topped with small perishable structures apparently serving as temples.

At Cuello, an early group of houses around a small courtyard was built by 900 B.C. and used for the next five hundred years (Hammond 1991). By at least 450 B.C. at Nakbe (Hansen 1991), Río Azul (Valdez 1993), and Altar de Sacrificios (Willey 1973:27) the Maya were building in stone and creating large terraced platforms, which probably supported small temples with stone walls and thatched roofs. Several very large platforms grouped about a courtyard have been found at Nakbe. This implies that the basic Maya architectonic unit of buildings around patios, courtyards, and plazas had been established by this time. Stone architecture was also well under development.

Nakbe was apparently abandoned about A.D. 150, and cultural activity in the region shifted north a few miles to a place called El Mirador, where there are immense Late Preclassic structures (Hansen, personal communication 1998). During the Late Preclassic, several centers in the southern lowlands were building such giant structures: Calakmul, Mirador, Tikal, Tayasal in the central zone, and Lamanai in the east. Calakmul, Tikal, and Mirador are located on the edges of vast swamps, and Calakmul and Tikal later became the largest cities of the Maya lowlands. Further north, the center of Edzna coordinated the building of a massive canal network in the Late Preclassic. Nearly all Classic period cities of the Maya area begin as Late

Preclassic regional centers. The period also witnessed surging population growth and the development of intensive agricultural techniques, which involved swamp drainage and raised field gardening.
This laid the economic basis for Maya civilization.

By A.D. 100 certain centers, including Nakbe, had adopted sculpture and writing. Several Maya centers show evidence for the presence
of divine kings, rulers whose ancestry was considered to originate
with the gods of creation. Ancestral figures peer down from the sky
at the ruler in certain sculptures. In most early sculpture, the ruler
also stands on a crushed human captive—a symbol of military conquest. Military competition among the elite groups of various centers
emerged and became more important. It is now apparent that this
militarism developed as part of the effort to build political units
larger than city-states. A number of scholars, myself included, believe
that regional states emerged in the Maya lowlands during the Early
Classic. One of the largest and most successful of these larger states
was the one headed by Tikal, already a city of about 25,000.
Calakmul to the northwest headed another regional state. Río Azul
is on the frontier between the two states. With the outside help of
Teotihuacan in central Mexico, Tikal expanded to the Río Azul zone,
conquered it, and established a stable boundary at that point (Fig.
1–3; Adams and Jones 1981, Fig. 1; Adams 1990).

Meanwhile, Maya culture flourished at dozens of small and large
cities over the whole Maya area. Temples rose higher and more
grandly and were decorated with elaborate frescoes, modeled stucco,
polychrome paints, and carved wooden elements. The elite lived in
relative luxury and splendor in stone and stucco palaces. These buildings were arranged around courtyards, which were paved with high-
quality stucco. The functions of this upper class were multiple and
included the planning and supervision of large-scale building, irriga-
tion-drainage systems, and road systems. The urban zones as well as
the countryside teemed with ever increasing numbers of people who
supported the expanding elite, along with their dependent artisans,
bureaucrats, retainers, servants, and other nonfarmers. Long-distance
trade, intermarriage, diplomacy, formal alliances, and other relationships tied the Maya states together politically and economically as well
as culturally. But a disaster ended the Early Classic period.

The time of troubles is called The Hiatus, generally a period of
about 60 years, although it now appears that even in the largest cities

Fig. 1–3. *Tikal Temple 1 and the North Acropolis, the possible Early Classic capital of a regional state that included Río Azul. (Photo courtesy of Alexandre Nikouline)*

the period of upset may have lasted as long as 150 years. A few exceptional sites, such as Altar de Sacrificios on the Pasión River, rode out the storm. As will be seen later, The Hiatus may have been a time of civil and interstate wars partially triggered by climatic and food crises on the one hand and dynastic crises on the other. There are very few sculptured monuments erected to rulers and very little major architecture from this period. Population may have decreased drastically, and certain centers seem to have been abandoned, never again becoming major players in the Maya game.

As many as three generations passed before Maya civilization stabilized, perhaps with the help of more favorable climatic conditions: rainier, warmer weather. By A.D. 650 many centers erected monuments again and constructed large buildings. Population seems to have grown at a rapid rate. In fact, much of Late Classic Maya culture appears almost megalomaniacal (Willey and Shimkin 1973: 484). Over the next hundred years (A.D. 650–750) Tikal grew to be the largest Maya city, with a population of between sixty and eighty thousand. A series of strong rulers, beginning about A.D. 680 (Jones 1977, 1987), reestablished the Tikal Regional State and expanded it, perhaps to the south. Río Azul in the north was reoccupied, and appears to have attempted to go it alone as an independent polity during the sixth century. Eventually, administrative functions passed to a newly created center nearby, Kinal. We are not certain that Río Azul ever again became a dependency of Tikal. La Milpa to the east was certainly a Late Classic power, but a diffusion of political authority to local nobility appears to have taken place in both eastern and western sectors of the region.

Because of excessive growth and resultant vulnerability, Maya civilization collapsed catastrophically during the period A.D. 840–900. The nature of the collapse has been well defined and the basic explanation for it has been advanced in a model that has been tested by twenty-five years of fieldwork and found to be fundamentally correct (Culbert 1973; Lowe 1985). Briefly, this model shows the interrelation among the factors of exponential population growth, intensive food production, endemic diseases, management overload, and other structural defects in Maya society. Warfare became an exacerbating element in the process of decline, and an enormous population loss resulted from increasing conflict and the associated factors of epidemic, enslavement, and agricultural-ecological disasters. With its economic and population bases destroyed, the superstructure of elite class culture and its architecture, art, rituals, political networks, and other features fell apart as well. The destruction of the environment due to overuse of land and excessive drainage of surface water meant that vast areas were abandoned and not reoccupied until the present day, 1,100 years later.

The disaster struck first and most severely in the southern and central lowlands, where it was over by A.D. 900. Indeed, there is a clear pattern of collapse from west to east. Copan, in its slow decline on the southeastern periphery, appears to have been an exception. The northern lowlands also suffered a collapse, but it occurred later and was less severe. Opportunistically, the northern cities and states raided southward into the troubled zones of Calakmul, Tikal, and other major centers. They possibly brought in military allies from the Gulf Coast and Central Highlands of Mexico—the Itza and the Toltecs. These mercenary-allies may have turned on their erstwhile employers and established themselves as competing political units. In any case it is certain that by A.D. 1000 the Toltecs and Itza had overthrown the last of the Maya Classic centers located at places like Uxmal, Kabah, and other cities of the Puuc region.

Early Postclassic Maya civilization was reoriented toward more secular and militaristic matters. With foreign elites in charge at some centers in northern Yucatan, and other areas apparently controlled by refugee or otherwise surviving Maya elites, intermittent conflict was a key feature of this period. Interestingly, the region became more open to trade, where Yucatan, unprepossessing as it may seem, had certain advantages. Salt from large-scale salt beds on the north coast, immense quantities of honey produced by stingless bees, cotton, and medicinal herbs were all highly desirable commodities traded widely into the rest of Mesoamerica. The Maya elites became more like merchant princes than divinely ordained rulers. Eventually, with the absorption of foreign elites into Maya culture and populace over several generations, Maya civilization stabilized into a political structure of small regional states. It also became much more like the rest of Mesoamerica and less unique in its features.

In the Late Postclassic, a Maya ruling family attempted to unify the regional states into a pan-Maya empire, according to contact-era accounts. At Mayapan, near what is now the modern city of Mérida, a capital was established where hostages from all the other ruling families of the northern lowlands were required to reside. This arrangement worked for about one hundred fifty years until 1446, when a bloody revolt overthrew the dominant Cocom family and the Maya returned to their more stable regionalized polities. When they arrived on the coasts of Yucatan in 1517, the Spaniards found sixteen regional states, each with a capital and at least one port on the coast through which the lifeblood of trade flowed.

The Spanish conquest of the Northern Maya was agonizingly long, lasting over forty years. Meanwhile, the central and southern cities of the Southern Maya lay abandoned and overgrown by forests except around the central lake district, where independent groups of Maya kept their cultural traditions alive until 1697. In that year Martín de Ursua y Arizmendi led an expedition that overthrew the last remnant of native American civilization in the New World.

Finally, it seems useful in this introduction to emphasize some of the latest insights about the nature of Maya civilization. For example, Maya civilization did not rise to its heights in the middle of an enclosing jungle. By the time the cities were built, the ancestors of the Maya had tamed the wilderness, and nearly every feature of the landscape was eventually modified. The Maya countryside would have been more like present-day Europe than an unmodified tropical forest. Another common misperception has been that the Maya region was sparsely populated. Certainly this was the case in the pioneer farming villages of the Middle Preclassic. However, by the beginning of the Classic period, there were thousands of people living together and scattered through many rural areas. After the recovery from the Hiatus crisis, populations became even larger, and we may speak of millions of people in the lowlands during the eighth century A.D. Clearly, such populations were not supported by the kind of slash-and-burn agriculture that is practiced today in the low-lands, since a slash-and-burn cultivation system depends on extensive farming of plentiful arable land with relatively small and scattered populations. By the beginning of the Late Preclassic, Maya popula-tions had outstripped the capacity of slash-and-burn agriculture and had turned to intensive forms of food production. They used drainage and raised field techniques to convert huge zones of swampland to wetland gardens and modified many other zones by extensive ter-racing of hillsides.

We are moving beyond the other-worldly image of Maya civiliza-tion fostered by many romantics, art historians, and archaeologists—that of a peaceful, mild, and intellectual people led by groups of philosopher-kings and their noble advisors. The reality is that the Maya could be as fully realistic, pragmatic, and at times, as unpleasant as the rest of humanity. Realpolitik, intrigue, deception, and warfare were all integral parts of Maya history. Politics, commerce, greed, avarice, competence, incompetence, and all the other admirable and lamentable traits seen in world history come through to us in our studies of the Maya, making them less mysterious and more interesting. Careful research and analysis is uncovering, not an indecipherable enigma from a jungle adventure story, but an extraordinarily rich early civilization that continues to enlighten us today.

CHAPTER 2

TIME AND ITS MEASUREMENTS

THREE ELEMENTS ARE CONSTANTLY JUGGLED by the archaeologist, time, space, and content. Of these perhaps time is the most crucial. Without excavation and chronometric techniques, it would often be difficult to know the order of events at a site and the length of time required for them to happen. The traditional process of sorting out time in archaeology begins with the establishment of a relative time scale. This can be done by stratigraphic excavation, which is based on the principle that the oldest material is the deepest and the most recent is on top. Ceramics in particular, but other artifacts as well, change through time, and these changes can be documented during excavation of stratified material and applied to unstratified material—debris in a room, for example. This produces a relative sequence, which is then dated by chronometric techniques, radiocarbon dating being the best known and one of the most widely used. Obsidian hydration dating is increasingly used as well. For any reader who wishes to understand the infinite complexities of these and other physical dating methods, there are a number of excellent introductions to archaeology that include this information (e.g., Renfrew and Bahn 1991).

The Classic Maya left us another chronometric tool, an indigenous calendar with hundreds of dates recorded on stone, in stucco, painted on tomb walls, and elsewhere and in other media. When absolute dates derived from this calendar and other methods are all applied to the relative sequence the total extension of the site chronology begins to appear. For example, radiocarbon dates were obtained on Tomb 19 at the Río Azul site, and thus the pottery in the tomb was also fixed in time. The resultant site sequence was compared to others established at other sites, especially those nearby. Minute comparisons can confirm a new sequence or point out differences and possible errors.

Río Azul is fortunately surrounded by several regions that have been or are now being intensively investigated and for which the sequences are well established. The North Belize zone to the east has been the focus of intense archaeological work since about 1975 (Hammond 1991). The Río Bec region to the north was investigated by several projects from 1969 to 1974 (Adams 1981). To the west and northwest lie the sites of Nakbe, El Mirador, and Calakmul, all recently or currently under investigation (Hansen 1990; Matheny 1980; Folan et al. 1995). Finally, and most important for our project, is the dedicated work of several groups of scientists at Tikal and Uaxactun to the southwest (Coe 1982; Kidder 1950). Meticulous work and extraordinary efforts have established detailed ceramic sequences to which we can refer and compare the Río Azul materials (R. E. Smith 1955; Culbert 1965; Ball 1977; Kosakowsky 1987; Valdez 1988).

Appendix 1 summarizes the evidence for time spans, and the cultural markers that we worked out for the various periods at Río Azul. Some of the major culture historical events are also noted. Dating by the Maya calendar has been a major aid in sorting out the sequence at Río Azul. The correlation of the Maya and Christian chronologies used here is one proposed by Martinez, commonly called the GMT correlation after its authors, Goodman, Martinez, and Thompson (Morley, Brainerd, Sharer 1983). A good example of the way we dealt with the problems of cultural chronology at Río Azul is the manner in which we dated the largest building complex at the site, A3. There are four tombs (1, 2, 7, 12) assigned to the fifth century A.D. by Maya dates painted on their walls. Two stone monuments, Stelae 1 and 3, are assignable to the late fourth century A.D., both by explicit dates as well as by styles. Stela 2 carries a date of A.D. 661. The only other stela at Río Azul is the aberrant and Terminal Classic monument, Stela 4, which is itself only dated by stratigraphy and style. Stucco glyphs on temple structure A-2 are Early Classic in style (Adams and Gatling 1964; Stuart 1986). By physical association with these monuments, temple complex A-3 is entirely Early Classic as confirmed by the pottery and stratigraphy.

Ceramics are plentiful, diverse, and nearly always associated with other remains. The pottery of Río Azul is almost entirely within the stylistic canons and traditions of the Tikal and Uaxactun sequences. These overlap and have some links to the sequences from sites to the west, north, and east of Río Azul, but the differences between them are significant, determined perhaps by commercial and political factors.

G. R. Willey has said that archaeology can be viewed as a great sampling game, and it is true that our conclusions are only as reliable as the sample. Thus we tried to obtain the widest possible distribution of excavated samples from throughout the site, and we were helped in a perverse way by the looters' excavations. We sampled nearly all of the 125 trenches and tunnels dug by the vandals. Because these diggings penetrated nearly every major and medium sized structure in the city, we could determine how often a building had been renovated and the periods to which construction phases belonged. This salvage of data was aided by a program of test pits distributed over the site in order to sample zones otherwise unexamined. Unfortunately, we could not complete the program, but we certainly have a better grasp of the history of regional urban development than otherwise would have been the case. The major gap in excavation control is in the large complex named Group E in the northern quarter of the city. This was scheduled for digging in 1987 but the work was scratched due to the shortened season. We have a very good idea of which structures were built during each period, thanks to the sampling of various sorts and especially the development of a ceramic chronology. This sampling of ceramics (content) with their temporal implications (time), from throughout the city (space), is an example of how the three elements mentioned at the beginning of this chapter came together in our operations. The effects of small samples on theory are briefly discussed in the next chapter.

Generally, our relative and absolute time scales comply with those established previously in the Maya Lowlands, with the following differences. Human populations seem to have been slow to settle and exploit the Río Azul zone, appearing no sooner than 900 B.C. compared to centuries and even thousands of years earlier in other regions. Thereafter the regional ceramic development seems to follow general sequences elsewhere until the last fifty years or so of the Late Preclassic. Indeed, nearly all of the Maya Lowlands had enjoyed a ceramic uniformity since about 600 B.C. The wares that dominated the Preclassic were lustrous monochromes, principally reds, blacks, and creams, in order of popularity. Recent work has revealed that this old monochrome pottery persisted later among the lower social classes than among the elite groups. The aristocrats, on the other hand, had adopted polychrome pottery—with an extraordinary multiplicity of designs and forms—partly in order to enhance their status. These two traditions, which were formerly thought to be mutually exclusive in time, are now known to overlap for perhaps 50 or 100 years (the Protoclassic period).

The Early Classic is traditionally divided into three phases, based on work at Uaxactun, where the first sequence was established. However, doubts about the validity of this division (Adams 1971:158) have been confirmed by work at Río Azul, which indicates that there are probably only two phases in the Early Classic at that site. Further, reanalysis of the Uaxactun material indicates that it also fits better into a two-phase scheme. This revision is more than a technicality; the major watershed in the Early Classic in the southern lowlands is the earliest evidence of Teotihuacan influence around A.D. 378 at Tikal. The two Early Classic ceramic phases seem to coincide comfortably with the pre-Teotihuacan and Teotihuacan phases.

The division between Early and Late Classic, The Hiatus, occurs at Río Azul, but appears to extend to about 130 years instead of the 60 years suggested by the Uaxactun work. I believe this reflects a genuine difference between the sites rather than being a function of incomplete data on the part of earlier investigators. As a secondary city, Río Azul probably suffered more from the political and military upset of The Hiatus and was slower to recover. The capital city of Tikal also experienced a long political disruption, but no apparent physical destruction or population loss. We can conclude that The Hiatus at Río Azul extends to about A.D. 650, and covers part of the period traditionally allotted to Late Classic 1.

The Late Classic 1 period is weak at Río Azul, and there is some doubt that it represents a real period of major activity at the urban center. No buildings were constructed, nor have any major events been identified with most of the period. Indeed, within the city the first signs of real recovery from The Hiatus may be as late as A.D. 660, nearly the beginning of the Late Classic 2 period. On the other hand, we do have good evidence for agricultural activity and rural residence construction in the nearby countryside. This demonstrates the difference between the larger-scale regional sequence for several cities and that of only one site. Clearly, things happened at a slower rate within the city than out in the countryside or, conceivably, at the nearby sister cities of Xultun and La Honradez.

The Late Classic 2 period can be divided into two segments, technically called facets. The first facet is one in which there is little outside influence, while the second shows strong northern Maya ceramic presence. Late Classic 3 was the period of military disaster, partial recovery, and the final collapse. It is an action-packed, relatively brief period, lasting about fifty years at Río Azul. The collapse was strung out a bit more at sites such as Tikal, perhaps because they had greater buffers against the multiple disasters of the period.

Chronological differences among sites may reflect important events in culture history. Classic period subdivisions tend to be of this variety. At other times, subdivisions are simply technical conveniences contrived to divide periods that would otherwise be excessively long. The division into Middle and Late Preclassic is this kind of distinction. Thus, although standard chronological divisions often reflect evolutionary trends and historical events, they are best regarded as arbitrary temporal markers against which we can measure whatever culture change we find.

CHAPTER 3

THE ARCHAEOLOGICAL RECORD, 1
The Data

CHAPTERS 3 AND 4 PRESENT THE archaeological data from Río Azul in a digested form. The chapters are supplemented by appendices where more detail can be found. I have arranged the material by topic in both chapters and in the appendices. Initially, the non-professional may find it somewhat confusing to be swept back into the past and then forward through a review of, say, architecture, only to repeat the process with ceramics. However, this is probably the clearest way of presentation and one rapidly becomes accustomed to the discussion of each category from its Early Preclassic appearance onward.

These chapters are preparation for the anthropological interpretations in chapter 5 and the final synthesis in chapter 6. In the latter, the trends and continuities of the Río Azul record are compared with the general Maya lowlands sequence. The reader should be able to find sufficient detail in chapters 3 and 4 about matters of special interest, tomb paintings for example, and be able to judge the validity of the interpretations on these matters in chapters 5 and 6. Some first-order interpretation is included in chapters 3 and 4, but is labeled as such. Finally, a great deal of information is placed in the appendices or referenced in the bibliography.

The topical organization used here moves from the economic and social infrastructure to the intellectual and religious superstructure. Thus, settlement patterns are reviewed early in the chapter and hieroglyphic writing later. The idea is that information on the physical arrangement of human populations will have broader implications for other aspects of culture than will information on, say, art or writing, which were so tied to elite class concerns that they reflect a very narrow view of Maya culture. Additionally, settlement pattern studies take an outsider's more objective perspective, whereas art and writing furnish an insider's perspective on Maya culture, and a limited one. Also, in contrast to the neutral and inclusive studies of communities and landscape, script was developed as an elite class tool of propaganda, and the information to be derived from its decipherment may even be suspect. The Maya aristocrats were not the first nor the last to skew the written record to their own benefit.

Settlement Patterns (Fig. 3–1; Plate 1; Appendix 2)

Communities

The Río Azul zone can be defined on the basis of two factors. One is the distribution of arable soils easily cultivated by early forms of agriculture, particularly slash-and-burn. These lands are largely confined to the zone east and south of the river. Land suitable for shifting cultivation is located west of the river, but it is 7 km distant and separated from the east bank by formidable periodic swamps. Only in the Late Classic were these difficult wetlands utilized for special forms of food production. There is no direct evidence that these distant farm lands were used by Río Azul even during the highest population maxima of the Late Classic. However, it is possible that commodities could have been shipped via the upper reaches of the Río Azul through satellite sites at BA-14 and BA-29 (Fig. 3–1).

The other factor that defines the Río Azul settlement zone is the inherent limitation of pre-Columbian transportation systems—by canoe on water or by porter overland. In both cases, the Maya may have made improvements. The Río Azul, for example, shows signs of having been dammed, deepened, and perhaps kept clean in ancient times. These improvements were probably in place by the Late Preclassic (ca. 250 B.C.). The river reportedly is navigable in the rainy season, but presents difficulties in the three or four dry months of the year when it shrinks into long lagoons. Even this problem might have been overcome by portages, damming, and organizational means, such as relay systems for travelers. In any case, various studies conclude that one moves across the landscape in the Maya lowlands at an average rate of about 37 km per day, by either water or land (Adams 1978), and, assuming a half day's walk as about the maximum that an average person will travel away from home, the figure of 19 km is reached. This is supported by the fact that many of the

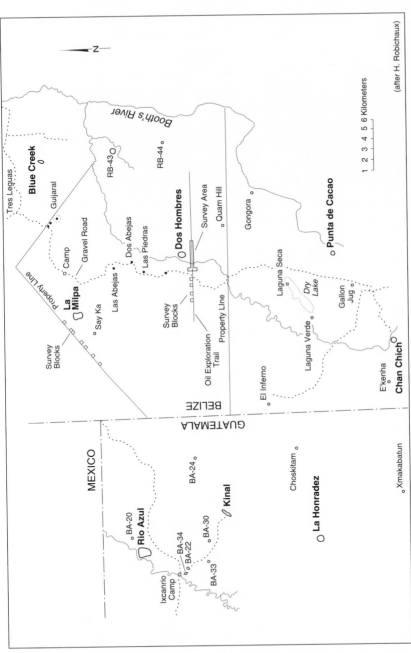

Fig. 3–1. Río Azul–La Milpa Region. This region is now called the Three Rivers Region after the Río Azul, Río Bravo, and Booth's River, which run through it. It comprises an area of about 2,000 sq. km and includes the major sites of Río Azul, La Milpa, and La Honradez. (See also Plate 1.) (Map by H. R. Robichaux, J. L. Gatling, and R. E. W. Adams)

cities of the Río Azul region are about 20 km apart—Río Azul and La Honradez, for example (Fig. 3–1). Calculating with these figures and swinging an arc that centers Río Azul in the zone east of the river, one reaches a theoretical zone of easy access of 1134 sq km. Given that about 40 percent of the surface in this part of the lowlands is one form of swamp or another, we are left with 60 percent of the area, or 680 sq km, suitable for residence, with much of the swamp zone used for cultivation. This is the theoretically defined heartland and support zone for Río Azul. The survey work of Hubert Robichaux (1995) and others in the Regional Project tends to confirm this conclusion.

Within this region the project found community types that ran the gamut from the simplest of farmsteads to the midsized cities mentioned above. Within and outside of the urban zones, we distinguished four classes of residence for Late Classic 2, the period of greatest complexity. All but the least significant houses (Class 4) were found in Early Classic. Class 1 structures, major palaces, were only found in cities. Class 2, comprises minor palaces with their auxiliary buildings, which were found in both the countryside and the cities. Class 3 structures were usually substantial farmhouses built on stone platforms and with auxiliary buildings. Class 4 houses were qualitatively distinct from Class 3 houses by their impoverishment, in architectural features and in artifacts, and their location in the least desirable zones. The status of the inhabitants was literally reflected by their housing elevation and, to a lesser degree, by space available. Class 1 palaces were elevated on major platforms, Class 2 palaces were lower and smaller. Class 3 and 4 housing was elevated more by placement in the terrain than by their artificial elevation on platforms. All of these perishable structures were placed on platforms, with the least prestigious and most uncomfortable zones being the lowest. Today, elevation gives relief from the heat through more breeze, as well as putting the residence above at least some of the voracious insects.

As the history of communities in the Río Azul Region shows, density and multiple functions generally increase as the size of communities increases. The first communities were small farming villages, soon supplemented by larger villages, which also contained religious structures and probably acted as regional markets. These developments took place in the Middle Preclassic (900–250 B.C. in the Río

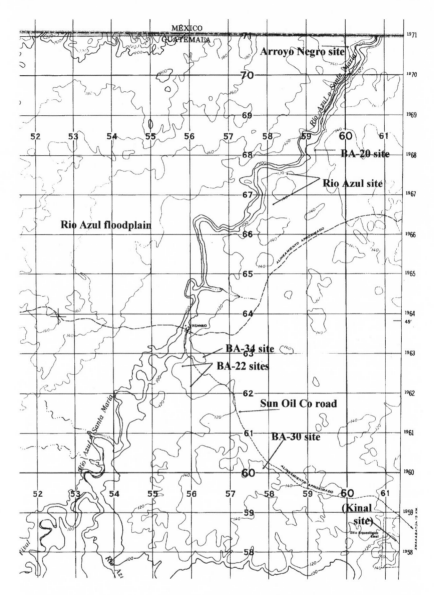

Fig. 3–2. Late Preclassic centers along the Río Azul. (Map by R. E. W. Adams)

Azul region), taking the form of nodes of higher density population and larger structures within a line of communities on the east side of the Río Azul itself (Fig. 3–2). By the beginning of the Classic, two very large regional centers existed, one around Río Azul Str. G-103 and the other about 8 km distant at Arroyo Negro. Neither center appears to have had the number of functions typical of an urban center, however.

The first true city in the region was the site of Río Azul itself, established in the Early Classic 2 period (ca. A.D. 390; Fig. 3–3). Studies have compared Río Azul with other contemporary cities in several ways, by size, by public and monumental hieroglyphic texts, and by estimated population. Their results will be discussed more thoroughly in another section. Suffice it to say that during the Early Classic 2–3 periods (ca. A.D. 390–550) La Milpa was about 40 km to the east and La Honradez about 20 km to the south of Río Azul (Fig. 3–1). During the Late Classic settlement patterns proliferated, and many more cities, both large and small, were in existence by A.D. 750 (see Fig. 1–2 and Appendix 1). Population had also surged, and rural population was at an all time high. After A.D. 900, communities of all sizes were abandoned, population declined disastrously, and most of the region was abandoned, except along the rivers.

Population history

In the above-defined zone of 680 sq km, general trends of population rise and fall are apparent. Middle Preclassic (900–250 B.C.) populations at Río Azul were sparse, with units perhaps as small as nuclear and extended families. Hamlets and villages from the period are unknown. The modern analogy would be the pioneer Kekchi families living isolated or in groups of two or three in the southern Petén until about twenty years ago. A guess of units of several dozen families, at most, is the best we can do for the early period from 900 to 500 B.C. Robichaux's detailed examination of transects 40 km to the east show the same lack of early population (1995). Population growth during the period is implied by the number of people needed to build the earliest temple (ca. A.D. 500), but again the figure can only be loosely estimated; perhaps six hundred able bodied males were required, which extrapolates to a total population of less than two thousand along the river.

Late Preclassic population estimates for the zone along the east bank of the river are somewhat insecure, given that we did not survey the entire strip. The length of the Late Preclassic is five hundred years or twenty generations, allowing twenty-five years per generation. Calculations are summarized in Appendix 2, Table 4. A maximum of about 17,500 people lived in the region's riverine zones

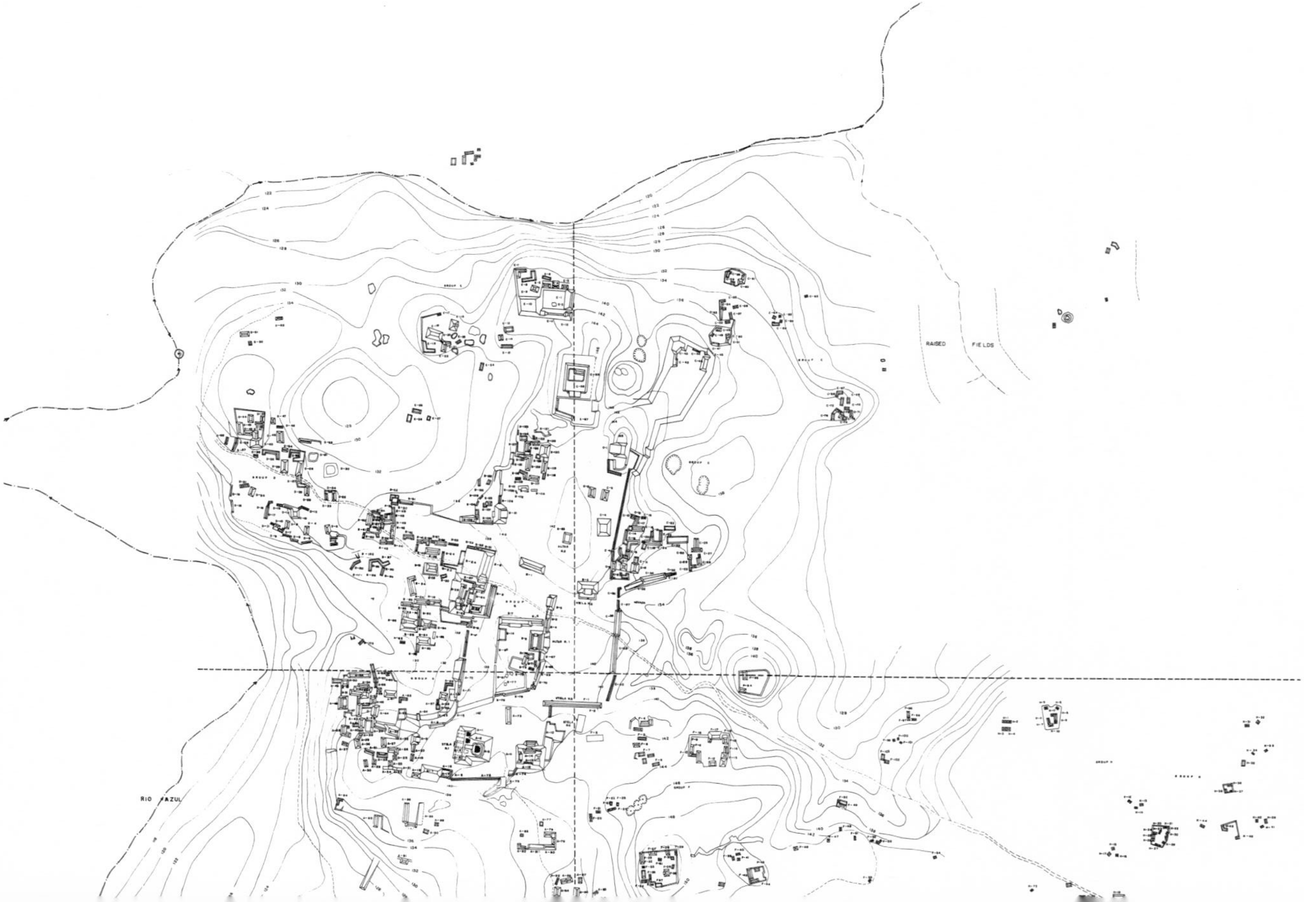
RAISED FIELDS
RIO AZUL

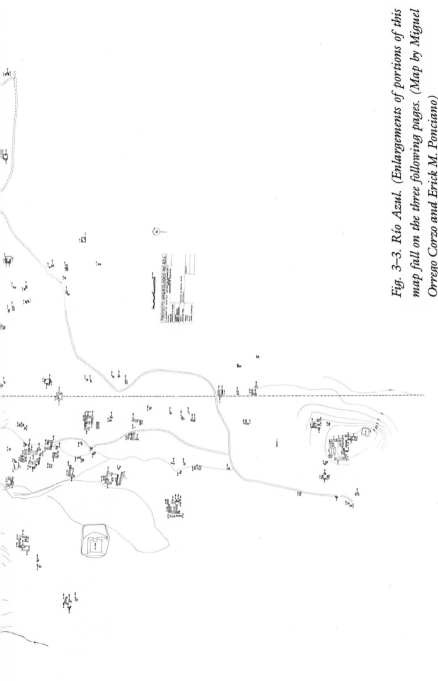

Fig. 3–3. Río Azul. (Enlargements of portions of this map fall on the three following pages. (Map by Miguel Orrego Corzo and Erick M. Ponciano)

Upper left portion of Fig. 3–3.

Upper right portion of Fig. 3–3.

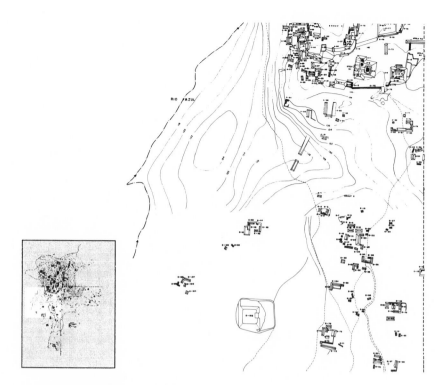

Middle left portion of Fig. 3–3.

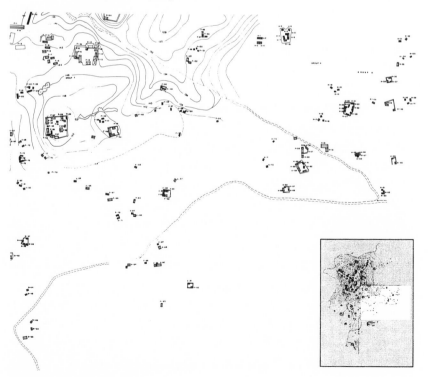

Middle right portion of Fig. 3–3.

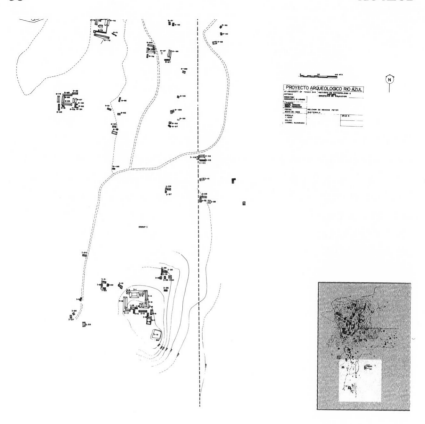

Lower portion of Fig. 3–3.

in the Late Preclassic. The Early Classic urban population of Río Azul is estimated as a little below 5,000 on the basis of water reservoir and covered space studies (Orrego 1987; Karbula 1989; Appendix 2, Table 3, Chart 2). This figure nearly matches that independently estimated from small structure survey work (4,965 people). Early Classic rural population seems to have dropped drastically, especially as it was soon consolidated into Río Azul. As Peter Dunham notes (personal communication 1997), the creation of the first cities by concentration of population into the new communities parallels the patterns from other early civilizations.

Out studies show that a drastic reduction of urban population occurred at The Hiatus—how drastic we don't yet know. Rural population appears to have been nearly nonexistent in this period. After the 130 years of regional hiatus, population growth surged strongly only in Late Classic 2 times. At this point regional population exceeded 400,000, which drove the development of sophisticated forms of wetland gardening. The latter were found at BA-20, between Ixcanrio and Kinal (Culbert, Levi, and Cruz 1989; Fig. 3–4), and are indicated by radar survey in the Bajo de Azúcar (Adams, Brown, and Culbert 1981) as well as swamps to the east. We estimate that as many as 200,000 people lived in the countryside, supporting a total urban population of more than 25,000 (7,500 in Río Azul and 4,500 in Kinal) with another 198,000 in intense interaction with the urban centers. To the east, around La Milpa and Dos Hombres, Robichaux's studies indicate rural densities of more than 177 people per sq km. Urban zone densities rose to about 820 per sq km. The period of maximum population was short, perhaps as little as sixty years, less than three generations, and ended abruptly with the military intrusion from the north about A.D. 840. Our data at the end of the sequence become vague and indicate perhaps a population level of only 12 percent of the preceding period—48,000 at around A.D. 1000. By A.D. 1200 the zone was nearly completely depopulated except for transient hunters and visitors to sacred buildings, such as Río Azul temple complex A-3.

Data derived from the population history include an indicator of ecological stress—firewood consumption. Demitri Shimkin long ago suggested this as a critical ecological factor (1973). Based on studies of our camp firewood consumption during the Río Azul Project and from observed consumption in contemporary Maya households, about a third of a cubic meter per person per week seems to be an average rate. With an early population of about 17,500, this works out to approximately 303,000 cubic meters, or about 6,900 tons, annually. This figure does not include any firewood consumption for the purpose of producing slaked lime, a necessary ingredient in the immense amounts of mortar used to build major structures.

Another measure of ecological stress is of the number of trees and materials required for construction of standard family housing (Fig. 3–5). Today's bush houses are built of poles for the walls and guano palm (*Acoelorrhaphe wrightii*) thatch for the roofs. R. Matheny (1983) estimates the use of an average of about fifty small trees per house. Seventeen thousand five hundred people living in 3,500 households (5 persons each), each having only one house, would use some 175,000 small trees for construction. With care, a house lasts

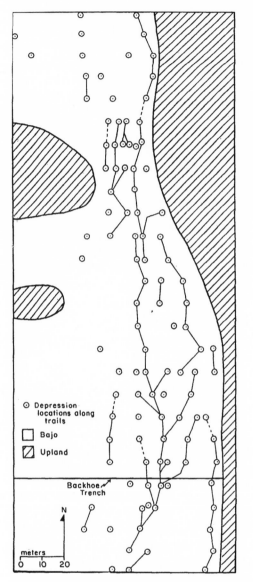

Figure 3–4. Drained field zone, BA-20, the northern suburb of Río Azul. (Map by T. P. Culbert, L. Levi, and L. Cruz)

⊙ Depression
   locations along
   trails

▢ Bajo

▨ Upland

Backhoe
Trench

N

meters
0   10   20

about twenty-five years and thus the estimated 175,000 small trees would be needed twenty times during a period as long as the Late Preclassic (five hundred years). The use of stone for parts of the walls in Late Preclassic housing at BA-20 is probably a response to scarcity of trees by that time. Thatching palm is even more rapidly exhausted, as proven by the experience in our own archaeological camp from 1984–1991. Supplying several large thatched structures that had to be repaired each year, the easily accessible guano palm was nearly

Fig. 3–5. Restoration drawing of ancient thatched-roofed, pole-walled houses at Colha, Belize, based on archaeological data. The house group was the residence of a group of flint knappers; hence the activity shown. (Drawing courtesy of J. D. Eaton)

exhausted by 1991. The substitute materials used in ancient times can only be guessed at, but probably included grass or cohune palm (*Orbignya cohune*) leaves.

Major Landscape Modification

Major leveling activities first appeared in the Late Preclassic. Large areas on the Río Azul ridge and in the BA-20 zone were flattened by cutting down into bedrock and using the debris to extend the leveled zones (Orrego 1987). At some point in the Late Preclassic these zones were paved with plaster floors underlain with grouting of small pebbles and grit.

Some slight evidence of river modification has been reported by Black and Suhler (1986:167–68), who located possible remnants of dams. Sinkholes (solution cavities) occur in the limestone bed of the river, and the function of the dams appears to have been to block off the drainage of the river into these underground cavities. The river may have changed its course in ancient times, making it somewhat closer to the site than it is now, but mainly it appears to be in its prehistoric location. If there are dams, their dating is unknown.

Swamp drainage on small and large scales also occurred in the Río Azul region; according to radar surveys (Adams, Brown, and Culbert 1981, 1993), the Bajo de Azúcar southwest of Río Azul (Fig. 3–1) is edged and perhaps filled with ancient drainage canals. These have not yet been ground confirmed, but a critique of the radar interpretation published by Pope and Dahlin (1989) has been answered (Adams, Culbert, Brown, Harrison, and Levi 1990). The controversy can only be completely resolved by further field work. The raised field system of the Bajo de Azúcar is estimated to be Late Classic, assuming that the larger drained/raised field systems would be of the same date as the smaller drained fields in the BA-20 site. Further, a line of seven Late Classic 2, Class 2 palaces were found along the edge of the Río Azul flood plain (Houk 1992).

Smaller systems of wetland cultivation have been located, mapped, and excavated in the drainage canals running through the BA-20 zone (Black and Suhler 1986; Black 1987; Culbert, Levi, and Cruz 1989; Fig. 3–4). The ceramic dating on these zones is firmly Late Classic 2 (Table 1). These low, wet, and clay-filled soils were modified by immense amounts of labor. The major features are drainage canals and large pits dug into the underlying caliche and filled with humus. We found at least one check dam, which would have functioned to slow water flow. The impression that most observers have is that some specialty crop was grown in these wetland gardens by utilizing these and other techniques and features. It is possible that the crop was cacao, which requires a moist, shady environment, but there are other possibilities (Culbert, Levi, and Cruz 1989:210–11).

There is also the possibility that a large quantity of the soil on the east side of the Río Azul was hauled in from elsewhere. Localities that are completely free of vegetation can be found on the western edge of the river and its flood plain. Such zones of thin or no vegetation are very unusual in the Petén, and perhaps it is from these zones that soil was carried in to enhance the poor soils of the eastern edge.

In sum, although leveling activities were carried out in Late Preclassic, the major modification took place during the Early Classic. Rural and food production modification apparently took place only in the Late Classic, presumedly in conjunction with the Late Classic 2 population peak.

Architecture

Middle Preclassic

The early temple G103 sub 2, with detailed designs incised in its stucco covering, is a surprisingly sophisticated feature of the Río Azul

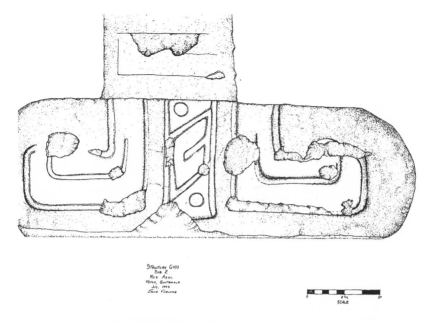

Structure G-103
Sub 2
Rio Azul
Petén, Guatemala
July, 1993
Juan Fedora

SCALE

Fig. 3–6. Middle Preclassic designs incised in plaster on Río Azul Str. G-103 sub 2; ca. 500 B.C. (Drawing by F. Valdez, Jr.)

sequence. The designs incised in the stucco covering are even more so (Fig. 3–6). At this point we can only say that the building faces south and probably consists of a single-room temple atop a terraced platform, with a total height of about six to eight meters above the ground.

Late Preclassic

Buildings from this period initially consisted of large platforms made of blocks of compacted lime powder, limestone rubble, and powdered caliche. Smaller platforms supporting perishable houses of wood and thatch were built atop the larger platforms. A series of inset stairways cut into a hillside was built at BA-20, locality 210 (Hendon 1989). Later in the period, more formal stone structures were built on plastered platforms. Two of these structures at BA-20, locality 206 had keyhole plans, and in one of them the floor was painted red (Hendon 1989:Fig. 7). A residential structure from the period had a less common quadrilateral plan, which included a separate kitchen. The very formal Late Preclassic structure, G-103 sub 1 (Valdez 1993), is a good example of the kind of architecture that dominated the city during the Classic period. Cut stone blocks faced a rubble core and were held together with mortar. Heavy coats of red-painted plaster covered the stone, providing weatherproofing and smoothing the lines of the building. From its plan, the structure appears to have combined the functions of elite residence and ritual center. No stucco was found on the building. The very Early Classic structure at BA-20, locality 205 is better preserved, and shows the typical plan of a two-room building with a roof comb, which is very typical of Classic temples. Modeled stucco decoration on the roof comb was enhanced with polychrome paints. All of these features were brought to full development soon after in structures such as the five temples in A-3 Complex.

Early Classic

Palace structures are defined as single or multistory buildings that contain residential rooms and administrative, storage, protocol, and other functional zones. These buildings do not appear in the Río Azul region until the Early Classic. The structures are oriented inward upon enclosed spaces, patios, or plazas. C-42 Complex was an early palace at Río Azul that appears to have been built in Early Classic 2 (Eaton and Farrior 1989). The courtyard around which it was constructed covers about 15,000 square meters in area. A still earlier (Early Classic 1) example is the set of rooms built around B-48 Patio in B-56 Complex (Ellis 1991). However, because this building is buried beneath two meters of debris, we did not get a good look at it. Generally, palace buildings become more complex and larger through the Classic, beginning with the Early Classic.

In contrast, temple architecture remains essentially the same throughout the Classic. It is the most conservative of architectural forms except for the increase in size, which seems to relate directly to the importance of the person being memorialized. The huge A-3 Complex consists of five temples on a very large platform with three major levels (Figs. 3–7, 3–8, 3–9). The calculated mass of A-3 Complex is over 200,000 cubic meters. Based on the work of Miguel Orrego, it appears to have been built in a fairly brisk series of construction projects beginning perhaps as early as A.D. 385 and reaching its final form by A.D. 500. The central temple, Str. A-3, is one of the tallest structures in the lowlands, anticipating in form and size the very large Tikal temples of the Late Classic. A-3

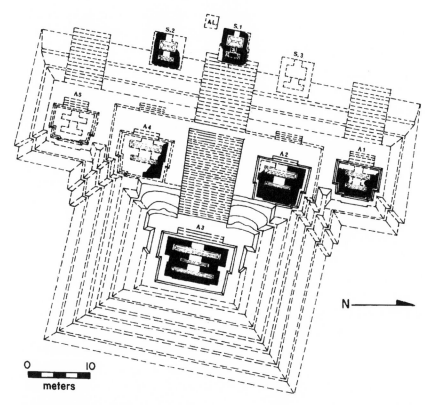

Fig. 3–7. Plan of Temple Complex A-3; A.D. 500, Early Classic. (Plan by Miguel Orrego Corzo)

Complex temples are entirely within the Tikal style of temple architecture.

In addition to the two forms mentioned above, there are a number of functionally differentiated types of buildings at Río Azul. Each palace complex seems to have one or more attached platforms, which are both lower and out of the way of the main traffic patterns. These appear to have been servants' quarters and/or kitchen areas, as in A-54 Complex (Ponciano and Foncea de Ponciano 1988) or the B-56 Complex (Ellis 1991; Fig. 3–10). Even country estates outside the center appear to have these features, as in Group I (Valdez 1990) or at BA-33 (Garcia 1990).

Still another category of buildings is what we term control or defensive structures. These are linear buildings that usually close off a complex, as do the western structures of B-5 Complex or the linear

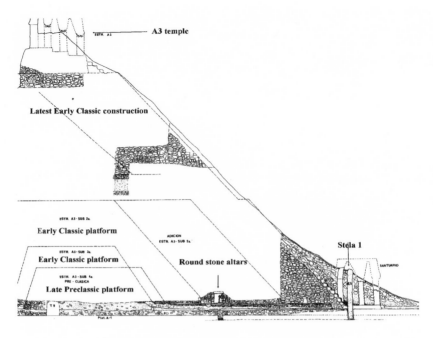

Fig. 3–8. Cross section of Temple Complex A-3; Early Classic, ca. A.D. 500. (Drawing by Miguel Orrego Corzo)

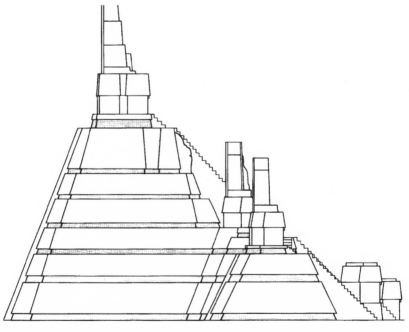

Fig. 3–9. Restoration drawing of A-3 Complex.(Drawing by W. Bruce Ellis, based on work of Karla Kletke Greer and Miguel Orrego Corzo)

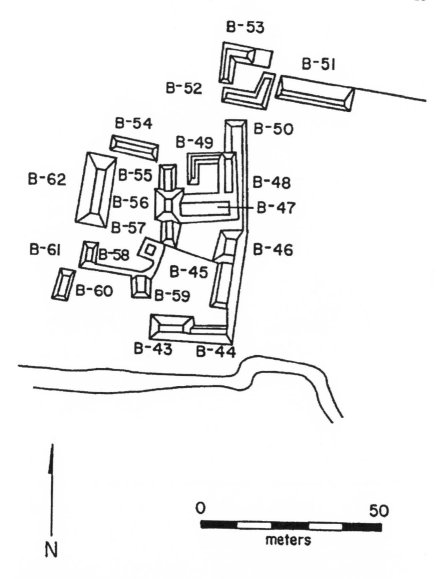

Fig. 3–10. Plan of B-56 Complex, a good example of Class II housing (small palaces) at Río Azul and further east. (Plan by W. Bruce Ellis)

buildings on the eastern side of the city. Some or all of these linear buildings were pass-through structures with narrow rooms where guards, porters, or other control personnel might be located. Other structures appear to have been simple parapets, such as those just east of Str. C-1.

Specialized and miscellaneous structures include the well-known (Late Classic) ball-court form (Strs. C2/C3), a pair of bridge abutments, and possible canoe docking zones north of E group and west of B-11 Complex. Raised causeways leading to the city are notably absent. This is probably because the river was the major route of access from outside. In this aspect, Río Azul differs from Nakbe, El Mirador, and El Güiro to the west, all of which were linked by Preclassic causeways.

When Río Azul assumed its final form during the Early Classic, all the features needed by a preindustrial city in the tropical lowlands were present, including two reservoirs. The East Reservoir was located east of C-7 Complex and has a capacity of about 5,550,000 gallons. The North Reservoir is located between C-47 and C-67 Complexes and has a capacity of about 6,450,000 gallons. Orrego calculates that the total is sufficient for about 5,000 persons in an average dry season of 120 days. (1987:50). This conforms to the independently estimated population of 5,000–7,500 people. The paved expanses of the zones between C-47 Complex and B-7 Complex were inclined toward the reservoirs, and breaks in the linear structures and parapets allowed water to drain into them. This area constitutes a water catchment area of about 72,000 sq meters.

Late Classic 2

After the disasters of The Hiatus and the abandonment, the refurbishment of Río Azul was the main architectural activity. In the worst cases, old structures were filled in and even belted with rough masonry to form solid substructures on which new buildings were constructed. Some palace buildings were constructed on top of filled-in buildings, as in the case of A-11 Complex, which is elevated and has a paved courtyard of about 300 sq meters (Fig. 3–11; Eaton 1987a). In other cases, it appears that the Maya were able to stabilize and repair walls, vaults, and interiors with mortar and plaster. The one major funerary temple known to have been built was that of Str. B-11/13, which stands immediately behind Stela 2. The Stela dates about A.D. 661, and it is probable that Str. B-11/13 was built by A.D. 665. It also appears probable that the rebuilding and repair of palaces was completed by that time.

Small-scale housing from the period has also been excavated. The most elaborate form of small-scale residential architecture is repre-

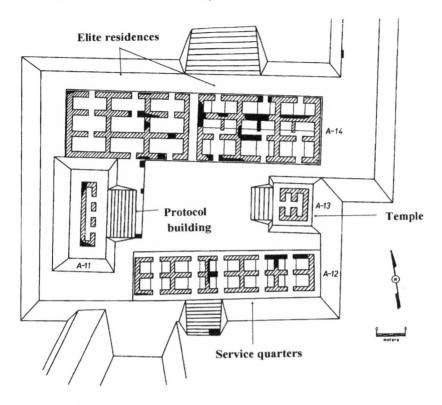

Fig. 3–11. Plan of A-11 Palace Complex; ca. A.D. 750, Late Classic. (Plan by J. D. Eaton and J. S. Farrior)

sented by C-63 group, which consists of four stone-walled and vaulted buildings arranged around a square. The nine rooms had an average of 13 sq meters of usable space. This complex was at a lower elevation than the adjacent C-42 palace complex and probably housed high-status retainers attached to the elite household. At BA-20, there are many single-family houses made of stone and perishable materials (Black and Suhler 1986). Adobe chinking and plaster probably filled in between the scarce poles used for walls and, again, we assume that grass or other palm-leaf substitutes were used for the roofs. These houses were mainly built on refurbished Preclassic and Early Classic platforms, which were finished with new plaster floors. Household water cisterns were built in at least some cases. Houses were typically built in clusters arranged loosely around small paved courtyards of 100 to 150 sq meters in size.

Terminal Classic (Late Classic 3)

The military raid of about A.D. 840 destroyed the city once again, bringing it briefly under the control of an intrusive northern Maya group. Simple, rectangular-plan structures from this period were uncovered in the mapping of Río Azul. These include Strs. F-2 and F-3, which are single-course stone building foundations with the upper walls made of perishable materials. They are apparently associated with nearby Stela 4, stylistically of north lowland derivation, and clearly a product of the Terminal Classic military intrusion. Similar structures of about the same date were found in the west plaza at Becan (Potter 1977). A more substantial building from this time is represented by ritual platform B-63 (Adams 1984 field notes), which consists of a two-terrace platform with four balustraded stairways. A tenoned serpent head was found at the base of one of the stairs, and probably was originally attached to the top of one of the balustrades. This form of architecture, which only appeared briefly at Río Azul, is much more common, larger in size, and later in time at northern sites such as Chichen Itza.

Reoccupation of Río Azul by the southern Maya led to a renewal of the city, but in the most limited possible form. Buildings were nearly all filled in solidly and used as platforms for perishable structures. The impression is that structures were spare, basic, and reduced in function. The plans of this last and most ephemeral construction have not been recovered. Because the platforms used were of the same dimensions as the maximum measurements of the Late Classic structures, it is assumed that the Terminal Classic buildings had about the same floor space. However, no information on spatial subdivision or functional differentiation was found.

Trends

As noted above, once it was developed in the Late Preclassic, the form of the funerary temple was the most conservative of the Maya structures. It varied only in size, location, and elaboration of decoration; all the essential elements had been present from the beginning and lasted until the collapse. This appears to be characteristic of structures dedicated to religious-ritual matters, whatever the civilization. The obvious comparative examples are those of the ancient Middle Eastern temples, Chinese temples, and Christian churches.

Palace structures do not appear as separate buildings until the Early Classic, when they undergo further interesting changes. Preclassic elite residences, of which G-103 sub 1 may be the best example from Río Azul, appear to have combined both ritual and residential functions. The recently excavated H Group palace at Uaxactun (J. A. Valdes 1988) is also a very good example of this type of structure carried into the Early Classic.

In the Early Classic, the palaces at Río Azul were somewhat rough-and-ready, with almost crude masonry and small rooms of irregular plan. They also lacked the masonry benches characteristic of later elite residential rooms (Eaton and Farrior 1989:172). In Late Classic 2, palaces became much more regular in plan, had larger numbers of more spacious rooms, and were furnished with built-in amenities, including benches for sleeping and sitting (Eaton 1987a; Adams 1974). Service rooms and servants' quarters were included in the complexes and appear to have followed a uniform plan (Eaton 1987a, Eaton and Farrior 1989). Functional differentiation is clear in palaces, as seen in the A-11 Complex, where there is a temple (A-13), an elite residence (A-14), an office-protocol structure (A-11), and a service/servants building (A-12) (See Fig. 3–11). Finally, it may be observed that the appearance of a clearly distinct elite residence structural type in the Early Classic probably signals the emergence of an hereditary leadership class. The continuation of functional differentiation through the Classic may well reflect changes and subdivisions of elite status and function in that period.

Burials (Tomb locations shown in Fig. 3–12).

Dealing with the deceased members of a social group always presents problems of physical disposal, ritually recognized departure, personal and social loss, inheritance, and memorialization. The Maya dealt with these problems in highly patterned ways, beginning in the Middle Preclassic. The following is not a complete and exhaustive description of the tombs and other burials of Río Azul. For that data the reader must turn to three articles by G. D. Hall (1984, 1986, 1987) and his unpublished doctoral thesis (1988). A summary article on the painted tombs has been published (Adams and Robichaux 1992), several other burials are described by Eaton (1989), and Tomb 25 is treated by Erick Ponciano (1989). The most complete study of the human skeletal remains is by Frank Saul and Julie Saul

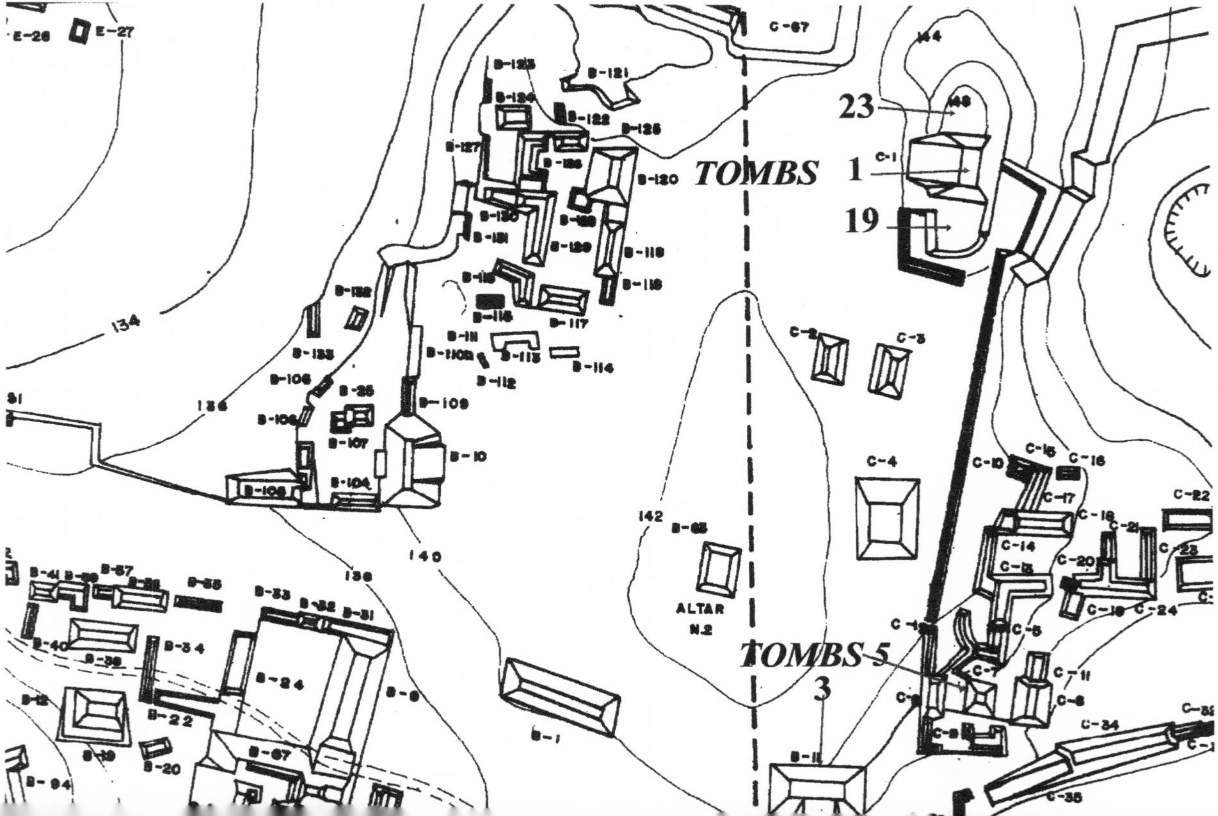
TOMBS
TOMBS
23
1
19
5
3
ALTAR N.2
C-1
C-4
B-24
B-10
B-1
E-27
C-67

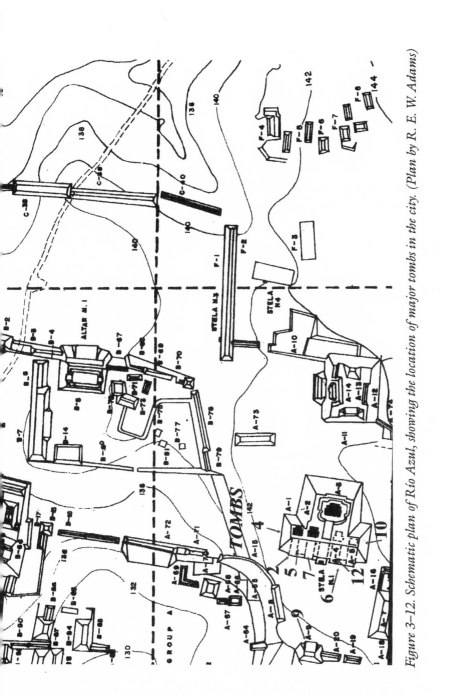

Figure 3–12. Schematic plan of Río Azul, showing the location of major tombs in the city. (Plan by R. E. W. Adams)

(1989), although it lacks some burials found in 1987 because the collections were unavailable. The skeletons from Tombs 19 and 23 are the subjects of intensive studies by D. Steele (1986, 1990).

Middle Preclassic

Although no direct evidence exists from the Río Azul zone for Middle Preclassic burial patterns, the regional centers of Cuello and Colha, 75 and 90 km to the east, have provided superb information on Middle Preclassic burials (Hammond 1991). In both cases, there were apparently cemeteries, located under paved floors in front of houses, and perhaps primitive shrines of the community. Pottery, presumably containing food, and other personal items, such as jewelry, were included in the inhumations. No clear status distinctions are apparent. We assume that the pioneer farmers of the Río Azul region did the best they could to follow such patterns and may have confined themselves to simple inhumations under and in front of the house of the deceased. No burials were found in association with the early temple, G103 sub 2.

Late Preclassic

In the Late Preclassic, there is direct although limited information from our region in the form of a burial from BA-20, locality 210 (Hendon 1989:125). It contains a body, probably that of an adolescent, and three pottery vessels. The person was laid in a flexed position on one of the steps of the Preclassic stairs at this locality. This burial may represent the earliest occurrence of dedicatory burial in the Río Azul zone. Such burials typically coincided with the beginning of a construction project and probably represent human sacrificial victims. This practice appears to originate during the Late Preclassic and continues until the end of the Classic.

Early Classic

As in life, so in death and burial the ancient Maya made clear distinctions among their members—through the ritual accorded them, the placement, size, and decoration of burial sites, and the number and quality of items that accompanied them. As in other cultures, the status of the survivors was a factor in the disposal of their dead. Thus, archaeologists habitually create classifications of burials, ranging them in type from the simplest to the most elaborate

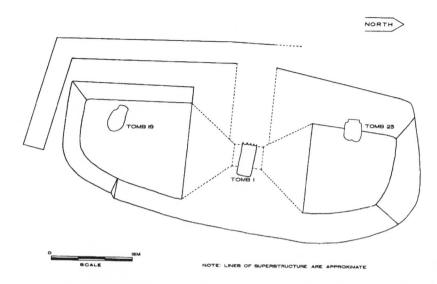

Fig. 3–13. Location of Tombs 1, 19, and 23 under Temple Str. C-1 and its two side platforms. (Plan by G. D. Hall)

forms. The entire range of burial types known from Río Azul came into existence suddenly and *de novo* at the beginning of the Early Classic. I will argue that these types reflect the social status in life of the principal human being buried.

The most elaborate burial category at Río Azul, Type 1, is that of a principal tomb accompanied by other tombs. Our only example is the group of tombs numbered 1, 19, and 23, all of which are under or to the sides of Str. C-1 (Figs. 3–12, 3–13; Plates 2, 3, 4, 6). Stratigraphic evidence indicates that the principal burial (Tomb 1) was made first, and the funerary temple (Str. C-1) was built over it. Burial of the two occupants of the accompanying Tombs 19 and 23 came later, strongly suggesting that the two individuals died later than the occupant of Tomb 1. The individuals in Tombs 19 and 23 appear to have been of high status. Their tombs were dug into the bedrock next to Str. C-1, and platforms supporting perishable temples were built over them. Dates of all these tombs are late fifth century A.D. based on Maya calendric as well as radiocarbon dates (Hall, 1987).

Tombs 19 and 23 were filled with pottery, carved jade items, carved wooden bowls, stucco-covered gourds, incised and carved shell pendants, obsidian blades, flint eccentrics, textiles, wooden litters and planks, kapok mattresses, wooden headdress armatures, feathers,

WITHDRAWN
4601 Mid Rivers Mall Drive
St. Peters, MO 63376

the remains of food and drink, and of course, the bones of the deceased. In the food and drink category only cacao has been definitely identified by chemical analysis (Hall, et al. 1990). However, judging by Maya art, corn (maize) tamales were another likely item (Taube 1989). Salvage work in Tomb 1 indicates that incense burners were also placed in that tomb, as well as a jade mosaic death mask (eighty pieces found), forty-nine perforated animal teeth from a necklace, mother-of-pearl fragments, and other items (Hall 1984:54).

The next most elaborate type of burial, Type 2, is that of the isolated tomb, located under a special structure. Tomb 5 under Str. C-7 and Tomb 9 under Str. A-9 are the only examples of this type at Río Azul, and both were looted. Tomb 5 dates to the fifth century A.D. We assume that elaborate burial offerings, including a mask for the deceased, were placed in the tomb, based on salvage of scraps of jade and mother-of-pearl mosaic, three jade beads, obsidian blades, and shell fragments, among other items (Hall 1984:57).

Tomb 9 is a large chamber with geometric painting on the walls and vault (Hall 1986:Fig. 25). A painted panel removed by looters may have had a geometric or hieroglyphic motif. The tomb is under Str. A-9, which is aligned with and faces the gigantic temple of Str. A-3 across the courtyard. Illegal excavation had emptied the tomb, but assuming the burial of a ruler in A-3, it may be that A-9 contains the burial of his consort. Unfortunately, the material salvaged by the archaeological project was very sparse and includes only a few frag- ments of shell, mother-of-pearl, and mosaic fragments. Again, a mask for the deceased is indicated by the remains.

Type 3 is the most common type of elaborate burial, of which thirteen were found at the site. It consists of clusters of bathtub- shaped tombs dug into the bedrock under a structure. Nearly all are decorated with murals. Unfortunately, all known examples of this kind of tomb had been looted by illegal excavations. At least two of these burials, Tombs 7 and 12, appear to have been those of rulers also memorialized by the temples built above them (Figs. 3–14, 3–15, 3–16). The hieroglyphic text on the east wall identifies the occupant of Tomb 12 as a certain person with the title of Six Sky (D. Stuart 1987:167; Figs. 3–15, 3–16). A piece of pottery from Tomb 12, now in the Detroit Institute of Fine Arts (Graham 1986:456), has a text on it that includes the title Six Sky and the emblem glyph

A

1

2

3

4

5

6

7

8

Figure 3–14. Tomb 7 painted text. Glyphs A1–4 are calendrical, and glyph A8 is probably the personal name of the tomb occupant. (Drawing by R. E. W. Adams)

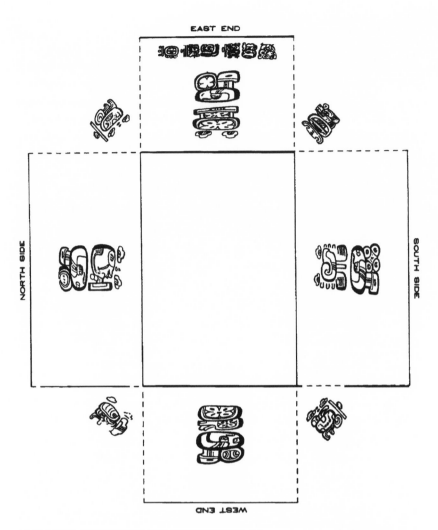

Fig. 3–15. Hieroglyphic texts from Tomb 12. The four large glyphs painted on the center of each wall designate the four cardinal directions, each associated with a major celestial body. The four glyphs in the corners are likely titles and names of the tomb occupant. The main text is on the east wall. (Glyph drawings by David Stuart; layout drawing by G. D. Hall)

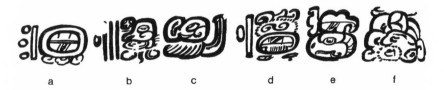

Fig. 3–16. The Tomb 12 main text (a-f), according to David Stuart, reads, "(On) 8 Ben 16 Kayab [ca. A.D. 449] was buried "6 Sky" [of Río Azul]." (Drawing by D. Stuart)

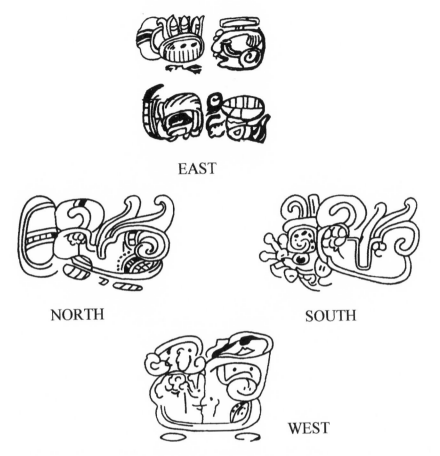

EAST

NORTH   SOUTH

WEST

Fig. 3–17. Tomb 6 murals include three variants of the witz *(mountain or major building) glyph and an undeciphered text on the east wall. A.D. 400–540. (Drawings by Barbara Cannell)*

of Río Azul. The date of burial is also given on the tomb wall—20 August, A.D. 450. Material salvaged from Tomb 12 includes human bones stained with red cinnabar, shells, jade beads, and a fragment of carved animal bone. Evidence of incense (copal) burning was found on the tomb floor (Hall 1987:148–49). Interestingly, there was no evidence of a death mask from this tomb, even though it appears to be a major burial, commemorated by Temple A-4 built over it.

Tomb 12 has an associated burial, nearby Tomb 6, which may be that of a family member who died later. Murals and a hieroglyphic text in the tomb may name the occupant and indicate family or dynastic affiliation (Fig. 3–17). The major motif in the murals is the

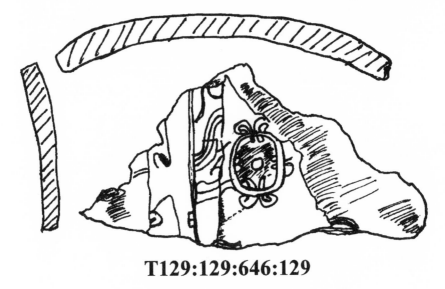

T129:129:646:129

Fig. 3–18. Wooden Bowl Fragment B; A.D. 450–500. (Drawing by R. E. W. Adams)

storm deity, a symbol found in several other tombs (i.e., Tombs 1, 2, 5). Jade and mother-of-pearl mosaic fragments, marine shells, copal incense fragments, and pieces of obsidian and slate were recovered by salvage work, which also uncovered evidence of a mask for the deceased.

Tomb 7 (Figs. 3–12, 3–14) is located under the Str. A-2 stairway and is evidently the principal tomb memorialized by that structure. Salvage work recovered jade beads, many jade and mother-of-pearl mosaic pieces, and carved Wooden Bowl Fragment B (Fig. 3–18). A single column of hieroglyphic text on the east wall gives a probable date of 21 October, A.D. 418 (Fig. 3–14; Robichaux 1990:40; Hall 1984:59–60; Adams 1984:Fig. 28; George Stuart, personal communication 1985). Surviving modeled stucco decoration on the overlying temple, Str. A-2, includes a hieroglyphic text on the south edge of the roof comb (Frontispiece; Fig. 3–19). The Río Azul emblem glyph appears at position B8a and is part of a title statement (Robichaux 1990; Adams and Gatling 1986:204–5; D. Stuart, personal communication 1984).

Tomb 2, a member of the Type 3 group, is located under the front stair of Temple Str. A-1. It appears to have been built after the construction of Tomb 4 and the funerary temple and therefore may

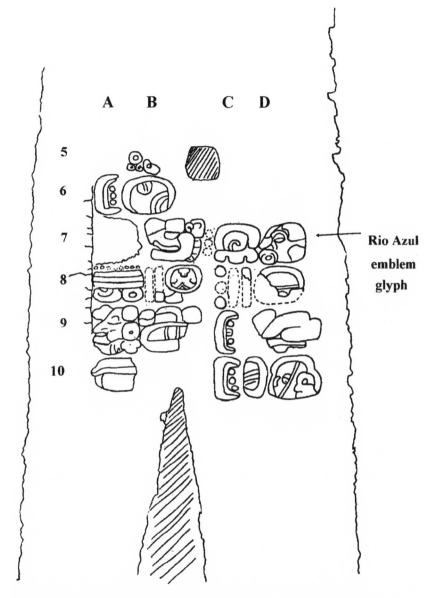

Fig. 3–19. Hieroglyphic text on Temple Str. A-2, south side. David Stuart identified glyph D7 as the ancient place-name of Río Azul. (See also Frontispiece.) (Drawing by R. E. W. Adams)

NORTH

WEST   EAST

Fig. 3–20. The murals of Tomb 2 are dominated by the images of the Storm God, albeit with a variable element in his headdress that is different in each of the three renditions. A possible date is on the right of the north wall, together with a "footprints of time" motif. A.D. 400–540. (Drawings by Barbara Cannell)

be that of a relative of the occupant of Tomb 4. Murals on the walls of Tomb 2 include the storm god motif as well as a possible Maya calendar round date 4 Ahau 14 Pop on the east wall (Fig. 3–20). The best reading of this text indicates a fifth century A.D. date. This tomb was swept clean by the looters and no salvage material was obtained by the archaeological project.

Type 4 burials are tombs located in the construction fill of platforms that once supported temples. Tombs 4 and 10 are truly enormous chambers associated with Temple Strs. A-1 and A-5 (Fig.

3–12). Their locations and the fact that the burials are the principal ones for each funerary temple lead us to think that they are probably the burials of rulers. Tomb 4 is a large vaulted chamber located above ground, in the body of the platform of Str. A-1. Unpainted, grayish-white plaster once covered the limestone walls and vault. Among the items recovered by salvage were pieces of slate-backed pyrite mirrors, fragments of jade, shell, and mother-of-pearl, and cinnabar chunks. The A-1 superstructure is badly collapsed, but it shows itself to have been a temple of the same sort as adjacent Str. A-2.

Tomb 10 is located under Str. A-5, whose superstructure is completely collapsed. This chamber tomb is entirely situated within the construction fill of A-5 Platform and is a very large vaulted masonry chamber. Among the items salvaged from the looters' backdirt and from the tomb chamber were many jade beads, over 100 shell beads, and jade and shell fragments of mosaic, as well as fragments of human bone.

Tomb 3 is a small vaulted tomb under and surrounded by the hearting or core wall of Str. B-11/13. It was badly damaged by the looters. The danger of collapse of tons of masonry kept us from working further in this burial chamber.

Tomb 25 was found intact within Str. B-56 and excavated by the archaeological project (Ponciano 1989). This was a woman's tomb (Saul and Saul 1989) containing seven pottery vessels, jade earplugs, and obsidian blades, among other things (Figs. 3–21, 3–22). The tomb is unusual in that it is oriented north-south, unlike most tombs, and is above and behind Tomb 8. The latter is a Type 3 burial and oriented east-west. We assume that the occupant of looted Tomb 8 was male, because all certain elite male burials found at Río Azul are east-west oriented (Tombs 19, 23, 1).

The clustering of several tomb burials in small mortuary structures that were the centers of their residential groups was a common pattern at Early Classic Río Azul, occurring in B-56, F-38, and D-4 Complexes. Tombs 30 and 31, found in Str. F-38, were small chambers in the hearting of the building platform. Both contained human bones and pottery that suggest that they date to the fifth century A.D. (Fig. 3–23).

Several other Early Classic burials of a simpler kind (Type 5) were found in palace rooms of C-42 Complex that had been converted to burial chambers (Eaton and Farrior 1989). Three burials were of

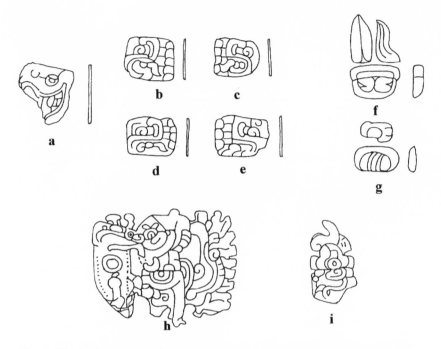

Fig. 3–21. Cache 3, Str. B-56. Forty-seven items, including those pictured here, were found inside a large cylinder jar. Carved jade and incised shell objects are from a fifth-century A.D. ritual deposit in Str. B-56. The objects in groups f and g are jade and combine to form a coat of arms that signifies the sun god. Items a-e are thin jade plaques incised with alligator designs. Items h and i are of shell, with serpent and bird elements incised on them. Item h was also embellished by small jade "buttons" that were attached to the nine serrations on the right of the object; A.D. 400–500. (Drawings by Vivian Broman Morales)

the simple inhumation type, while the fourth was radically distinct. This burial (PD-4) was an incomplete cremation associated with sherds of both Teotihuacan and Early Classic Maya pottery. Aside from cave burials, cremation was not a Classic or Preclassic Maya custom, but was a normal practice at the Mexican highland city of Teotihuacan.

Type 6 burials were placed in crypts built into stairways and under floors of temples. They represent burials of persons who were either not important enough to rate a massive renovation of the temple, or who died when the resources were simply not available for such renovation. One such burial was found under the floor of the Early

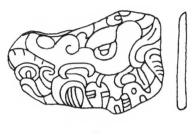 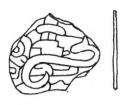

a   **b**

c

Fig. 3–22. Cache 6, Str. B-56. Twenty-nine objects were found inside a large cylinder jar, including those pictured here. Items a and b are thin jade plaques incised with alligator motifs. Item c, which is of shell, depicts what George Stuart has interpreted as ". . . probably . . . a long beaked cormorant, its body curving around the face of a man" (Adams 1986b:449). A.D. 400–500. (Drawings by Vivian Broman Morales)

Fig. 3–23. Black on White bowl from Early Classic 2–3 Tomb 30, F38 Group; ca. A.D. 390–500. (Drawing by Leonel Alvarado)

Classic 2 temple, Str. B-56. It contained human bones and a reworked piece of Teotihuacan pottery, but little else. The ceramic is of unusual interest because of the hieroglyph that is painted on it, which will be discussed in the section on written texts (Fig. 3–40). Unfortunately, we found no nonelite burials from Early Classic at Río Azul.

Late Classic

All Late Classic burials are either from phases 2 or 3.

Late Classic 2 burials are represented by a set of very simplified practices. The only elite burials known from the period come from rather small elite residential buildings or are Type 6 crypts placed into the stairways or terraces of A-3 Complex. There is a likelihood of a very large Type 2 elite burial within Temple Str. B-11/13, but none was apparently found by the looters, and the project did not excavate this building. A secondary burial was found inside a bench of a Late Classic remodeled palace (D-29).

Type 7 inhumations with little in the way of burial offerings became the pattern in Late Classic 3. Burials were made with little of the major construction effort that had characterized earlier elite burials. A Type 6 crypt was created under the plaza floor between what was even then an ancient mausoleum (B-56) and a small palace building (B-62). A bench burial was found in B-48 Patio of the same complex. An intrusive burial was made in the old C-42 Palace; a reused Early Classic room was cleared, stripped of its red painted plaster, and a Late Classic burial placed in it with a large number of pots. This burial is the exception, however, since it appears that for most people in Terminal Classic times, burial distinctions among classes had become vague except for location.

Artifacts

The products of human hands are customarily labeled *artifacts* in archaeological reports. One could regard architecture as a kind of giant artifact, but a building is a product of a group effort and is immovable, while an artifact is usually the product of one person, often a skilled artisan, and is portable. Pottery is the most common artifact type found on Maya sites, but stone tools, or lithics, are also often encountered in high frequencies. These two kinds of materials are the most common because both survive well and both were used by all classes of people for multiple purposes. Among the Maya pottery was used to contain liquids, foods, incense, and other substances. Stone tools were essential to the basic Maya technology, since what little metal the Maya had was late and nonutilitarian. No metal objects were found at Río Azul. Because of their high frequency, relatively rapid change over time, and variety in space, ceramics are used as chronological markers, as explained in chapter 2.

Undoubtedly there were many other artifacts in use that we do not find, principally because they decay so rapidly. These were items of wood, shell, feathers, bone, and textiles. Under exceptional conditions, such as the airtight environments of the Río Azul tombs, we did find traces of these fabrications. Appendix 4 provides more detail on nonceramic artifacts.

Much of this book's descriptive material on artifacts is placed in Appendices 3 and 4, making some of the bases for interpretation available. Here I shall outline some of the more significant trends in artifact styles and usages at Río Azul and its surrounding region.

Ceramics (See also Appendix 3)

The Preclassic

Pottery appeared in Mesoamerica by 2200 B.C. and in the Maya lowlands by about 1200 B.C. Thus, the earliest Maya materials were already sophisticated in form and decoration. At Río Azul the earliest pottery dated about 900 B.C., was present only in very small samples that were very similar to contemporary pottery from surrounding regions. Small bowls with gourd forms, flat, open pans, round bowls, and water jars with necks and roughened surfaces were all used both at this time and later. Cooking vessels are probably represented by the round bowls and flat pans. Food service pottery was finished with a color coating called a *slip*. Most preclassic ceramics are either uncolored or slipped in single colors or monochromes, dark red being the favorite. Black and cream were also used as finishes. The water jars were unslipped, and their rough surfaces enabled people to keep a grip on them even when they were wet and slippery. A few Preclassic Maya ceramics have different forms, such as effigies of animals or humans like those found east of Río Azul at Cuello and Colha (Kosakowsky 1987; Valdez 1988). None of the effigy pottery has been found at Río Azul.

In the Late Preclassic, the Río Azul region appears to have adopted most of the ceramic standards of surrounding zones, especially the Tikal-Uaxactun region. As noted in chapter 2, recent ceramic analysis in the Belize sites (Kosakowsky 1987; Valdez 1988) and in the Río Azul region (Adams and Adams 1991) has indicated that the older traditional Preclassic monochromes continued in use among the rural population even as the newer forms of decoration were adopted among the elite classes.

The Early Classic

The earliest polychromes appear in the Maya lowlands at the beginning of the Classic and even in the Terminal Preclassic. This category includes three- or four-colored, brightly painted ceramics with distinctive motifs and vessel forms. It has become apparent at Río Azul that in some cases the motifs relate to families or dynasties of rulers and serve as coats of arms. This would explain why the appearance of polychromes was delayed among rural and nonelite families. These motifs were human, animal, geometric, or abstract, and combinations of parts of these motifs make up a set of abstractions that blend into Maya writing. Symbolic scenes, themselves made up of symbols, led to more abstract and efficient ways of transmitting messages. Thus, early examples of polychrome pottery at Río Azul serve to express worldview, identify the possessor with aspects of the supernatural, and in some cases, identify the owner as a person of superior status (Fig. 3–24). Fairly rapidly, the possession of polychrome pottery became an index of social status, and the more excellent the piece, the higher the possessor's status.

In Early Classic 2, a series of incised and carved types appeared, many of which are very elaborate. These ceramics are mainly monochrome in coloring, although their forms may differ drastically from those of the older Preclassic monochromes (Fig. 3–23). Much of this pottery appears to have been influenced in form and decoration by central Mexican ceramics from Teotihuacan. Some of it is a blend of the two traditions, while other undecorated monochromes show outside influence only in their vessel forms, particularly that of cylindrical jars with tripod feet and lids (Fig. 3–25). Occasionally, these cylinder tripods were decorated with a thin coating of stucco painted in bright colors. Huge water jars, which must have been made and

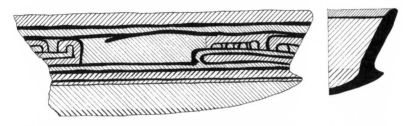

Fig. 3–24. Early Classic polychrome basal flange bowls; probable elite "tableware" for food service; ca. A.D. 350. (Drawing by Leonel Alvarado).

used in place, and very large monochrome food service bowls imply meals served to large numbers of people.

The tombs of Early Classic 2 were packed with pottery containing food and liquids. A kind of black pottery, the Balanza Black Group, was especially favored for such use in tombs, as was another monochrome called Águila Orange (Fig. 3–26). Unique ceramic objects were likely to come from these proveniences, of which the best example is Vessel 15 from Tomb 19, called The Chocolate Pot (Fig. 3–27; Plate 6), is the best example of unique ceramic objects likely to come from these style groups. (The Chocolate Pot is discussed further in chapter 4.)

As in the Preclassic, the Early Classic complexes were stylistically linked to contemporary pottery of Tikal and Uaxactun, even sharing their assimilation of outside influences from central Mexico. For example, the ubiquitous brown-black cylinder tripod vessel with a lid was locally imitated in both sites. Stylistic analysis shows that there were also definite imports, such as pottery stamped with the image of Tlaloc, the Mexican version of the rain god.

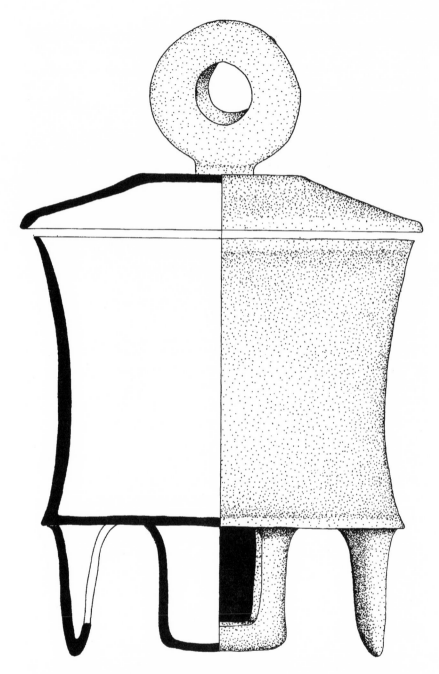

Fig. 3–25. Early Classic cylinder tripod vase; a mark of Teotihuacan presence at Río Azul. From Tomb 31, F38 Group; ca. A.D. *400. (Drawing by Leonel Alvarado)*

Fig. 3–26. Early Classic Aguila Orange bowl from a looted tomb. Note the incised design with short hieroglyphic text and a glyph on the pot in the depiction. Ca. A.D. 390–500. (Photo by R. E. W. Adams)

Fig. 3–27. Chocolate Pot (Vessel 15) from Tomb 19; ca. A.D. 480. The hieroglyphic text on the lid gives the function of the vessel as a "chocolate pot," and the text on the body states that the owner was the "counselor of a prince," according to the readings by David Stuart. (Photo by R. E. W. Adams)

Late Classic 1

Our samples of pottery from the Late Classic 1 period at Río Azul are weak. We have concluded that this relative scarcity is due to the extension of The Hiatus into Late Classic 1 in the region. The little pottery we recovered from the complex is again unexceptional compared with that of the Tikal and Uaxactun sequences.

Late Classic 2

Huge amounts of pottery recovered from this period allow us to define it with confidence. We found the same proliferation of elaborate forms as at Tikal and Uaxactun, indicating broader and stronger demand for polychrome and incised-carved pottery (Fig. 3–28). Some very attractive local innovations were developed, including one type that emphasizes a glassy black rippled surface. Another distinctive type is a sort of pink polychrome. Water jars in the Late Classic became larger, some reaching truly gigantic proportions. The latter must have been made in place and contained up to 150 gallons of water each. N. Hammond suggests that *chicha* or corn beer might have been brewed in these large jars (personal communication 1994). Individual food service bowls supplemented very large serving vessels.

Late Classic 3

The Terminal Classic was a period of significant change, outside influence, and discontinuity in our sequence. Roughened water jars and orange and red monochromes met most household needs for containers, cooking vessels, and food service pots. The proliferation of decorated types continued and a bewildering amount and variety of imported and local polychromes was found in all classes of housing. Even the water jars had elaborate rims and at least four types were developed.

Samples of potsherds from Late Classic large palace complexes (Class 1 housing) typically produce 12–16 percent polychrome pottery, while minor palaces (Class 2 housing) possess only 8–12 percent. "Middle-class" housing (Class 3) will have roughly 4–6 percent polychrome pottery, and the most impoverished housing (Class 4) have only 1–2 percent. Quality and variety also diminishes down the scale as might be expected.

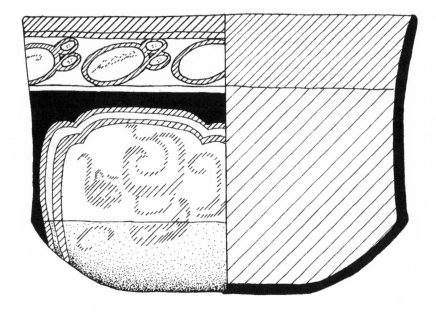

Fig. 3–28. Late Classic polychrome bowl; ca. A.D. 800. (Drawing by Leonel Alvarado)

Outside influences from the Puuc hill region of northern Yucatan can be seen in the appearance of Trickle Ware and Slate Ware jars and small polychrome cups decorated in northern style. We found Fine Orange (Fig. 3–29) and Fine Gray pottery from the lower Gulf of Mexico, as well as lead-colored Plumbate ceramics from the south coast of Guatemala.

Toward the end of the period, the repertoire of pottery was apparently reduced to the most utilitarian types: water jars, cooking vessels, and food service pots. Incense burners dating from A.D. 1000, in one case (Fig. 3–30), and from the nineteenth-century Maya in another, are indicators of visitors. Río Azul had been abandoned in the ninth century, and by the time the first incense burners were placed in Temple Str. A-3, it was falling into ruins and overgrown.

Lithics

Stone tools reflect the utilitarian needs of the ancient Maya, largely those of the lower classes. Woodworking, forest clearance, agricul-

Fig. 3–29. Fine Orange jar found in a shallow deposit in F-38 group. A trade piece from the Chontal area, perhaps via N. Yucatan; ca. A.D. 840. (Drawing by Leonel Alvarado)

tural tasks, and construction jobs all required large numbers of stone tools. Most of the tools were made of local chert, but limited use also was made of obsidian imported from the Maya highlands. It is likely that obsidian importation was controlled by the regional capital at Tikal during the Early Classic and then through the eastern sites in Belize in Late Classic times.

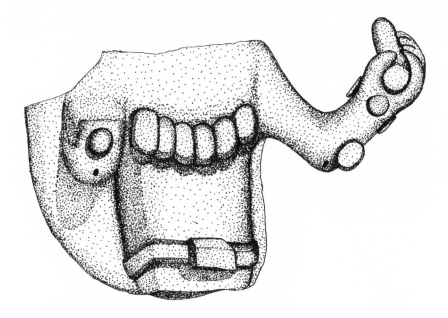

Fig. 3–30 Fragment of Postclassic incense burner; found in debris atop Temple Str. A-3. (Drawing by Leonel Alvarado)

Art and Iconography.

Preclassic

The relationship between Maya art and writing has often been remarked upon (Coggins 1979; Marcus 1992) and is evident at Río Azul, where tomb murals and sculpture were mainly supplemental to hieroglyphic texts. However, there is also a significant body of art from ceramics and other media that apparently is independent of both written records and funerary contexts.

Complex art appeared in quantity at the beginning of the Early Classic. Unlike many other sites such as Nakbe, El Mirador, Lamanai, and Cerros in the Maya Lowlands, there is only one example of Preclassic art at Río Azul, the incised stucco on Str. G103 sub 2 (Fig. 3–6). This is not surprising, given the relative isolation and marginal nature of the Río Azul region, which appears not to have been an innovative zone for Maya civilization.

The incised mirror and flanking "J" symbols on G103 sub 2 are nearly identical with elements common to the Middle and Late Preclassic Izapan style (Fig. 3–6; Quirarte 1973:Figs 2, 8; 1976).

The dating on the Río Azul structure is still insecure and could plausibly date anytime between 500 and 50 B.C. The dating on most Izapan sculpture is now placed in the period 300–50 B.C. (Lowe et al. 1982:17, 23, Fig. 2.1). Given the lack of evidence for any innovative role in the development of early Maya art at Río Azul, it is likely that the origin of these elements is from contact with the Izapan area, the south coast of Guatemala, and the Isthmus of Tehuantepec. This makes 300 B.C. the earliest probable date for G103 sub 2. The meaning of the combined elements is somewhat enigmatic, but the "J" elements may be examples of what Jacinto Quirarte has identified as the "bifurcated tongue" (1976:79), since the central element (perhaps a loincloth) is associated with the tongue in at least one other case (Quirarte 1976:Fig. 4f). The total image may be a symbolic representation of one of the creator "dragons" or serpents that overhang scenes in so much of Izapan art.

Although Str. G-103 sub 1 is Late Preclassic and certainly a ritually important building, we have thus far not been able to locate any decorative art—masks, painting, or the like—associated with it. Possibly the earliest Classic period example of complex art is that of the modeled stucco masks on the temple at BA-20 (205 sub 1). These masks are not exposed enough to reveal their subject matter with any certainty, but they may be personified wind god references (Black 1987:Fig. 49), which also may have the meaning of "breath of life" derived from the Ik day sign symbol (Thompson 1950:73).

The round masonry column-altars set in front of Str. A-3 sub 3 date between A.D. 360 and 393, based on stratigraphy and the date of Stela 1 (Figs. 3–31, 3–32). Three altars were found by Miguel Orrego by using lateral passages dug outward from the main looters' tunnel under A-3. These altars are decorated with stucco modeled into the bas-relief forms of nude male human figures (Fig. 3–33). Five of these human figures were found, although it is probable that there were originally six or eight. Safety considerations inside the deep tunnels under A-3 made it inadvisable to remove any more of the material around the altars.

All of these human figures are presented in the same pose—down on one knee with the appearance of being pulled off balance or falling. Blood is depicted flowing in a large stream from each man's head to the ground. The heads have disheveled hair, no headdress, and mutilated ears without earplugs. Each figure is bound with rope

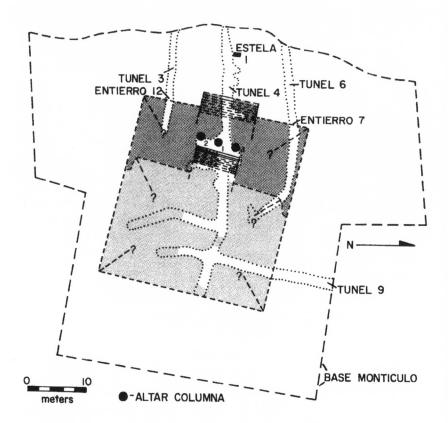

Fig. 3–31. A-3 Temple Complex, plan of buildings showing the column altar locations. (Drawing by Miguel Orrego Corzo)

around the wrists. Male genitalia are clearly depicted in each case, and the total effect is that each person has been stripped of his clothing and jewelry and exposed to ridicule. In spite of the similarity of poses, each face is individualized. Their eyes and mouths are wide open, giving the appearance of terror. An elaborate and unique glyph is bound by rope or cloth to each person's back. From each glyph falls a cloth with two tails. These glyphs have all the epigraphic characteristics of personal names and will be discussed in the next section. Incense had been burned on the tops of the altars. A ceremonial deposit (Cache 16), consisting of a flared-sided orange bowl containing a bundle of nineteen laurel leaf-shaped flint knives wrapped in rough cloth, was placed behind the altars when they were finally covered by new construction. Based on stratigraphy, associated pottery,

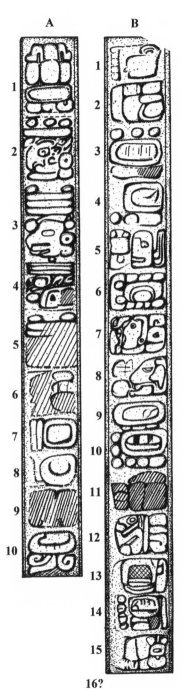

Fig. 3–32. Río Azul Stela 1, north (A, B) and south (C, D) sides, The Maya date (A1–10) and the name of Río Azul ruler Zak Balam (B8) are included in this text. (Drawing by R. E. W. Adams and Cathy Dodt Ellis)

Fig. 3–33. Modeled stucco decoration on Temple Complex A-3 altars, showing execution of Río Azul rulers. Letters designate the individual persons depicted; note the individualized glyph on each man's back. (Drawings by Miguel Orrego Corzo)

and style of rendition, the estimated date of the altars is between A.D. 380 and 392.

Comparative materials are rare, but there are other sculptures in the Maya highlands and lowlands that show captive figures in the same pose. The most important parallel is a modeled stucco frieze from the rear of an Early Classic temple at Tikal, Str. 5D86-6 (LaPorte and Vega de Zea 1988:127–40, figure on p. 139). The frieze depicts a row of nude human figures, each on one knee, with hands bound, and name glyphs on their backs. It dates between A.D. 200 and 300 and therefore is earlier than the Río Azul altars by at least eighty years, making the specific iconography of conquest and humiliation established at Tikal well before it appeared at Río Azul. An example from much farther away is an unpublished Early Classic sculpture now in the National Museum of Guatemala. It is from Kaminaljuyu, the huge site now under Guatemala City, and it shows individual captives, each confronted by a finely dressed person seated on a cushion or throne. As at Río Azul, the captives are nude, male, bound, down on one knee, and identified by associated glyphs.

Early Classic Stelae

Stela 1, a sculpted stone monument in front of Str. A-3, is chronologically the next piece of art from Río Azul. It was erected after the altars were in place and probably after an enlargement of the platform and temple. The monument has texts on the two narrow north and south sides (Fig. 3–32). At some time after the monument's erection it was deliberately battered and burnt on the front. The back side, facing east, is uncarved. On the main broad side facing west a standing figure is visible from the knees down, and at its feet a captive human figure lies prone on its stomach. The text indicates that the principal figure was a ruler of Río Azul, Zak Balam. The Maya date on Stela 1 correlates to A.D. 393.

Stela 3 is a badly damaged, large stone monument on which the carving is eroded from all but about the lowest meter. Enough remains to show that it also faced west and depicted a principal figure standing in the stiff, "at attention" pose characteristic of early Cycle 9 monuments in the lowlands. A seated, bound captive figure with personal name glyphs in his hair is seen in the lower left corner. The sides of the monument are carved with glyphs, most of which are badly damaged by weather and deliberate battering. Based on style, location, and stratigraphy, we estimate the date of Stela 3 to be between A.D. 400 and 420. It is located near two large (Class 1) residential compounds both of which existed in the Early Classic and therefore were contemporary with the monument. Later, in

Late Classic 2, the monument was incorporated into a long, linear structure, which may have been a deliberate act of disrespect or sacrilege.

Tomb Murals

All murals from Río Azul were found in tombs dating from the years between ca. A.D. 440 and 520. There are eleven painted tombs. It is noteworthy that in six tombs mural subject matter is a combination of hieroglyphic and iconographic material, four painting sets are exclusively hieroglyphic, and only one mural is exclusively iconographic. Therefore, in the Río Azul tomb murals, depictive material is supplementary to hieroglyphic symbolism.

The most elaborate of the murals are those in Tomb 1 (Fig. 3–34; Plates 2, 3). The hieroglyphic text dominates the scene because of its placement and states the birthday of the occupant, an individual who we have designated Governor X. More detail about the text is given in the section on hieroglyphic writing. The text is flanked by two pairs of elaborated mask motifs. Based on the usual stela text formula, the birthday of the principal individual mentioned is often followed by a genealogical statement. I have interpreted the masks to be a kind of "coat of arms" that designates Governor X's illustrious ancestry.

These ancestral figures can be more specifically identified given that the iconography of the upper left mask is close to that of the contemporary Tikal ruler called Stormy Sky. While a full comparative statement is beyond the scope of this book, the storm god, or the Classic equivalent of Chac, appears to have been the special patron of this Tikal ruler (Jones and Satterthwaite 1982:Fig. 41; W. R. Coe 1990:Fig. 182). Further, the tomb of Stormy Sky at Tikal is the only known Early Classic painted tomb at that site. Finally, the consort of Stormy Sky is known to have been a woman nicknamed by epigraphers Bird-Claw (Jones and Satterthwaite 1982: Tables 5 and 6); the lower left-hand mask in Tomb 1 is clearly a bird and is associated with the Stormy Sky mask above it. To the right of the stela-like text in Tomb 1 are two more masks. The lower mask bears a close resemblance to the hieroglyphic rendition of the Tikal ruler Curl Nose (Jones and Satterthwaite 1982:Fig. 41). Finally, the upper mask is clearly that of the Sun God.

All of these elements appear to be much more than happenstance correlations, especially given the historical timing. Stormy Sky is

Fig. 3–34. Black and white photograph of Tomb 1 murals. The view is toward the eastern end of the tomb, with the birth date of the tomb occupant, 29 September A.D. 417, as well as the name of the tomb occupant, Ruler X, noted. The probable "coats of arms" of the parents of Ruler X flank the text on the left, and the emblems of a grandfather (below) and of the sun god (above) are on the right. Symbols of the watery underworld decorate the rest of the tomb. (See also Plates 2 and 3.) (Photo by R. E. W. Adams)

estimated to have ruled at Tikal from A.D. 426-457 (Jones and Satterthwaite 1982:Table 6). Governor X was born in A.D. 417. Thus, the person buried in Tomb 1 appears to make a claim to parentage from Tikal ruler Stormy Sky and his consort Bird Claw. Further, Governor X, as we now call him, also claims ancestry from Curl Nose, the father of Stormy Sky, and ultimately from the sun god. Stormy Sky's successor at Tikal was named Kan Boar, and may have been his eldest son. Governor X's identification as a son of Stormy Sky and Bird Claw and his rule at a city much smaller than Tikal would seem to indicate his status as a younger son, not the heir to the Tikal throne.

The rest of the tomb up to the doorway is decorated with symbols for water, deluge, rain clouds, serpents, jade, and flood. The doorway to the tomb is flanked by two vertical panels representing mats. The iconographic symbols of water refer to the watery underworld that is passed through after death. The mat is the traditional symbol of rulership. A sixteenth-century title of rulership was *ah holpop*, or "head of the mat" (Roys 1972:63–64). There are nine panels on the walls of the tomb, each separated from the other by broad, dark red bands. Nine was a sacred number for the Maya and usually referred to the nine levels and lords of the underworld, entirely appropriate symbolism for a tomb. Red was a sacred color because of its identification with human blood and therefore with genealogical matters. All other painted tombs at Río Azul were painted with similar red stripes demarcating the corners, wall bases, and wall tops. The stripes were occasionally given emphasis with black parallel lines, as in the case of Tomb 12.

Tombs 2, 5, 6, and 25 combine hieroglyphs with storm god or mountain (*witz*) symbols as the main iconographic referents. In the section on hieroglyphic texts, I will argue that these are symbols of kinship (lineage) or of a dynasty (Figures 3–20, 3–43, 3–17, and 3–39).

Tomb 9 possessed the only painting of a completely nonhieroglyphic nature. However, even this painting may have originally been partly hieroglyphic. It has already been noted that a painted panel with an unknown motif was removed by the looters. The remaining paintings are entirely geometric and cover three walls—west, south, and north. Bands of dark red outline the walls and delimit panels on the walls which are solid rectangles, an empty rectangle, and a boxed rectangle.

Early Classic Modeled Stucco Architectural Decoration

Str. A-2, the temple memorializing Tomb 7, retains portions of modeled stucco decoration, which originally covered the entire building. J. L. Gatling and I (1964) noted that one can discern the remains of a giant seated human figure on the front or west side of the roof comb, but that it is so damaged that no details can be seen. On the south side of the roof comb is a hieroglyphic text, which will be discussed in the next section. On the rear or east side of the building is a very large standing figure with the body presented full front and the head turned in profile to the observer's left. As we observed in 1964:

An apparent speech scroll issues from the figure's mouth. It can be seen that a small (human) head is held in the figure's hand in front of his face, although the arm has largely disappeared. Remains of stucco scrolls and costume detail indicate that the principal figure was dressed in ceremonial regalia similar to that found in stela depictions. Finally, at the base of the wall there are remnants of at least one and possibly two serpent heads upon which it seems that the human figure stood or sat. The earplug of the principal figure is of the scroll type. Unfortunately the figure is too badly damaged in critical areas to permit style dating by Proskouriakoff's (1950) method, although the general impression to Adams is that of earliness. (Adams and Gatling 1964:205)

Recessed panels on the sides of the temple were decorated with modeled stucco. The motifs on the north and south sides are the same and allow a complete restoration of the design, which is that of a goggle-eyed, tusked, full front mask. The reconstructed masks shows a certain resemblance to Teotihuacan depictions of Tlaloc, the central Mexican version of the rain god.

A section of a very large Early Classic painted and modeled stucco facade was cut through by the looter's trench into the west side of A-2. This very complex facade, with an estimated height of about fifteen meters, is associated with Tomb 7 and belongs to the earliest construction phase of Temple A-2. It was anciently covered by an extension of the temple to the west. We left it unexcavated because exposing it would have made it too difficult to preserve, and our attempt to raise funds for the purpose of excavation, stabilization, and protection failed. Unfortunately, Guatemalan government funds allocated for this and other work were used for other purposes.

A very damaged large modeled stucco mask and its armature are exposed about three-quarters of the way up on the south side of the stairway to Str. A-3. There are also fragments of scrolls and modeled stucco in the debris.

The fragmentary remains of the modeled stucco on A-2 and A-3 indicate that they are only parts of a much larger program of decoration, which must have been extraordinary in size and complexity. George Stuart has produced a tentative reconstruction of the A-3 complex, giving an excellent impression of its probable original appearance (Plate 7). The only change made necessary by further

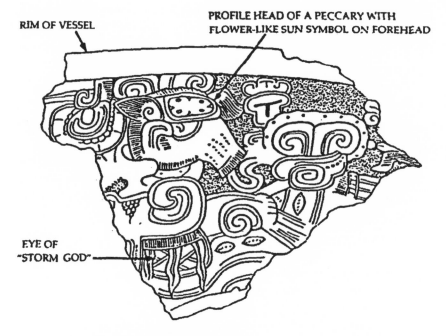

RIM OF VESSEL

PROFILE HEAD OF A PECCARY WITH
FLOWER-LIKE SUN SYMBOL ON FOREHEAD

EYE OF
"STORM GOD"

CARVED WOODEN BOWL FRAGMENT

Fig. 3–35. Wooden Bowl Fragment A; found abandoned in looters' camp. Probably from Tomb 1, based on similarities between the bowl motif and those in the murals of the tomb. Ca. A.D. 460. (Drawing by George E. Stuart)

investigation is that we now know that the inner small temples (A-2 and A-4) did not have independent stairways (Fig. 3–9).

Items of Wood

Carved Wooden Bowl Fragments A and B are excellent examples of Early Classic art in this medium. The subject matter on Fragment A appears to be that of the storm god, Chac, on whose head appears the head of a peccary or deer (Fig. 3–35). A sun symbol is on the forehead of the animal head and an Ik, or wind, sign is in front of it. Fragment B appears to depict a glyph (Ik) hanging like fruit on a tree branch (Fig. 3–18).

Ceramic Art

Elaborately decorated pottery appeared in profusion at the beginning of the Early Classic, although it was first introduced during the

Terminal Late Preclassic. Of the possible methods of decoration, polychrome painting was always the favored method in the southern lowlands, but at times carved and related techniques were very popular. The earliest polychrome at Río Azul is a type called Ixcanrio Orange Polychrome, which was made into bowls with feet that are clearly representations of human female breasts.

During the Early Classic, decoration was mainly placed on food service and mortuary vessels. Polychrome motifs range from animal and bird forms to highly stylized geometric and curvilinear designs. One of the most complete examples of Early Classic I polychromes is a water jar that we found under about ten meters of ballast in a court-yard of B-56 building complex, a Small Palace (Class 2) residential complex. The jar was restored from sherd material and is now about 75 percent complete. Fortunately the painted scene on it is about 95 percent complete (Fig. 3–36). The following summarizes the analysis of the scene done by Jane Jackson Adams (1990) with advice from Professor Jacinto Quirarte.

Briefly, the scene is that of four Cauac monsters, which appear to represent the four directions of the universe. The monsters are arranged on the jar so that they are opposed to one another. Each of two opposed Cauac monsters is associated with a parrot and a motmot bird. The other monsters are associated with a monkey on one mask, and a composite, feline creature on the other. The scene is complex and includes two monkeys, seven birds (parrots, motmots, and waterbirds), and one composite feline creature, together with vegetation and abstract symbols.

The core of the interpretation made by Jackson Adams is that the scene probably represents activity in the afterlife. Both the celestial world and the underworld are present, linked through the Cauac monsters. The vessel therefore appears to be a cosmic diagram in which various roles are assigned to various creatures. No overtly human figure is to be seen, although humanity might be represented by one or more of the birds or the composite animal. A tentative suggestion is that the birds and animal may represent totemic creatures associated with patrilineages. This would accord with the generally agreed upon theme of ancestor worship in Classic Maya religion as well as the concept of the "way" (animal spirit companions) that has been detected by David Stuart and Stephen Houston (1989).

RED
ORANGE
BLACK
WHITE
BROWN

*Fig. 3–36. Early Classic polychorme decorated jar—the "Cosmogram Pot"; ca.
A.D. 350. (Drawing by Leonel Alvarado)*

The archaeological context of this jar indicates that it held a liquid
that was poured out as a libation over a small courtyard altar, after
which the jar was smashed over the altar as an additional termination
offering. Finally, the altar was buried under new construction. The
interpretation of the scene lends some credence to Proskouriakoff's
idea that Early Classic religion was more impersonal and animistic
than it became in the Late Classic. The lack of iconographic referents
and human figures are in strong contrast to the importance of these
aspects in Late Classic polychrome ceramic decoration.

This tendency to more abstract ceramic art in the Early Classic 1
period gave way in Early Classic 2 to a use of symbols possibly associated with families and other kinship units. The best example from
Río Azul is that of a motif that we call Caal Red Polychrome Motif
No. 1, or simply Caal Motif No. 1 (Fig. 3–37). The shape of the
motif suggests the body of a snake. The motif is invariably painted
on the sides of elaborate food service dishes called basal-flanged

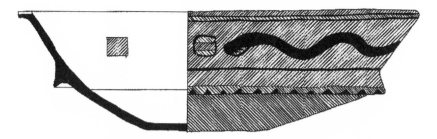

Fig. 3–37. Caal Red Polychrome Motif No. 1. (Drawing by Leonel Alvarado)

bowls. Several sherds from this type of bowl and bearing the motif were found at Río Azul, along with a complete vessel found in the tomb of an a aristocratic woman (Tomb 25). A very similar polychrome vessel was found in a woman's tomb (Burial C2) of similar date at the city of Uaxactun, near Tikal (A. L. Smith 1950:Table 6; R. E. Smith 1955:Fig. 13b). It is possible that these women belonged to the same kinship group, perhaps a lineage or a clan.

Late Classic Art and Iconography

We found no Late Classic architectonic art in the form of modeled stucco or painted surfaces. Judging by contemporary temple structures at Tikal and elsewhere, Temple Str. B11-13 was probably decorated with masks and other media but is so destroyed that nothing is now visible. No evidence for stucco decoration was found at the Late Classic 2 palace of A-11 complex, although the buildings were undoubtedly painted (Eaton 1987a). All Late Classic tombs were unpainted.

The major evidence for Late Classic art is in the form of ceramics. As mentioned before, one of the functions of highly decorated pottery during the Classic period was as status material for the aristocracy, since elaborate pottery was a valuable possession not easily available to everyone in Maya society.

There is great diversity in ceramic decoration from Late Classic 2 in Río Azul (A.D. 680–840). At one elite residential compound, I Group, twenty-four separate types of polychrome were found in a sample of twenty-six sherds. Again, there is evidence of the use of ceramics as documents of the possessors' social status; more hieroglyphic texts occur on the brightly colored vessels, the mythological linkages of families with the gods are shown, and actual historical scenes occur (Adams 1971:59–78). In some highly customized pieces, the owners of vessels are named and their titles given, and even the painter of a vessel may be identified (Fig. 3–28; Houk and Robichaux 1991).

It has been noted repeatedly that polychrome decoration of the Late Classic is highly regionalized, and that therefore certain types of pottery can be identified as coming from certain zones (Adams 1971:117–37). A few of these zones are represented in the Río Azul region. The appearance of regional styles in tombs far away from their zones of origin has been interpreted as the result of a pattern of aristocratic funerary visits. Thus, on the occasion of the death of an important family member, other members would travel long distances to be present at the funeral and bring with them offerings, including pottery (Adams 1971:59–78). Evidence of such a pattern from Río Azul is especially strong in the Early Classic, but also occurs in the Late Classic.

An interesting and significant negative example is that of the Late Classic polychrome style defined as Codex Style pottery (Robicsek and Hales 1981). None was found in Río Azul. Based on recent work by R. D. Hansen and his colleagues (1991) at Nakbe, 60 km to the west, it is now known that this pottery was made in a small part of the otherwise abandoned city of Nakbe, to the west (Hansen 1991). These codex style polychromes occur within the area defined as the Calakmul Regional State (Adams and Jones 1981:Fig. 1). Río Azul, while not certainly part of the Late Classic Tikal Regional State, was part of the economic and social sphere of influence of Tikal, within which clearly defined status items circulated among the elite.

On the positive side, pieces of ceramics from the smaller city of Holmul to the south have been found; they appear to depict elite persons in ritual settings (Fig. 3–38). Many of the pieces from the Late Classic, both imported and of local manufacture, are of exquisite quality—from very good to excellent—in brushwork, color, and execution (Fig. 3–28). They are true works of art. Most were probably burial offerings inasmuch as they were found only in collections salvaged from looter digging.

In Late Classic 3, there was a definite decline, both in the quality of polychrome pottery and in the diversity of types. Particularly interesting is the appearance of a local type of polychrome bowl with

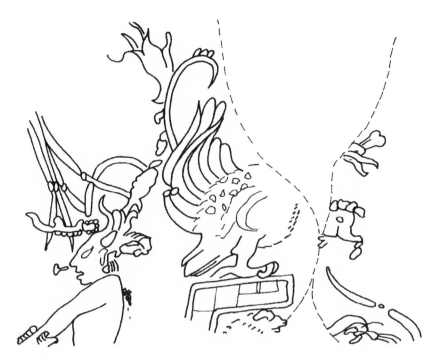

Fig. 3–38. Fragment of a ninth-century A.D. polychrome cylinder jar similar to those found at Holmul about thirty-two miles south of Río Azul. Recovered from looters' discard. (Drawing by Leonel Alvarado)

a standardized motif. The bowl is usually orange in background color with the motif in red or black. The elements are invariably a "darkened sun" symbol with a raptorial bird (eagle or buzzard) flying toward it. This symbolism may indicate the advent of a new ideology, associated with the sun and perhaps the epi-Classic "sacred war" concept. These ideas seem to have been present earlier at Uxmal, likely the regional state capital of the Puuc Hills zone in the northern lowlands. Ultimately, the origin of the new worldview appears to have been central Mexico, perhaps with the Toltecs.

Compared to the Early Classic, the body of art from Late Classic Río Azul appears to be impoverished, except for the polychrome pottery of the Late Classic 2 period. This 150-year florescence produced some highly creditable ceramics, but it must be remembered that many of the best pieces may have been imports from other zones. At Río Azul imported polychromes from northern Yucatan include small drinking vessels that are mainly geometric in

motif. Carved pottery, with an emphasis on hieroglyphs and geo-
metrics, also makes a strong appearance. Much of this material seems
to come from centers in the east in what is now Belize.

Hieroglyphic Texts

Of all the thousands of people who lived in and around Río Azul
during its six hundred years of history, only about twenty-five are
known to us by name (Robichaux 1990:113–16). All members of
the elite class, they owe their relative immortality to the fact that they
were mentioned in written texts found at Río Azul.

The sophistication of the Maya writing system distinguishes Maya
culture from any other civilization in Mesoamerica, even the entire
New World. All other Mesoamerican writings were either supplemental to illustrations, or limited in the amount of information they
could convey. Either limitation made an oral or artistic explanation
necessary to get the full meaning. For many of their neighbors, like
the Zapotecs, writing depended on a combination of writing and art,
with the texts largely limited to pictographs. Only a small amount of
phonetic information could be transcribed by this means. Only in the
case of the Maya could a complete message be transcribed without
the need for exegetical aids. A discussion of New World writing
systems is beyond the scope of this book. However, the major
differences between the Maya and other Mesoamerican writing was
that the former had developed a way of directly and completely
transcribing the sounds of their language into written form (Adams
1991:179–87; Marcus 1992).

Tatiana Proskouriakoff defined the content of Maya writing in a
brilliant effort (1960, 1961, 1963) and provided the means of seeing
a part of Maya culture from the inside. Many other scholars rushed in
to build on her work. We can now read many Maya texts completely,
and others yield at least their general meanings to us (Houston
1989). We now know, for example, that Maya texts are entirely con-
cerned with elite class matters: politics, war, ruling class genealogy,
accession rituals, and related affairs. At Río Azul, therefore, the
twenty-five "immortals" are mentioned because they were important
enough to figure in such texts.

The extant Río Azul texts cluster into two periods. One falls into
the Early Classic, from about A.D. 372 to perhaps 525. The other
cluster of written materials falls into the middle and late parts of the

Late Classic, from about A.D. 680 to 840. Texts are found on the walls of tombs, sculpted in stone, painted and carved on pottery and wood, and modeled in stucco on large buildings. Hubert Robichaux made a comprehensive study of all twenty-eight texts that were found by the project or which appear to be from Río Azul (1990). David Stuart (1986, 1987), Stephen Houston (1986), Clemency Coggins (1988), and Michael Closs (1988a, b) all have published short or comparative studies of Río Azul hieroglyphic materials.

It should be noted that the surviving body of written data from Río Azul is but a small part of the original. An example of the wealth now lost to us is the fragmentary text from the Str. A2 roof comb (Frontispiece; Fig. 3–19). Nineteen glyphs are presently intact on the south edge of this building, but it is calculated that there is enough space for twenty-four more glyphs above the intact text, for a total of about forty-four glyphs. There was undoubtedly a complementary text on the north edge of the roof comb, for a possible total of eighty-eight glyphs on Str. A2. The three other small temple buildings of A3 Complex undoubtedly carried texts as well. Assuming that their texts were as long as that of A2, this yields a total of 352 glyphs originally on Strs. A1, A2, A4, and A5. A3 is a much larger building and its assumed text would probably have been much longer, perhaps as many as 100 glyphs. Thus the total number of glyphs in texts on the A3 Complex may once have been on the order of 452, of which only the 19 on A2 have survived—a mere 4 percent of the estimated original number. This calculation does not include any of the other, contemporary temple structures at Río Azul, which probably also carried hieroglyphic texts.

Early Classic

The earliest "texts" at Río Azul may be the name glyphs on the modeled stucco altars under Str. A3, depicting the execution of five high-status men, and dating between A.D. 360 and 393. Each of the men shown bears a large and very distinctive glyph on his back (Fig. 3–33). Unfortunately, none of the putative names of the captives also occur on the stelae at Río Azul or in the known texts at any other city.

Proskouriakoff has definitively demonstrated that stelae are historical monuments that record the major events in the lives of Maya rulers (1960). Two of the four Río Azul stelae, Stelae 1 and 3, date from the Early Classic. Stela 1 (Fig. 3–7, 3–32) is directly in front of the most important temple at Río Azul, Str. A3. The text gives a date of 26 March, A.D. 393 (8.17.16.12.2) and mentions two people who may be rulers. Federico Fahsen (1998) has identified one of these people as Zak Balam (White Jaguar), who may have been a ruler of Río Azul. A contemporary ruler of Uaxactun (or Tikal), Smoking Frog, is also mentioned. The name Zak Balam also appears on the back of the "Phoenix Mask" (Mayer 1987), which is a fuschite mask apparently looted from Río Azul. A color illustration of the front of this mask can be found on the cover of *National Geographic Magazine* for April 1986.

Stela 1 is a conquest monument, judging by the captive figure at the feet of the principal person shown on the front. The monument is somewhat later than the nearby stucco covered altars, but may refer to the conquest that led to the execution of the five persons shown on the altars. The date of A.D. 393 is shortly after the takeover of Tikal about A.D. 378 by a usurping ruler, Curl Nose, who may have allied or identified himself with the central Mexican power of Teotihuacan.

Stela 3, although very weathered from standing in the open, can be dated by its style. It has the remnants of a long text on its sides, and some calendrical material appears to be present, but erosion has erased most of the details. The monument is again a conquest memorial, with a captive figure seated in the one corner of the front panel.

As noted above, modeled stucco glyphs on the south side of Str. A2 represent about half of the original text on the south side of the building's roof comb (Frontispiece; Fig. 3–19). The front of the roof comb originally presented a huge modeled stucco portrait of a human, the general outlines of which can still be seen. The rear of the roof comb also presents a very large standing human figure with a human head resting on its right hand. The text probably explicated these scenes. Although no glyphs are now visible on the north edge of the roof comb, they were probably there originally, judging by texts from other similar Maya buildings such as those at Tikal.

The surviving text from Str. A2 has been read by Robichaux as naming a ruler who appears to have included the phrase, "the younger," in his name. A fragmentary calendrical calculation and the Río Azul emblem glyph make up the majority of the remaining text (Robichaux 1990:35–38; Frontispiece).

Plate 1. Mosaic section of synthetic aperture radar imagery of the western sector of the Three Rivers Region. (Courtesy of NASA-JPL.)

Arroyo Negro site

BA-20 site

Rio Azul site

Rio Azul floodplain

Ixcanrio Camp

BA-22 sites

Rio Azul watercourse

swamp

Kinal

Plate 2. *Río Azul Tomb 1. (Courtesy of George F. Mobley/National Geographic Image Collection)*

Plate 3. Tomb 1 Murals. (Photos by R. E. W. Adams)

Bird Claw

Storm God; Curl Nose

8.19.1.9.13 4 Ben 16 Mol

Plate 4. View of Tomb 19. (Courtesy of George F. Mobley/National Geographic Image Collection)

Plate 5. Chocolate Pot (Vessel 15) from Tomb 19. (All rights reserved, Photo Archives, Denver Museum of Natural History)

Plate 6. View of Tomb 23. (Courtesy of George F. Mobley/National Geographic Image Collection)

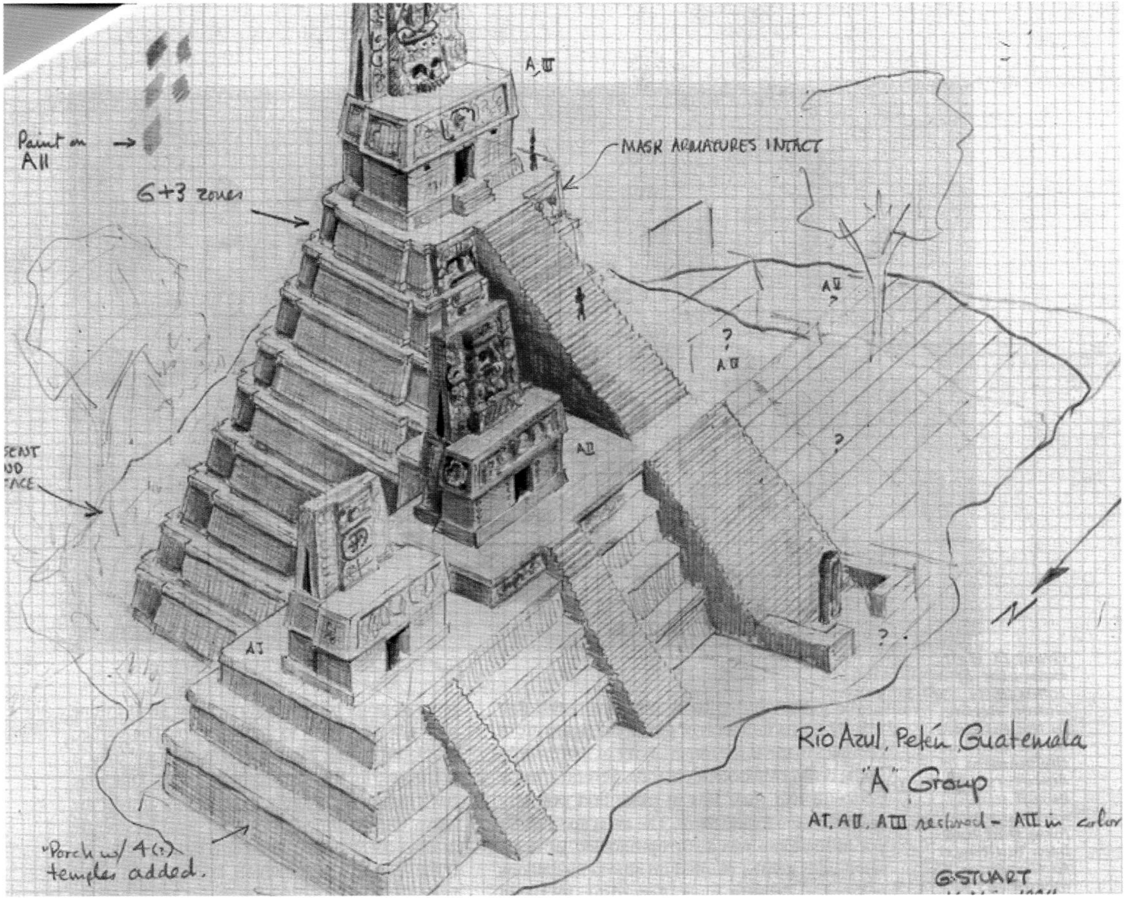

Plate 7. Color restoration drawing of A-3 Temple Complex. (Courtesy of George E. Stuart, National Geographic Society)

Río Azul, Petén, Guatemala
"A" Group

AI, AII, AIII restored — AIII in color

©STUART

Plate 8. A Late Classic vase reconstructed from fragments found in a looters' discard pile. An example of the damage that illegal and unprofessional excavation does to individual artifacts and the cultural patrimony of millions. (Photo by R. E. W. Adams)

The series of eleven painted tombs discussed earlier can be dated to the Early Classic and moreover, can be narrowly assigned to the fifth century A.D. Tombs 7, 12, 6, and 2 are all painted with texts and all are under the associated temples of A3 Complex. The function of many Maya temples being funerary, there is a special interest in the burial below Str. A2, Tomb 7. Unfortunately, Tomb 7 was looted, but there remains a text on the east wall, which appears to name a certain "Three Monkey" and to give a date of 21 October, A.D. 418, apparently the date of death or interment (Fig. 3–14). Perhaps Three Monkey was a governor of Río Azul or a member of the ruler's family. Robichaux (1990:116–17) remarks that the common use of the eastern walls of Río Azul tombs for statements of names and even of birth is probably significant. Arthur Miller has suggested that for the Maya, the rising of the sun, the moon, and Venus in the east represented a rebirth after the death of night and darkness (1974:45–49).

Tomb 12 has at least five separate texts with an additional four isolated glyphs (Figs. 3–15, 3–16). David Stuart has deciphered most of the inscriptions (1987). Each of the four walls of the tomb bears a glyphic compound that corresponds to a world direction—north, south, east, or west. On the east wall is a glyph for the sun, and on the west wall is a glyph for the night sun, or darkness. The north wall bears the moon glyph, and the south wall the glyph for Venus.

Some controversy has been generated between two groups of scholars who interpret the directional glyphs differently. Michael Closs (1988a) and Hubert Robichaux (1990:45) prefer the simpler explanation that each glyphic compound represents a cardinal direction. Clemency Coggins (1988) and V. R. Bricker (1988) prefer an interpretation in which the so-called north glyph really represents the zenith or "up," and the south glyph symbolizes the nadir or "down." The major text on the east wall has been read by David Stuart as: "(On) (18 March, A.D. 450) was buried Six Caan (Sky) [last part of name], (member of the ruling family of) Río Azul" (1987:167). The four isolated corner glyphs appear to be additional names or titles for the person buried in Tomb 12.

Tomb 12 was looted before the archaeological project arrived, and we found little confirming evidence from it. However, a vase acquired by the Detroit Institute of Arts likely originates from this tomb. It is both carved and covered with brightly colored stucco, with eleven glyphs painted on the stucco. Justin Kerr has published a rollout photograph of the vase (1989:5). Robichaux's reading of the text is that the three glyphs on the lid describe the vessel's function—a container for strong cacao drinks (Robichaux 1990:46–49). The main text on the pot seems to be a statement of ownership by a titled lord of Río Azul, one of whose parents is also named. Given the occurrence of the Río Azul emblem glyph and the name of Six Sky, it is likely that the vessel came from Tomb 12 at Río Azul.

Two jade earflares now in a Brussels collection (Mayer 1987) have incised texts that include the Río Azul emblem glyph on one, and a hieroglyphic phrase similar to one on the "Detroit Vase." The original (Maya) owner of the earflares was apparently a titled lord of Río Azul and possibly the occupant of Tomb 12. The tomb is directly under Str. A4, a temple that therefore probably memorialized Six Sky.

Tomb 6 is physically associated with but later than Str. A4 and Tomb 12, sometime between A.D. 450 and 525. The burial in Tomb 6 was looted, but all four walls were painted with hieroglyphic texts (Fig. 3–17). On the east wall is what is probably a personal name, which Robichaux reads as North Ceiba (1990:51). The ceiba was the sacred tree of the Maya. As Peter Dunham notes, "indeed, the ceiba mediated between (the) heavens, our world, and (the) underworld" (personal communication 1997). On the other walls are rather enigmatic glyphs, the main sign of which is apparently the witz or mountain sign, according to David Stuart's reading (1987b:18). Robichaux suggests that the witz may refer to buildings or locations at Río Azul. Perhaps the tomb occupant was thus symbolically surrounded by sacred geography.

Tomb 2 is located under the front of Str. A1, the northernmost temple in A3 Complex (Fig. 3–12). It is a secondary tomb, the principal burial associated with this temple being the very large, unpainted Tomb 4. Both tombs were looted, but based on size and location it is likely that Tomb 4 held the principal person being buried, while Tomb 2 was the resting place of a relative.

Tomb 2 (Fig 3–20) was originally decorated with paintings on all four walls, but the south wall painting was nearly destroyed by the looters. On each wall is a depiction of a monster face, which Eduard Seler named The Lightning Beast (1960,4:549–52). It is probably a Classic period version of the Maya rain god, Chac.

EAST

NORTH

SOUTH

WEST

Fig. 3–39. Tomb 25 texts are placed one glyph to each of the four walls and appear to refer to the witz, *which is the mountain or major structure in which the tomb is located. (Drawings by Erick and Carolina Ponciano)*

The dating of Tomb 2 is particularly difficult. The possible dates on the walls make no calendrical sense in known Maya systems. It is possible that a different system was used, or that a mistake was made by the artist-scribe. However, most "mistakes" detected in Maya calendrics have turned out to be deliberate manipulations of the calendric base date, which may be the case here (Peter Dunham, personal communication 1997). Stratigraphically, the tomb ought to date between A.D. 450 and 525.

Tomb 25 (Figs. 3–10, 3–39) is located in a small temple building (B-56) surrounded by Class 2 (small palace) residences. Two tombs, 8 and 13, were looted from B-56 by the vandals. Tomb 25 is the only burial at Río Azul that we know to be that of an elite woman (Saul and Saul 1989). The tomb is oriented along a north-south axis. Four glyphs are painted on each of the four walls of the burial chamber. Three of the glyphs refer to the witz, or mountain glyph, which also has associations with the Chac rain god. The east wall carries a distinctive glyphic compound, which Robichaux has read as possibly meaning "Nine Darkness," and which may be the name of the individual buried in Tomb 25. The glyphs are similar to those in Tomb 6, but better executed. Again, as Robichaux suggests (1997 personal communication), the witz glyphs may refer to specific locations within Río Azul.

Tomb 24 (Fig. 3–10) is a burial under the floor of the rear room in the temple at the top of Str. B-56. A vase from the tomb shows strong evidence of being an heirloom piece. The vessel is of a type of pottery called Balanza Black. The pot originally had three feet, but these have been broken off. This sort of vessel invariably has a lid also, but the lid was missing in this case. The original black monochrome finish of the vase had been altered by a thin coat of cream stucco, which had been painted with brown-black paint. The two glyphs painted on the vessel are highly aberrant in Maya writing style (Fig. 3–40). Five separate elements make up each glyph, and each glyph is a duplicate of the other. The five components include an inverted sky glyph with a spear passing diagonally behind it as well as possible jaguar spots and a shell element. No interpretation of this glyph has been made to date. It is as if someone unfamiliar with Maya writing had set down all the right elements, but did not know the Maya technique of integrating them into a single compound.

Tombs 1, 19, and 23 (Figs. 3–12, 3–13) are all physically associated with one another and with Structure C1, a large temple building. All these burials contain glyphic material, either painted on the walls or on pottery. Tomb 1 (Fig. 3–34 and Plates 2, 3) was looted and, unfortunately, we found only a small amount of material from the floor of the burial chamber. The hieroglyphs are framed in the manner of a stela text (Plate 2) on the east wall of the tomb and present a Maya date which is equivalent to 27 September, A.D. 417. Some lunar information is also given. The text states that the date is that of the birth of a certain person whose name is given. There is controversy among the epigraphers about the exact phonetic equivalent of this name, and therefore I have simply called him Governor X. As noted before, the elaborated masks on either side of the main text probably represent the parents, the grandfather, and the sun god ancestor of Governor X. Its identical symbolism suggests that Wooden Bowl Fragment A (Fig. 3–35) probably comes from Tomb 1.

Fig. 3–40. Photo of hieroglyphic text from modified (heirloom) Balanza Black pot from Tomb 24, under the temple floor of Str. B-56. (Photo by R. E. W. Adams)

Fortunately, a text from associated Tomb 19 gives more data about Governor X. Tomb 19 was discovered, undisturbed, by the archaeological project. Symbols of rulership and power were painted on the tomb's walls (Plate 4), but the major text from Tomb 19 is found on Vessel 15, The Chocolate Pot (Plate 5, Figs. 3–27, 3–41). This ceramic vessel is of unusual form. It is a small jar with a lid, which has a flange lock in it. The lid had six stucco medallions on it, each painted with a glyph. On the body were originally nine stucco medallions painted with glyphs, of which seven remain. David Stuart (1986, 1987) has interpreted the text in the following manner. The lid text can be paraphrased as: "This vessel is for the containing of two kinds of chocolate drink." Analysis of brown powder from the closed vessel by chemists at Hershey Foods Corporation confirms that the powder was definitely the residue of cacao, or chocolate (Hall et al. 1990). The text on the jar is less clear. It refers to "an advisor to a prince" as the owner of the pot. This is taken to mean that the owner of the pot was the occupant of Tomb 19. The prince referred to is probably Governor X, who is buried in adjacent Tomb 1.

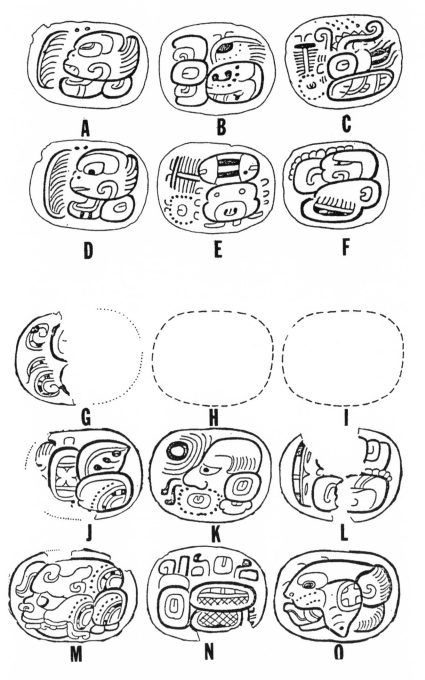

Fig. 3–41. Tomb 19 Vessel 15 text; Chocolate Pot texts. (See legend for Fig. 3–27.) (Drawings by George and David Stuart)

Tomb 19 also contained Vessel 17, a gourd covered with an eggshell-thin coating of blue-tinted stucco. Six glyphs were delicately painted on the stucco (Fig. 3–42). The text is extremely difficult to deal with, but Robichaux thinks that the general import concerns a ritual having to do with an anniversary date (1990: 89–91). The vessel itself may have been intended to hold blood or incense pellets.

Tomb 23, on the other side of Governor X's burial, contained only two glyphic elements, both painted on a rock protruding from the ceiling of the chamber (Plate 6). Following George Stuart (Adams 1987a:24), Robichaux (1990:96) interprets these elements as the portraits of the Moon Goddess above and the Earth Monster below.

A small temple building similar to B-56, Str. C-7, contains Tomb 5. This is a very deep shaft-and-chamber tomb with nine glyph groups painted on the walls (Fig. 3–43). Considerable damage was caused to the texts by the looters. Stratigraphic and comparative evidence dates Tomb 5 to between A.D. 400 and 450. No Maya date is discernible in the confused mélange of affixes, small heads, painted representations of human footprints, and Maya numerals spattered on the walls. The west wall displays a Lightning Beast with the mountain glyph in its headdress. Robichaux suggests that abbreviated forms of the mountain glyph may be a reference to Chac, the rain god (1990:99). To the left of the Chac is a glyphic symbol that is generally used to designate the half-Katun, or ten-year period ending, but is also occasionally used to mark the half-Baktun, or two hundred-year period. If the former is meant, there is a possibility that a date of 30 January, A.D. 426 is referred to.

Tomb 17 is a small tomb in a small temple structure in a Class 2, or small palace, residential compound. Looters emptied it prior to 1981. A badly faded text is on the east wall of the burial chamber (Fig. 3–44). Robichaux reads it tentatively as "Stormy Sky, Lord . . . Sky Bone" (1990:102–3). This may be a person's name, as is the case with the other Río Azul tombs in which personal name phrases were placed on the east wall. That the tomb was painted and evidence from some diagnostic pottery salvaged from the looting of the burial indicates a fifth century A.D. date.

Fig. 3–42. An elegant but enigmatic set of glyphs painted on stucco medallions that were originally on a gourd vessel (Vessel 17) in Tomb 19. (Drawing by G. D. Hall)

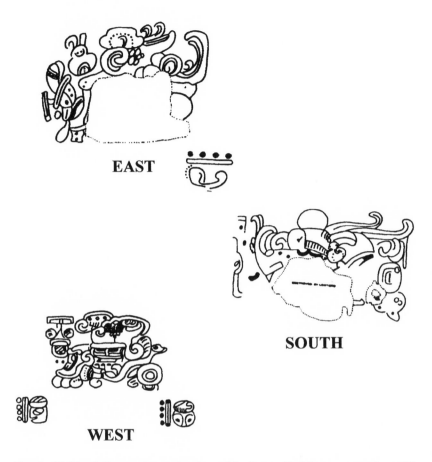

Fig. 3–43. Tomb 5 murals are dominated by Storm God images, together with enigmatic glyphs and numerical coefficients; A.D. 400–450. (Drawings by Barbara Cannell)

Late Classic

Stela 2 stands in front of Str. B11-13—inside a shrine at the foot of the stairway of this massive temple. The stela is carved on all four sides (Figs. 3–45, 3–46). The monument was discovered, recorded and partially published by Ian Graham (1984). Graham furnished his finished drawings to Robichaux, who has worked on the complete text. S. D. Houston (1986) partially deciphered the text but did not do a comprehensive analysis of the whole inscription.

The monument is of very soft limestone, and the sculpted scene on the south side has especially suffered from exposure to the elements.

EAST

Fig. 3–44. The Tomb 17 test is on the east wall of the tomb in a building in a remote part of Río Azul. The text is enigmatic, but the upper left glyph appears to refer to the sky. Early Classic period. (Drawing by R. E. W. Adams)

Graham found pieces of modeled stucco from the stela, which indicated that even when it was new, it was necessary to fill in defective or especially soft parts of the stone shaft. The remains of the scene on the south face show a standing male figure with a prostrate captive at his feet. The west, east, and north sides are carved with hieroglyphs. Robichaux calculates that there is space for a total of thirty-two glyphs on the east and west sides, but notes that only nineteen glyphs remain. The north side has twenty-two glyphs, all of which are readable.

Houston (1986:Fig. 8) has read the date of the monument to be 8 December, A.D. 661, but this now seems likely to be the birthdate of the ruler mentioned later in the text (Robichaux 1997). The

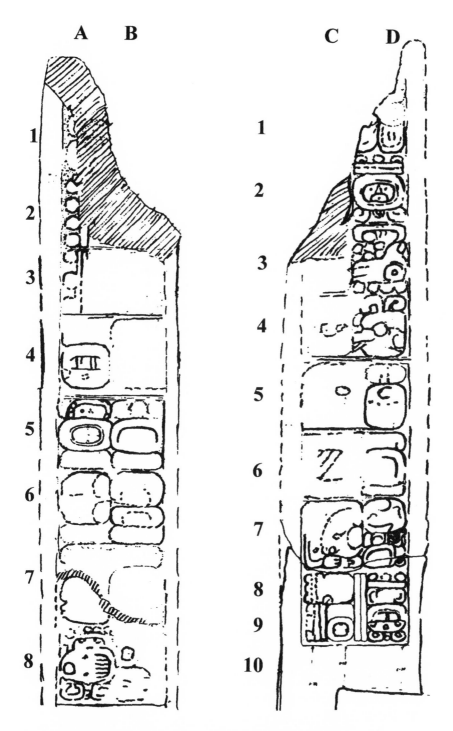

Fig. 3–45. Stela 2 hieroglyphic texts from the north (A–B) and south (C–D) sides. (Drawings by Ian Graham, from controlled-light photos)

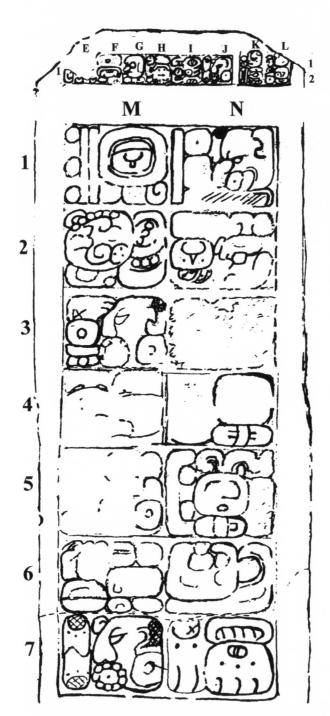

Fig. 3–46. Stela 2 text on the rear (north) of the monument. The text is long and difficult, but Robichaux considers that the A.D. 661 date on the monument is likely the birth day of the ruler depicted on the front. The Stela was probably erected later, perhaps as late as ca. A.D. 690. (Drawings by Ian Graham, from controlled-light photos)

dedicatory date, however, is surely after this, since the activities of the ruler are also mentioned. Robichaux suggests that the dedicatory date may be c.a. A.D. 690. The text appears to record the accession to power of a local ruler, who we call Governor Z, and to give data on his genealogy. The ruler is named, as are his father and his mother. Robichaux notes that a visit from a personage of La Milpa, 40 km to the east, is also mentioned on the stela (1997). The sculptor of the monument is named as Ah Zactel, or He of the White-Crested Bird, perhaps indicating that the artist himself was a member of the nobility. The Río Azul ruler is referred to by the title of *u-ha-chi'l* or His Utmost. Governor Z also is referred to as a *Batab*, a Maya title for a subordinate ruler, and his name is associated with the Río Azul emblem glyph. This ruler was possibly attempting to establish himself as an independent ruler, but, alternatively, may have been allied to the ruler of La Milpa. No mention is made of either the Tikal dynastic record or the contemporary ruler of Tikal (Robichaux 1997).

Kerr Vessel #1383 is a ceramic vessel apparently looted from Río Azul and now in a private collection. A rollout photograph has been published by Justin Kerr (1989:5). S. D. Houston (1986) has linked the text on the vase to that of Stela 2 because of the appearance of Governor Z's mother's name on the vase. Her mother, the grandmother of Governor Z, is also mentioned, extending the genealogy back another generation. Legitimacy of rulership was part of the reason for such emphasis on specification of kinship among the Classic Maya.

Stela 4 is the final monument at Río Azul and, although crude in execution, is of great interest because of its possible association with the art style common at the Early Postclassic city of Chichen Itza, to the north. Two glyphs are incised on the monument and these are similar to a glyph that appears at Chichen Itza (Fig. 3–47; Kelley 1976:Fig. 72, 73).

Summary

Of the twenty-eight texts presently known to be from Río Azul, many more are from the Early Classic than from the Late Classic. This fits very well with the other evidence from the site and region for an especially strong Early Classic florescence. Given that the hieroglyphic texts from Río Azul probably represent less than 5 percent of the

Fig. 3–47. Río Azul Stela 4 is a very late Late Classic monument, ca. A.D. *840 or later. The style of the monument owes more to the Early Postclassic style of Chichen Itza than to the Late Classic monuments of the Petén. (Drawing by R. E. W. Adams and Cathy Dodt Ellis)*

original body of material, it is not surprising that we can reconstruct only an incomplete and ambiguous history. This cautionary tale should warn us against reconstructions of Maya culture that are almost exclusively based on decipherments of hieroglyphic texts. The reconciliation of *all* data is needed for proper reconstruction; such an exercise is the subject of the next chapter.

CHAPTER 4

THE ARCHAEOLOGICAL RECORD, 2
Primary Implications

IT MAY APPEAR TO BE an act of hubris to attempt an anthropology of Río Azul and its people, given the limitations of the archaeological record. Yet if we do not make such attempts, archaeology as a part of anthropology can only be seen as a very limited, highly technical study of material culture and its evolution. In any given instance, we must go beyond those limitations and attempt to breath life into the culture that created the material remains.

Like the man who had been speaking prose without knowing it, most people in civilized societies unknowingly spend their energies creating and operating cultural institutions. The concept is one which is familiar in a kind of folk classification which we all use: politics, society, religion, and so forth. Anthropology has formalized these categories into institutions which, taken together, form the whole of any culture. I will use this device to examine the various kinds of ancient activities that we have found at Río Azul and to come up with a few basic institutions, based on evidential logic, analogy, and historical parallelisms.

Kinship

The most basic of cultural institutions is that of the family and the larger groups based on it. Our evidence for kinship organization comes from three sources: ethnology, archaeology, and linguistics. The Maya were and are a patrilineal society, its families tracing their descent through the father's line. This was as true in the colonial period (1540–1821) (Roys 1972:33–36) as it is in the ethnographic villages of today. William Haviland has made several studies of the data from Tikal (1968, 1977) and has concluded that all information indicates that the Maya were patrilineal through the Classic period. This seems to have been the case both for the elite and the commoners. N. A. Hopkins has reached the same conclusion from his studies of Maya languages (1988), although he suggests considerable variability, especially among elites who maximized legitimacy from both sides of their ancestry.

The record at Río Azul also indicates that, for the elite, information from both sides of the family was recorded. Governors X and Z both mention their mothers, and Governor Z's mother's mother is also mentioned in another text. This goes against the received wisdom that the elite were strictly patrilineal, but it may be that this practice was more widespread than we had supposed. When power is involved, all possible buttresses to legitimacy will be called upon. However, it should be noted that all known rulers at Río Azul were males. Elsewhere we do find women rulers, but we do not yet know whether they were political leaders in their own right or regents standing in for young sons, nor do we understand what impact their status may have had on elite geneologies.

Clues about how they traced their lineage can be found in the Maya organization of living space. Minor palace groups such as B-56 have as many as twenty-two small platforms that supported buildings having a variety of functions. Food preparation, storage, religious activities, mortuary, and residential are all included, but the latter function was predominant. Excavations elsewhere suggest that each small platform and residential building represented a household and, likely, a family. Perhaps as many as ten or twelve families lived together in B-56 group. This seems to include servant and artisan families, who appear to have lived near elite groups, albeit on the outskirts of the elite housing groups.

In any case, allowing for about an equal number of servants for each elite family we can estimate that perhaps as many as five or six related families lived together. This is a pattern typical of kinship groups that emphasize unilineality in their genealogical reckoning, regardless of whether they emphasize the fathers' or mothers' lines. Since the Maya are patrilineal today, in the colonial period, and in the Late Postclassic, it seems probable that they had the same kinship arrangements in the Classic period, as Haviland has argued.

The small groups of house platforms in the Maya lowland countryside show the same pattern of groupings ranging from three to six in number. Artifacts dug from these platforms indicate commoner status. It is assumed that there were few, if any, servants attached to these groups, which suggests that they were patrilineal descent groups.

Social Structure

Fred Valdez's discovery of the Middle Preclassic pyramid at Río Azul has several implications. It indicates that the organization of Maya society was sufficient to build a sophisticated temple structure by at least 300 B.C. It also suggests that society had already evolved beyond an egalitarian, ranked society in which people gained status by their achievements. Indeed, there is evidence that status was already being ascribed to people based on their family backgrounds, which is the basis for an aristocratic society. Maya social structure was certainly headed by a hereditary aristocracy by the Late Preclassic, and perhaps even by the Middle Preclassic as Hansen's findings at Nakbe (1991) and Valdez's at Río Azul (1993) suggest. In any case, by the time of the Late Preclassic, Maya social structure had assumed the basic form it would hold for the next seven hundred years.

Classic-period social structure appears to have been a mixture of a caste and class society (Adams 1970). A caste is a frozen class into which one enters only by birth. This was the case with the hereditary elite. It was impossible for a member of any other class to join it, sealing the elite class off from the rest of Maya society. The seal was created by the identification of elite ancestors with certain gods, as is shown in the genealogy of Governor X. Within the elite, there were apparently subdivisions based on whether one belonged to the current ruling family or not. A family distinguished merely by collateral ancestry would have been second-level aristocrats. We know from historical records from Yucatan that such lower nobility were used to fill political positions, such as state administrators or regional and district governors (Roys 1972).

All social divisions are ultimately based on status groupings. The next levels of this society were exalted because of their associations with the elite class. Such people may have been persons of nonelite birth, but who had certain esteemed talents, such as abilities in mathematics, in writing, or in the creation of prized works of art. Thus sculptors, ceramists, scribes, mathematicians, and others of ability might rise to higher status. Likewise, counselors and lower-level administrators might achieve status through their careers.

Personal servants and other service personnel attached to large palaces and religious establishments may have formed a third class. They also profited by virtue of their connection to the elite classes.

Housing for service people attached to the Late Classic 2 A-11 Palace Complex was relatively sumptuous (Eaton 1987a:83–84). Service specialities that we know of from chronicles, but for which there is no direct archaeological evidence, include herbal healers and diviners, who may have been the same people. They may have fit into the third level as well.

The mass of the population formed the fourth class, which was largely made up of farmers and part-time construction workers. The skills needed to make dwellings from jungle materials are readily adaptable to creating scaffolding for construction projects. Moving masses of materials, mixing mortar, quarrying stone and shaping it, building walls of stone and mortar, plastering, and the myriad other construction tasks would have been well within most Maya men's capabilities. Specialized tasks, such as laying out the structure, planning and supervising the construction, and building vaults, were presumably higher-status jobs. Hunters may have also been specialists, and it is possible that guides and hunters, something like Scottish *ghillies*, were attached to noble households. Perhaps such specialties created subdivisions within the fourth social class.

A fifth social class appears to have been the impoverished, who may have done the inevitably dirty, dangerous, or brute tasks for society. Such work would have included acting as porters, litter bearers, diggers of ditches, haulers of water, paddlers of canoes, and gatherers of firewood. Collectors of nightsoil for fertilizer were evidently a despised class among the Aztecs, and might well have existed among the Maya.

Economics

There were several classes of economic activity among the Maya. The basic categories fall into the general class of subsistence activities—the raising and gathering of food. As we have seen, early on these tasks became specialized, soon ranging from the relatively simple cycle of slash-and-burn to the infinitely more complex forms of irrigation cultivation. Perhaps 75 percent of the Maya population was involved in this work during the Classic period.

Specialty crops probably evolved early in the Maya lowlands, particularly cacao, incense (copal), and medicinal herbs, all of which could be used for local consumption. Later the cultivation of these crops expanded on the basis of long-distance trade and became export items.

Marketing and exchange systems developed rapidly during the Preclassic. Many items not native to the Maya lowlands were introduced, including obsidian from the Guatemalan Highlands and jade from the Motagua River zone. Perishable materials must have been imported also, including quantities of cacao, which grows more easily in the southeastern lowlands.

Thus, there were two exchange systems, the most basic being the internal redistribution of common agricultural commodities: corn, beans, squash, fruits, roots, herbs, firewood, and other products and gathered materials. Locally manufactured items, such as utility pottery, simple wooden furniture, mats, basketry, net bags, and common cloth, also would have circulated through villages and hamlets. There is no firm evidence on the nature of such exchange early in the Preclassic. Itinerant merchants may have traveled from village to village, or regional markets may have centered on the larger villages. Both patterns are found in the Maya Highlands today.

There is little doubt that by the time of the Late Preclassic, there were formal markets operated in association with religious structures. These newer exchange centers did not supersede, but complemented the older village markets, probably handling the more exotic materials and most of the imports, such as salt from the north Yucatec coast and dried fish and ornamental shells from the seas around the peninsula, as well as the previously mentioned materials. It is likely that the new markets were sponsored by the elite.

By the time the elites and new markets appeared, there had also emerged a group of artisans who made most of their livelihood by their skilled labor. These craft specialties began in the Late Preclassic and possibly earlier. Most of the Classic period specialties were extant by the Late Preclassic, although some, such as makers of polychrome pottery, were only to blossom in the Classic.

A crucial question about these artisans is how they were organized in society. Were they artisan families attached to noble families? Were they independent operators living in relatively affluent, but nonelite circumstances? Were there independent artisan villages, such as exist today in the highlands of Guatemala and Chiapas?

In the Late Classic Río Azul region, we find lower-class housing bunched near elite palaces. Further, these humbler residences show evidence of considerable artisan activity such as polychrome pottery making. This suggests that artisans may have been attached to noble households in a patron-client relationship. Reciprocal obligations between classes are typical of generalized feudal societies (Adams and Smith 1981; Coulborn 1956), where the horizontal relationships tend to be along kinship lines within classes. Thus it is not out of the question to imagine a period of feudal society for the Classic Maya.

Assuming this were so, then the products of skilled artisans in Maya society would be tightly controlled by patron elite families. Therefore work might be initiated on the basis of commission rather than on the basis of supply-demand market operations.

Archaeological work at Río Azul detected one building complex that appears to have been suitable for a formal market/warehouse area. This is Group E in the northern edge of the site (Fig. 3–3), a series of quadrangles formed by major buildings. Unfortunately, we neither tested nor otherwise excavated this area, but we can tell that it is similar to the probable market building at Tikal, Str. 5E-32 (W. R. Coe 1967:map). Its location also suggests such a function; it is on the river at the first point where a canoe coming from Chetumal Bay on the Caribbean coast would enter the city. Black and Suhler (1986:168) noted some broad stone stairs descending from the level of the main buildings to the river. These could have made a suitable landing for both people and cargo. The major buildings could have been permanent warehousing and administrative offices, with space in the courtyards for thatched roof shelters and secure storage.

There is little doubt that the state and its political units controlled external trade during the Classic period. Group E at Río Azul, with its major community construction investment, conforms to the expectations of such a model of Maya exchange systems. Linkage to the social structure is of course apparent, in that it is certain that the aristocracy controlled both political and economic structures. Thus, it is to political organization that we now turn.

Political Structures

Politics provide for the allocation of authority and power within a society. Administration is a mechanism through which authority and power is exercised. Therefore, if administrative arrangements can be defined archaeologically, it is also possible to also define the political system.

A major function of cities is to serve as administrative centers. In civilized societies, the principle of hierarchy is well-developed. Generally speaking, ever larger cities wield ever more power in modern and historical cultures, and there is reason to believe that it was so in the prehistoric past. However, it is not necessary to appeal solely to a principle of uniformitarianism to confirm this parallel. Because one of the major ways authority and power are exercised is through communal projects, major building aggregates, cities, reflect the former relative power and wealth of both individual communities and groups of communities. There appears to be no historical exception to this pattern. According to all our data from Río Azul and elsewhere, neither are the Classic Maya an exception to this rule.

The various measures of urban hierarchies that have been worked out for Maya cities all directly reflect political relationships, among other things (Hammond 1974; Flannery 1972; Adams 1981; Turner, Turner, and Adams 1981; Adams and Jones 1981). Although such relationships were complicated by changing historical circumstances, the nature of Maya political arrangements can be defined fairly specifically in many cases. Individual urban centers can only be fully understood as parts of a greater whole. Even if they were independent political units, the various infrastructures that sustained them must be defined. Thus, political relationships at Río Azul might be understood in the context of a larger political unit. But there is a controversy over the nature of Classic Maya states. The two major alternatives are to interpret the data as indicating either city-state or regional state units. This book argues that the weight of the evidence is in favor of the regional state model for the Classic period. Putting aside this controversy for the moment, we should examine Río Azul in terms of its local political structure.

The Preclassic Period

The political structures of the Preclassic are the most obscure, but we must begin there. Rather surprisingly, Valdez's large stucco-decorated temple at G103 sub 2 is evidence of a Middle Preclassic community integrated enough to build such a structure. The design of the building indicates that it was probably a religious structure, and its decoration confirms this (Fig. 3–6). The use of specific iconography such as the "mirror" (or loincloth) sign and the paired "J" elements flanking the mirror are very close to the symbolism of later glyphic writing. The "J" signs have been interpreted as a bifid serpent tongue (Quirarte 1973, 1976). The combination of elements is also reminiscent of the lower part of a day sign, but we cannot see enough of the image to be certain. In any case, this temple tells us that large religious structures decorated with iconography or writing in modeled stucco were possibly present ca. 500 B.C. and certainly by 300 B.C. The size of the building is estimated at around 40,000 cubic meters, a much larger structure than can reasonably have been built by a single village effort. This implies that construction was done by the population of the region and that a coordinating agency was present to plan and execute the project.

Ethnographic analogy suggests that it is quite possible that such coordination at this early date was achieved by consensus, a council of village headmen being the most likely form. On the other hand, it is also possible that the coordination of community affairs was already in the hands of a single individual, a chief. The Preclassic-period evidence presently available does not permit a clear choice between these two alternatives. We do know that later Classic-period Maya rulers were certainly despotic and aristocratic, suggesting the appearance of a nascent hierarchy in early times. Regional coordination being needed for such enterprises, it appears that the most likely administrative hierarchy that can be suggested for the Middle Preclassic along the Río Azul has at least two tiers: the village and regional levels. It is also possible that long-distance imports such as obsidian were obtained by regional arrangements. Thus, basic economic and religious functions may have been the stimuli for the evolution of the complex political structures that eventually appeared.

Descriptions of political life in other ancient civilizations can give us further clues. The criterion developed by H. T. Wright and G. A. Johnson (1975) to define the appearance of state-level political systems in the Middle East are particularly compelling. Civilizations are characterized by hierarchical structure throughout, and the Wright-Johnson scheme can be used to describe a subordinate part of a civilization, namely, politics. The Wright-Johnson archaeological criterion of three or four administrative levels is arguably a valid indicator of the threshold of complex political systems in Mesoamerica.

In our region, three or four levels of administration can be seen in the community levels of hamlet, village, town, and city, which come to exist in the Río Azul zone no sooner than A.D. 390 (Appendix 1). Thus, the ultimate form of centralized political control, the state, emerged late in the Río Azul zone in comparison with the Tikal or

Calakmul regions, where it seems to have appeared at least by 150
B.C. Further, it seems to appear *de novo* at Río Azul, rather than by
gradual evolution. Such a sudden appearance in itself would argue
for the introduction of the system from elsewhere. Recall the prob-
ability of conquest of the Río Azul region by Tikal about A.D. 380.
In this case, it is worth noting that political reorganization to a new
level of complexity was a direct result of such conquest.

The Classic Period

Classic-period political structure is less difficult to outline. As we
have noted, various studies have described patterns typical of more or
less centralized relationships among the various cities of the southern
and central Maya Lowlands (e.g., Adams and Jones 1981). The
means of analysis used to rank and order the ancient cities are those
applied by geographers to modern urban centers. Briefly, three
patterns can be seen among groups of modern cities by using the
Rank-Size Rule. One of these, the lognormal pattern, reflects a high
degree of centralization of power. This is the pattern shown by
analysis of the cities near and around Tikal (Figs. 1–2, 4–1). This
analysis shows that Río Azul was probably a part of the Tikal Classic
grouping of cities. Further, the map generated by such an analysis
indicates that Río Azul was on the northwestern frontier of what we
have called the Tikal Regional State. The Calakmul Regional State
was to the northwest of a buffer zone which averages 20 km wide
and at least 80 km long (Fig. 1–2). Hammond's prior (1974)
analysis by single-link contour planning shows the same patterning.
Presumably these regional states were competitive at times, as recent
hieroglyphic decipherment confirms (Folan et al. 1995:325–329).

Río Azul's location and its fortifications make sense only in light of
the suggested regional political structures of the Classic period. The
alternative interpretation should also be examined, however. If Río
Azul is considered as an independent city-state, then certain other
difficulties of explanation arise. One must explain why the city arises
de novo within a relatively short period of time, seventy-five years.
The labor source to build and maintain the city must also be identified, since the immediate region was not densely populated enough
to provide such a construction force. The interlocking of the dynastic
records of Early Classic Río Azul with those of Tikal presents a
further difficulty. Why do the Río Azul records only mention the

Early Classic rulers of Tikal, and not those of the major cities of La Milpa, Xultun, and La Honradez, all of which are within 20 km of Río Azul? If Río Azul was an independent entity, why is the immense city of Calakmul to the northwest not mentioned? Río Azul's location is itself a difficulty. As noted before, the soils are poor, and no other obvious natural resources call for the establishment of a large city, except for the presence of the river. But the presence of a significant city on the river makes sense only if the city were able to use the river as a route for communication and long-distance trade as well as its obvious use as a source of subsistence for its population. If Río Azul was independent, La Milpa to the east could have blocked its river access to the Caribbean.

All of these and other difficulties can be explained with a complex and torturous set of theories. However, science and scholarship in general follows the logical rule of Occam's Razor: the simplest (most elegant) explanation to account for all the facts is likely to be the correct one. All of the primary and most of the minor difficulties disappear if we describe Río Azul as a part of a regional state rather than as an independent polity. In other words, as part of the Early Classic Tikal Regional State, Río Azul becomes a fortified city on the frontier with the Río Bec and the Calakmul Regional States (Fig. 1–2). The location becomes strategic both politically and militarily and has economic significance in terms of long-distance trade access to the Caribbean. Construction crews could be imported from the south and east and logistical support furnished from the greater resources available to Tikal. The appearance of the Tikal rulers in the dynastic records at Río Azul become comprehensible, because Río Azul rulers were members of the ruling families of Tikal.

The Late Classic political structure is at once more complicated and more obscure. Rank-size analysis indicates that Río Azul may still have been a member of the Tikal Regional State. However, the one stela that includes a lengthy text, Stela 2, does not mention Tikal or its rulers. Its date of A.D. 690 is relatively late in the Late Classic, and after the great and dynamic Tikal ruler Ah Cacau, who came to power in A.D. 681.

Robichaux has deciphered a clause on Stela 2 indicating that the ruler of La Milpa may have paid a visit to Río Azul. This suggests that in the aftermath of the Hiatus events, a ruler of Río Azul attempted to establish an independent state in alliance with the neighboring

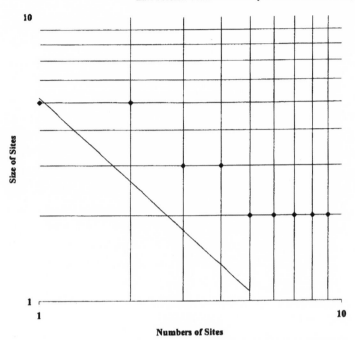

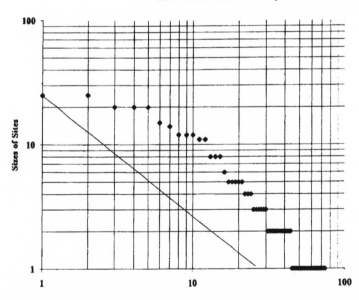

Fig. 4–1. Rank-size analysis of Three Rivers urban centers by courtyard count and by period. The three periods of maximum cultural development were chosen: Late Preclassic, Early Classic 2–3, and Late Classic 2. Sample sizes are 8, 8, and 74, respectively. For the Late Classic 2 period, the Three Rivers sites were melded with the Tikal region sites for a total sample size of 147. Low-size pluralism is evident in the Late Preclassic, indicating the lack of hierarchical structure or urbanism. Early Classic 2–3 shows a primate pattern, with Río

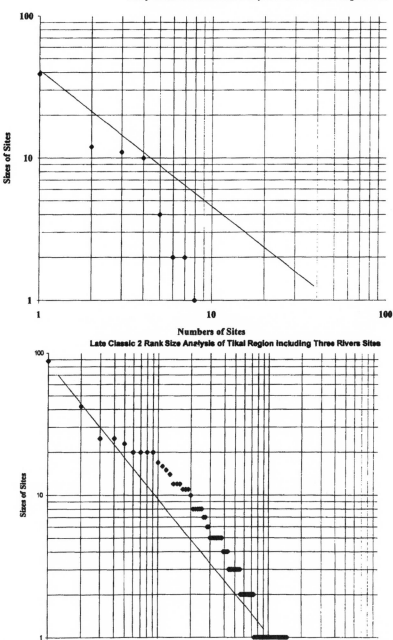

Early Classic 2-3 Rank Size Analysis of Three Rivers Region Sites

Sizes of Sites

Numbers of Sites

Late Classic 2 Rank Size Analysis of Tikal Region Including Three Rivers Sites

Sizes of Sites

Azul clearly dominant over other sites in its region (including La Milpa) and, based on its size, an urban center. In the Late Classic pluralism is again evident, but among many urban centers, the Río Azul has lost its primacy. If Tikal is assumed to have regained control over the Three Rivers Region, then the sample shows a log-normal distribution. The latter is that of mature, well-integrated political and economic structures within a regional state. (Chart by R. E. W. Adams) ruler of La Milpa, with Río Azul subordinate to La Milpa. It is noteworthy that the Kinal fortress was built well after the date of Ah Cacau's succession and that there are no more Classic stelae at Río Azul after A.D. 690. The questions remain open as to whether Río Azul was ever reintegrated into the Tikal Regional State or whether it and Kinal were part of a new regional state headed by La Milpa. The role of La Honradez, about 20 km to the south, is unknown. The disintegration of all forms of unified states after A.D. 850 is implied by the events of the military intrusion and the subsequent rural depopulation of the Río Azul region.

Urban Structure (See Figs. 3–3, 3–12)

Although we have already begun to examine the city of Río Azul as it relates to the economy and politics of the region, it is necessary to examine the urban character of the city as a phenomenon in itself. For this I will draw upon the information and insights derived from the mapping and architectural work of the Project Associate Director, Miguel Orrego C. (1987).

The city was laid out on a ridge that runs more or less north-south. The river flows north along the western length of the ridge, bending around the northern end and continuing far to the east before it turns north again, eventually to join with the Río Hondo.

Like most Mesoamerican cities, Río Azul is composed of functional units called courtyard groups. This is in contrast to the later Spanish colonial pattern of a civic square (or squares) at the center of a residential grid of houses facing onto streets. Maya architecture is oriented inward upon enclosed plazas, or courtyards, which are often square or rectangular in form (although irregularities do occur). The city is composed of 729 separate formal buildings center on several large plazas, which are paved with heavy plaster floors covering about 197,000 square meters (48.6 acres) (Fig. 3–3). A number of subsidiary or smaller independent plaza groups round out the courtyard count for Río Azul to a final adjusted total of thirty-nine.

Due to the relatively rapid construction of the city during the late fourth and early fifth centuries, the initial plan is relatively clear and unobscured by later building. Further, there are recurrent components in each group, large or small. I have already introduced the architectural elements and functional units and described the four classes of housing. Recall that these residential classes are associated with other functional units such as temples or mausolea, kitchens, servants quarters, and so forth. (These functional assignments are based on sample and salvage excavations with extrapolation to unexcavated buildings.) Thus we have enough information to see Río Azul in terms of its people and their various degrees of status.

The largest palaces are connected to the largest temples. The B-8 Palace Complex forms an acropolis of elevated residential buildings, which not only overlook the whole city but provide views west over the river and to the ridges 5 to 8 km distant. This palace complex is physically connected by a paved causeway to the largest temples, the A-3 Complex, approximately 150 meters distant (Fig. 3–7). A-3 Complex sits in the middle of a paved area on the highest point of the ridge with its temples towering up to 34 meters (115 feet) in the air. Another major palace is located east of it, A-11 Complex (Fig. 3–11). Whether the ruling family of Río Azul lived in B-8 or A-11 complexes is impossible to determine at the present, because we were unable to dig into the B-8 building for lack of time.

The causeway from B-8 to A-3 passes immediately in front of the B-5 Complex, which appears to be an administrative group. B-5 buildings include elite residences, but the major feature of the group is that it encloses a great space with a kind of large podium in its center. The main entrance to B-5 is from the west, through the protective buildings that line the western edge. This entrance also forms one end of an east-west axis with the river at the other end. There is an open corridor, free of buildings, between the river and the very large staircase that stands before the entrance to B-5 enclosure. Thus this is the main entrance to the city from the river, its features being suitable for the sort of status ritual appropriate for elite visitors to the city. In fact, there is only one other accessible entry to the city and that is on the north side at E Group, which is located on the edge of the river (Fig. 3–3). Therefore, the north-south and east-west axes intersect in front of the entrance to B-5 Complex, emphasizing the importance of the various buildings along these avenues.

To the east of B-8 palace complex is the city's largest plaza, an immense paved zone of approximately 62,450 sq meters (15.5 acres), about one-third of the paved area in the city. While this Early Classic plaza was originally rectangular in plan, it now contains certain Late Classic additions that break it up—Structures B-11/13, the ball court (C2-3), a small platform (Str. B-63), and a few other buildings. In the original Early Classic plan there was simply a very large space with no obstructions, defined on the east by long linear buildings that were defensive in nature. At the north end of this great plaza is C-67 Complex, built in the Late Preclassic and modified in Late Classic times.

A large group of Early Classic palaces are on the northwest side of the plaza, and another elite Early Classic residential group, C-5 Group, is on the east side, but external to the plaza, forming a salient out from the city itself. Both groups are Class 1 residences probably housing rulers and their collateral relatives and descendants.

The early funerary temple, Str. C-1, with Tombs 1, 19, and 23, is located on the northeast corner of the great plaza (Fig. 3–13). From that temple building a causeway leads northeast to a separate and important palace group, C-42 Complex. Although modest in size, this appears to have been the residential compound of Ruler X. Its small scale compared to later Class 1 residences is probably due to its early date.

The northernmost major group, E Group, is a major palace. Although the idea is untested, it may also be more of a warehouse zone than a simple elite residential-administrative complex. I have offered a speculative reconstruction of its warehousing and marketing functions in a previous section (p. 113). Thus E Group is possibly either a Class 1 residence or a functionally unique group.

Late Classic Class 1 residences include B-8, which was refurbished, A-11 Complex, which was also revamped, and a very large building, A-1 Complex. All of these are impressive buildings, but their construction falls far short of that represented by the major Early Classic residences.

Class 2 residences probably housed lower-level nobility, persons of high status but who clearly were not rulers. B-56 Complex is the most thoroughly explored of these groups (Ellis 1991). It appears that it comprised a long-occupied set of residential courts oriented around a mausoleum. The burial structure (B-56) was enlarged and new burials put in at intervals. There is strong evidence of domestic function. The life of the complex runs from approximately A.D. 250 to A.D. 830 or slightly later. Generations of presumably related families occupied the group.

There are sixteen such groups within Río Azul. An additional fifteen Class 2 housing groups are located within 1 km of the city

limits. All of the nine tested or salvaged Class 2 groups were originally built in the Early Classic. During the Late Classic 2 period,
Class 2 housing evidently spread over the countryside, being found
throughout the six-kilometer range that marks the maximum distance possible from all urban sites during this time. Most of the Class
2 groups were occupied in both the Early and Late Classic. These
complexes are clearly set apart from one another, both within the city
and nearby. F-38 Complex is an example of the latter.

In an apparent exception to this pattern, a huge complex of small
palace (Class 2) structures lies about nine meters below and to the
west of the A-3 Temples. These structures are associated with the A-3
Temple Complex, but are very much smaller and less elaborate than
the larger B-8 and A-11 palaces. However, upon close examination
and excavation of part of the group, it was found that the zone
represents an aggregation of Class 2 housing. Various lines of evidence suggest that these residences represent the housing of collateral
relatives of rulers buried in the temples above. Excavations in these
buildings revealed elite residences, kitchens, and other domestic
features. Platforms that appear to have supported perishable housing
were probably servants' quarters as well as utility spaces, as Hendon
has shown at Copan (1991). An estimated 600 people lived in this
group of small palaces during the Early Classic and perhaps half that
number in the Late Classic (Karbula 1989:181). The proportion of
elite to commoners is 432:167 or 2.6:1. Clearly service personnel
from elsewhere must have commuted in to take care of some of the
maintenance and cleaning tasks in Group A palaces.

Approximately 85 percent of Class 3 and 4 housing can be associated with Class 2 residences. These smaller buildings, made partly
of perishable materials, apparently housed commoner families that
were often, if not always, bound by patron-client relationships to the
elite families. The remaining 15 percent may have been housing for
commoners who were also attached to elite families, but this cannot
be demonstrated. It is possible that these persons were on call for
service in the Group A palaces, which, as noted above, were short on
commoners.

A Functional View of Río Azul

The functions of Río Azul fit those of any urban center at the top
of hierarchially arranged cultural institutions. Economically, it was a

regional market with connections to other regions and to foreign places and their commodities. Politically, it served as an administrative center for the region and for the resident population. From about A.D. 380 to 550 Río Azul was a third-level administrative center in a political system dominated by Tikal.

The social structure at Río Azul appears to have been somewhat different from what researchers have outlined for Tikal or Uaxactun, where society was characterized by the classic and clichéd pyramidal shape. In these central Petén sites, the dominant social classes constituted perhaps only 5 percent of the population (Adams 1974, 1981). In the greater Three Rivers Region, the elite was less than 4 percent (Appendix 2). At Río Azul, however, the elite made up a much greater fraction of the total population, perhaps as much as 25 percent. The suggested frontier military and commercial functions explain this disproportionate ratio. Construction labor demands would be met by temporarily imported work forces rather than permanent residents. As we have seen, the Río Azul elite lived in large and small palaces inside and nearby the city. Intermediate and lower ranks of society supported the elite and most often were housed nearby. Artisan families and, presumably, important bureaucrats also tended to reside near patron elite families. The likelihood of patrilineal lineages and clans suggests that the lower-class families may have been members of lower-ranking lineages, while belonging to the same clan as the leading elite families. This linkage would form an indestructible social bond among the social classes as well as carrying inherent obligations.

The city's functions shifted and were modified through time. It was always in an intermediate position, whether it was a member of a larger political unit or not. Initially Río Azul was probably created as a frontier administrative-commercial fortress for the Tikal Regional State. When that regional state underwent a severe crisis during the sixth century A.D., Río Azul was at least partially abandoned. In any case, it ceased to perform the functions for which it had been designed originally. The city's late and sudden recovery in the late seventh century was perhaps as an independent city-state. A reincorporation into the Tikal Regional State by A.D. 700 is possible, in which case Río Azul once more became an important subordinate administrative unit. However, as noted before, it may have become a unit in a new regional state with the capital at La Milpa. A substantial increase in rural population during the eighth century A.D. coincides with dispersal of the elite class over the landscape in the "manor-house" pattern. The rebuilt city may have become much more important as a means of social and political integration during this period. The military intrusion and destruction of Río Azul around A.D. 830 definitely led to the abandonment of much of the city and its conversion to a military outpost. The fortress of Kinal, 12 km distant, was built in the eighth century A.D. and seems to have been an elite refuge at this time. The military intrusion from the north appears to have been brief, and afterward Río Azul was reoccupied. These late residents, however, were only a surviving remnant of the city's population, camped among ruins. The Kinal fortress survived these events, but both city and fortress were abandoned gradually in the general Classic Maya collapse.

Militarism and Warfare

Three major episodes at Río Azul seem to reflect a history of militarism. First, the Early Classic presence of Teotihuacan is in some way connected with warfare. Second, The Hiatus seems to have been a period of violence, but there is less evidence for war in this episode than in the others. Third, the Late Classic (Tepeu 2–3) sequence of events is tied up with trade, the northern Maya, and a devastating raid. Material evidence for militarism lies in Río Azul's defensible location on a ridge on the east side of a river fronted by an extensive swamp, its defenses enhanced by linear defensive structures and dry moats, examples of which are found in the southeast edge of the city. All these fortification features at Río Azul are Early Classic. The Late Classic fortress at Kinal is even stronger and was never overrun (Adams 1991). The defensive features at Kinal include location on the highest ridge in the vicinity, a series of vertical terraces, each about seven meters high, an interior acropolis, or citadel, which rises about fifteen meters above the surrounding pavement, and assured water supplies within the citadel (Robichaux and S. C. W. Adams 1993; Scarborough 1993).

Taken together, the evidence from the entire Maya Lowlands region indicates that Maya campaigns were short and swift, employing the strategy of the surprise raid. In this, they were different only in degree from Aztec warfare, as recently studied by Hassig (1988). Given even minimal warning, populations—especially elite people—

could have taken refuge rapidly within defensive zones, in this case Río Azul and, later, Kinal. Defense against raids must have included several kinds of "early-warning" systems. Traditionally, farmers living in buffer zones have been counted on for such warning. Formal outposts, lookouts, and patrols are traditional features as well. All of these imperatives as well as the fortifications themselves argue for a more systematic militarism than we previously have allowed the Maya. In a more rationalized military structure, Río Azul assumes its place as part of the defensive structure of a larger political system, the Tikal Regional State. The unusually high percentage of elite families at Río Azul makes sense in a framework of military necessity. There may have been more professional soldiery and fewer militia present than we had previously thought, but there is little doubt that the prime movers and leaders in Maya warfare were the aristocrats.

Strategically, Río Azul in the Early Classic was probably supported by military strength from elsewhere in the Tikal Regional State. An analogy may be the Tikal fortifications themselves, which enclose a zone of about 300 sq km. The north and south fortification lines have an aggregate length of about 25 km (Puleston and Callendar 1967; Puleston 1983). The most efficient way to hold such a line is with forward listening posts, patrols, and strong points backed up with "fire brigades." The solution to the larger strategic problem of defending the Tikal Regional State territory is somewhat the same. The buffer zone beyond Río Azul would have been the forward listening zone, Río Azul a strong point, and the whole system backed up with major military units from deeper within the Regional State.

If such a system existed, it appears to have failed at least twice— once during the putative civil wars of The Hiatus and again at about A.D. 830 when the northern raid occurred. The Hiatus events may have been partially an inside job with elements of betrayal and uprising. The Late Classic raid, however, probably owed at least part of its success to surprise, shock, and perhaps new tactics and weapons. It did not defeat Kinal, however, which seems to have weathered the storm, even if later it "withered on the vine."

Religion

Maya religion has become a revitalized subject in the past twenty years. Much controversial material has been developed on the basis of enthusiastic readings of symbols, art, and fluid decipherments of written texts. But iconography is such an ambiguous business that it calls into question any otherwise unsupported interpretations. Thus, we will continue to rely most heavily on data that is confirmed from several sources.

Preclassic forms of religion probably were analogous to the shamanistic practices of Maya groups today. In these relatively simple societies, everyday religious activities are carried out by the individual, who is assisted in times of crisis by a community specialist, a shaman. The shaman has certain characteristics that call him to be a curer of disease as well as of mental disturbance; disease, illness, and accident are all looked upon in these societies as being at least partially due to supernatural causes (Colby and van den Berghe 1969).

We have relatively sparse data on religious practice from Río Azul during the Preclassic period. A few fragments of clay human figurines, some "mushroom" effigy pot parts, and some small jade pieces all suggest that the inhabitants of the Río Azul region shared the same general beliefs as their lowland neighbors. Based on much more evidence available from other sites, these religious beliefs appear to have emphasized the continuity of human life through a fertility cult, which used the small female figurines. The mushroom stands may have been used in rituals that used a mildly hallucinogenic experience to establish closer contact with the powers of creation. Jade was not only a status symbol, but also a sacred substance that represented water, living plants, and, therefore, life. Using analogies to contemporary Maya societies, we can reconstruct a community in which household, family, lineage, and clan were the basic units of worship.

Religion below the elite level is even less accessible because of the lack of formal art and other evidence. However, we may posit that there were curing ceremonies for all the ills and accidents that plague humanity. These may have been carried out at more or less elaborate levels, as appropriate to the social status of the patient. Further, we can use the considerable body of anthropological knowledge about how modern Maya curers operate to build a testable reconstruction of ancient medicine. A fundamental feature of all traditional Maya medicine is the blend of what might be called psychologically therapeutic with physiological treatment in the process of healing. Mind, spirit, and body were all healed in one operation through a process of individual prayer, herbal treatment, sweatbaths, short pilgrimages, group prayer, and other techniques.

This reconstruction applies to the Classic period Maya at Río Azul, but there is considerable evidence that nearly all of these elements were in place by the Middle Preclassic. Proskouriakoff said some time ago (1964b) that she believed that the developmental path of symbolic art and writing indicated that the elite Classic Maya gradually shifted from animistic to anthropomorphic forms of belief. By this she meant that in the Early Classic, and probably the Middle and Late Preclassic, the Maya were more interested in the manifold expressions of the supernatural in whatever form: rocks, trees, lightning, storms, clouds, and so forth. The shift noted above occurred during the Early Classic, placing an emphasis on the gods as manifested in human forms, and on ancestral figures as assuming roles of supernatural beings. Ancestor worship seems to have appeared at least by the end of the Preclassic in Río Azul and even earlier elsewhere, as shown in the Izapan style art of the Guatemalan south coast and the Maya highlands (Adams 1991:Figs. 4–7, 4–8). The earliest direct evidence for this practice in the lowlands comes from Burial 22 at Cuello, Belize, which dates around 400 B.C. (Hammond 1991:245).

The subjects of donation, invention, and diffusion are reserved for the next chapter. I will say that the Maya Lowlands were in contact and had significant interaction with other parts of Mesoamerica by the Middle and Late Preclassic. They shared a pattern of reverence for ancestors early in the Preclassic. The Izapa and early Maya sculptures indicate another aspect of this belief system—that the gods legitimated supreme political power through ancestral sanction. This particular twist meant that the Maya rulers became divinely sanctioned. Whether they also became divine rulers in the sense that they were gods on earth is a question we will consider later.

By the Early Classic there is little doubt that the Maya were revering their ancestors and that the rulers used this as a legitimating device for succession to power. However, even on the lower levels of the elite and perhaps among the commoners, such ancestor worship took firm hold. The B-56 mausoleum has at least two and perhaps three "meditation" rooms which abut the bulk of the temple structure precisely against the location of the important tombs. These rooms also have niches on the abutting walls, which show signs of repeated incense burning. The rooms are furnished with benches for seating and perhaps sleeping (Ellis 1991). Hammond has suggested that perhaps this practise of communing with the ancestral spirits is what is shown on Piedras Negras Stela 40 (personal communication 1994).

The well-known Maya habit of burying people inside benches in palaces perhaps reflects a desire to keep family members nearby even after death. We found several such burials in large and small (Classes 1 and 2) Early and Late Classic palaces.

The dedication and termination ceremonies that appear to have begun and ended the construction projects of the Maya, at Río Azul and elsewhere, perhaps had everything to do with the disturbance of ancestral resting places. Many burials from years gone by were evidently remembered, because the Maya appeared to have gone to some lengths to avoid disturbing them. The formal tombs have layers of flint or chert chips above them; perhaps this was a warning to construction crews.

The iconography of Classic polychrome pottery appears to reflect not only the ancestor theme, but others as well. It has already been argued that the Early Classic "Creation Vessel" (J. J. Adams 1990) is more animistic than anthropomorphic. Indeed, it is a highly elaborated graphic expression of mythical themes with symbolic referents to important animals, plants, birds, and composite monsters. Such thematic expression is fairly common on polychrome pottery during the Early Classic, but becomes more simplified in motif and symbolism during the Late Classic. Again, it has been argued that much of the symbolism on this status pottery was kinship linked.

As nearly as our reconstructions can tell, religious rituals at Río Azul fall principally into two categories. One is the ceremony for deceased elite personages (or funerals). The other is that of commemorative liturgy. Most of our data is from the Early Classic, particularly from the fifth century A.D.

Elite class funerals can be largely reconstructed from the elements involved. While the sequence of events is reasonably certain and the liturgy somewhat accessible, the symbolism is least understood of all. Final obsequies involved physical preparation of the deceased, who were dressed in fine clothing and jewelry. Appropriate headdresses were included in some cases, as shown by the remains of wooden armatures in Tombs 19 and 23 (Hall 1988). The bodies were apparently not always eviscerated or drained of body fluids, judging by the explosive decomposition that took place after the closure of the tombs (Gentry Steele, personal communication 1985). After dressing, the bodies were wrapped in cloth, first with several layers of a fine material and then with an outer wrapping of a kind of a burlap. In the case of rulers and possibly their near kin, mosaic mask images of their features were placed on the shrouded bodies. The corpse was then put onto a stretcher, which was padded with a mattress.

We assume that dressing and preparation of the corpse was carried out in the privacy of the deceased's residential compound. Therefore the next likely event was a formal procession from residence to tomb. Such processions were an important part of major Maya rituals, judging by their frequent appearance on polychrome vessels. Grave-side ritual included the rapid painting of symbolic material on the walls of the tomb, placement of the body on its litter inside the tomb, the offering of food and drink in pottery vessels, and the burning of incense. We can infer the probable offering of prayers in all these stages. The final occurrence was the closure of the tomb, which might be a wall, as in the case of the lateral cell tombs, or might involve the construction of a vault, as in the case of the tombs in Str. A-3. In the latter case, the body and the funerary offering were protected from falling debris by a net of finely woven fabric. Impressions of these nets were found in the mud plaster of the walls.

We presume that after this "funeral" ceremony, the major activities relating to the deceased were commemorative and had several pur-poses. One might have been grief assuagement. Another appears to have been communicative, as the "meditation rooms" of B-56 Com-plex suggest. Communication with the dead is also suggested by the repetitive relationships between buildings within a group, where a principal structure is oriented so a person seated on a bench in the central doorway would have faced the temple of the group. This is the case in the Late Classic A-11 Complex (Eaton 1987a) as well as in the Early Classic B-56 Complex (Ellis 1991). Many other such temple-meditation axes were noted in the site, and perhaps all of the Class 2 compounds were laid out in this way. Assuming that the persons seated in the meditation locations were communicating with the persons buried in the temple being viewed, then the question arises, to what purpose?

Formalized communication with the supernatural is an invariable part of all religious practices. We know that it occurred in Meso-america, generally in order to divine the future, or to consult with divine spirits on matters of importance. It is noteworthy that the larger temples of A-3 Complex can be viewed not only from the auxiliary buildings opposite them, but from a smaller temple (Str. A-9). Temple building Str. A-9 is centered on temple building Str. A-3 as well. This pattern anticipates that of the Late Classic opposing Great Temples I and II in the Great Plaza at Tikal.

CHAPTER 5

THE CULTURE HISTORY
OF RÍO AZUL

The Middle Preclassic 1: Pioneer Farmers, 900–500 B.C.

THERE ARE UNDOUBTEDLY EARLIER REMAINS in the Río Azul zone than those we have found. Several finds only 60 km to the east of our region indicate early occupation by hunting and gathering peoples, perhaps by 11,000 B.C. (Hester et al. 1981; Hester, personal communication 1995). MacNeish has found a series of sites in what is now northern Belize that seems to indicate the presence of people who intensively exploited wild foods, including shellfish from rivers (MacNeish et al. 1980). Suggested dates on these sites range from about 8000 to 2000 B.C.

The earliest farmers detected thus far in the Maya lowlands date from about 2500 B.C., based largely on evidence of forest clearance and maize pollen (Hammond 1991:5). From the first, small villages appear to have been the community pattern of these early farmers, who raised corn, beans, squashes, and other vegetables. They supplemented their diets heavily with the same wild foods that their ancestors had extracted from the environment.

Techniques worked out over thousands of years and dozens of generations were applied or adapted to the new forms of food production. Foods can be processed in many of the same ways whether they are from wild or domesticated sources. Thus, grinding stones such as mullers, mortars, pounders, and other variants were in existence long before the domestication of plants in the Maya lowlands and continue to be used up to the present day. In fact, much of the technology the Maya used until the time of the Spanish conquest, essentially a set of stone and wooden implements, was inherited from the Archaic period. For example, the methods and efficiencies of building houses from jungle materials were developed long ago and

have continued unchanged to today. Indeed, much of the archaeological camp near Río Azul was built using the time-honored techniques of pole walling and palmleaf thatching for roofs. The first
villages were clusters of such pole-and-thatch houses, each housing a
single family (Fig. 3–5). These small social groups were the basic
building blocks of Mesoamerican society, no less in the Maya Lowlands than elsewhere. Then, perhaps by 600 B.C., zones were set aside
in the early Belize villages for elevated, more formally built structures,
which may have had ritual importance (Hammond 1991:240). It was
during this time that we find the first traces of human occupation
along the Río Azul.

If the Río Azul zone was indeed late in its development for human
use, it may have been due to the sparseness of arable soils. The
eastern side of the river is the best zone for slash-and-burn agriculture, the prevalent technique in use at the time, but even so, much of
the area is very thinly and poorly covered with humus. West of the
river is an area of floodplain and periodic swamp, again an unpro-
mising zone for extensive agriculture.

Thus our first traces of human culture are a few sherds of Middle
Preclassic pottery, some imitating the shapes of gourds, and others
shaped into flat pans, perhaps in the same forms as earlier wooden
containers. The distribution of pottery from this period is spotty but
widespread. At Str. C-69 we found extensive debris from the period
as well as a small cache of thin chert blades. These all-purpose tools
were likely knives and slicing instruments. C-69 is located on a rise in
bedrock around which the river flows. It is a superior place to live,
having the advantages of drainage in tropical downpours as well as
cooling breezes which blow away insects. We assume that these
remains were left by people living in villages or single family households, but there is no direct evidence from Río Azul, and we are
extrapolating from remains 60 to 80 km away in Belize.

As Black indicates (1987:216), the original jungle had likely been
transformed by this time into a mosaic of secondary growth, recovery
forest, and islands of original tropical forest.

The Middle Preclassic 2:
Río Azul as a Small Regional Center, 500–250 B.C.

By 300 B.C., and perhaps as early as 500 B.C., a terraced, masonry
and mortar, plastered platform about five meters high was built at

Río Azul (G-103 sub 2). The platform is oriented to the south and
has space on top for only a single structure. Decorative motifs are
incised in plaster and consist of "J" elements flanking a decorated
loincloth motif (Fig. 3–6). The section uncovered thus far is approximately four meters long by two meters high. Fred Valdez, the
discoverer, deals with the structure's implications in a formal paper
(Valdez 1993). Two points are worth noting here. One is that the
design motifs are identical to those found in Izapan art on the south
coast of Guatemala, 350 km distant. The second is that all indications are that the people who built and supported this temple were
from immediately surrounding farmsteads and villages.

The Late Preclassic: Medium-sized Regional Centers along the Río Azul; 250 B.C.–A.D. 250 (Fig. 3–2)

Some of the largest and most sophisticated Late Preclassic construction at Río Azul lies on a hilltop in the southern part of the site,
the same place that Valdez's Structure G-103 sub 2 was built about
500 B.C. The entire structure was later covered with an immense
platform (around 97,000 cubic meters) that was built of rubble,
faced with cut stone, and finished with a heavy plaster coating. The
much larger temples at Mirador, 60 kilometers to the west, are
contemporary with this structure at Río Azul. There they occur in
groups of threes—the triad pattern—and face east or west (Hansen
1990:117, Fig. 64). The Río Azul Late Preclassic temple faces north
and is a solitary structure.

We have evidence for pole-and-thatch housing in a site called BA-
20, about 2 km northeast of what would later be Río Azul. By the
time that this village appears, however, society had become stratified.
Hendon (1989) found evidence for two and possibly three levels of
society based on the remains of differential housing. In the simplest
level of housing, single-family houses were built on a large level zone
that seems to be a part of a very large platform supporting several
houses. Based on data from BA-20 (Str. 3, 206D), these houses were
largely made of pole and thatch but had partial masonry walls and
well-made plaster floors. Food preparation areas were located inside
the houses.

A more sophisticated and complex form of architecture appears in
two other structures from the same zone (Strs. 1 and 2, 206I), which
are roughly contemporary with Str. 3. These are single-roomed

buildings with masonry walls, built on low platforms and keyhole shaped in plan. The latest building, Str. 1, also had a red-painted plaster floor. Given their unusual plan and the red floor, Hendon concludes that the structures may have had a ceremonial or ritual purpose (1989:131).

However, similar Late Preclassic house platforms at Uaxactun and Santa Rita were certainly domestic in function. Farther afield, in her excavations in the Maya zone of the Early Classic Merchants' Barrio at Teotihuacan, E. C. Rattray (1987) found *only* keyhole shaped structures, and these buildings were apparently residential. Late Classic palace residential rooms at Kinal were painted red, although admittedly this example is much later than Hendon's house platforms. The most substantial indication that the keyhole buildings may be residential is that elsewhere along the river, and within BA-20 itself, there are much larger and more sophisticated constructions suitable for ritual purposes.

BA-20 includes other large platforms that apparently supported clusters of both residential and ritual buildings, especially in the area to the west of the 206 residential zone. The 209 and 210 excavation zones represent a set of very large connected platforms. These were built on leveled and paved hilltops and, in at least one case, a series of staircases were carved from the hillside, ascending by degrees to landings and finally to the top, onto a plaza with buildings on three sides. Hendon's work demonstrated that the hillside staircases were Late Preclassic. A burial of the same date was also found on the stairs. The stairs and burial were covered up with a floor and a structure. The frontally terraced hill may have been designed to give it a pyramidal appearance.

The most developed and complete example of Maya architecture from this period may be the temple building in the Operation 205 locality. This small Late Preclassic building possibly had only one room and was built on a plaster floor. Ceremonial deposits in the form of two caches of pottery vessels were sealed and placed under the floor. Such ceramic vessels are usually empty when found, but probably contained perishable materials: liquid, fiber, cloth, or other substances.

This small building was subsequently sealed in the Late Preclassic and covered by a much larger temple building with a volume of about 7,000 cubic meters. A very large platform was built of rubble, covered with a casing of cut limestone, and then coated with lime plaster. A single-roomed superstructure with a roof comb was built on the platform. The roof comb and probably the temple itself were decorated with modeled stucco and a red wash. The roof comb is vaulted with wooden beam supports. In other words, all the formal features of later Maya architecture are present in this Late Preclassic building. The structure was in use for long enough to be replastered three times. The temple room was then converted into a burial chamber and sealed. A yet more massive temple was built over it in the very Early Classic (Black 1987:216). After the Late Preclassic, parts of the zone were abandoned and not used during later periods.

Contemporary with the BA-20 material are some very large platforms and temple structures located both north and south of the zone. At Arroyo Negro, about 7 km north where the Río Azul now exits Guatemala into Mexico, there is a very large mound which produced only Late Preclassic pottery. The construction of the platform-mound is probably also Late Preclassic, as indicated by excavated samples from similar and more sophisticated platforms at Río Azul itself. For example, Str. C-67 Complex lies in the northern part of Río Azul on high ground where bedrock rises near the river. In fact, it covers the remains of some of the earliest (Middle Preclassic) occupation found at Río Azul. A large Late Preclassic rectangular platform supports at least three higher platform-terraces. The bulk of the complex amounts to about 17,000 cubic meters (Adams 1987b). The zone to the south of C-67 Complex, including the underlying temple building C-1, is paved with a vast, well-made floor of hard stucco, its full extent still undetermined. Other plaster floors of Late Preclassic date were found under A-3 Complex in the southern part of Río Azul (Miguel Orrego, 1988). Elsewhere in the region, at Kinal, scanty Late Preclassic debris underlies some of the later construction. A cache of a standard Red Ware pot was found placed in the bedrock in front of a much later structure, which may have replaced an earlier building.

The amounts of construction, the widespread and massive distribution of Late Preclassic pottery, and the increasing sophistication of all aspects of culture throughout the period have several important implications. One is that population grew substantially during the 500 years of the Late Preclassic. Large numbers of people were required to level hilltops, build large platforms and superstructures, and support the activities for which these buildings acted as the settings. Another implication is that society was stratified, at least economically, and was probably divided socially as well. The Classic features of Maya funerary temples seem to be anticipated by the Phase 2 temple at BA-20, locality 205 as well as by Structure G-103 sub 1. Such temples were later ancestor veneration centers and there is reason to believe that the earlier examples, with the same formal qualities, had the same function. Politically, the Late Preclassic material from the Arroyo Negro–Río Azul zone suggests that there was no centralized control over the region. However, there do seem to have been certain elite families who lived in better quarters, which were usually elevated and associated with ritual buildings. The supporting population of these ritual-elite clusters was spread over the countryside adjacent to them. If we posit that each of the temple clusters indicates a local ruler, then there may have been as many as four political segments to the riverine zone, each with independent political leadership. Centralization may have also been a tendency in the Late Preclassic. If, as appears possible from the ceramics, the latest constructions are the two largest temples, BA-20, locality 205 temple and G-103, there may have been a reduction from four units to two. Judging by size, the most important temple center by the end of the Late Preclassic was undoubtedly G-103 sub 1.

Based on population growth and a consequent shift to intensive agriculture, S. L. Black (1987:217) argues for a serious ecological crisis at the end of the period. However, intensive agriculture only appears around Río Azul in the eighth century A.D. (Black and Suhler 1986:189). Intensive food production may indeed have appeared in the Formative (Adams 1986a), but there is no direct evidence for this at Río Azul. As we will see, calculations indicate a total average population of about 17,500 living within a half-day's walk of the four large platform sites. A modern bush house lasts about twenty-five years with care and renovation, but requires about fifty small trees. Perhaps the use of stone for the lower walls in the Late Preclassic houses at BA-20 reflects a scarcity of poles for walls. Firewood consumption is significant for a household, averaging about two cubic meters per week, which would mean about 7,000 cubic meters of wood fuel burned each week in the region. This calculation ignores the use of wood for construction or other purposes. Thus, the great numbers of trees needed for house building as well as for firewood, and amounts of thatching material for roofing, over a period of five hundred years may well have caused an ecological crisis.

The Early Classic: Florescence and Apogee, A.D. 250–550

The transformation from Late Preclassic to Early Classic civilization at Río Azul may have been one of gradualism up to a certain point. The temple centers at G-103 and BA-20, locality 205 continued in use. The BA-20 temple was rebuilt in a larger version and may have been in use longer than G-103. Debris, which includes basal flanged polychrome bowls, is spread around its skirts. This distinctive form of pottery is typical of the Early Classic of Uaxactun and Tikal.

A more drastic transformation of Río Azul took place at the estimated date of A.D. 385. Three matching, round altars with modeled stucco decoration show the deaths of eight elite-class persons. They are all males, stripped of finery, with blood streaming from their foreheads, their hands tied with rope. Each with an individual name glyph on his back (Fig. 3–33). The altars were placed in the open air in front of a low, terraced platform, which probably supported a temple. This ritual structure, with its monuments in front, was the earliest temple of Structure A-3. The stuccoed monuments show little evidence of weathering, and they must have stood outside for only a few years, we estimate fewer than five.

A much larger temple, Str. A-3, sub 2, was then constructed over the earlier temple, and Stela 1 was erected in front it in A.D. 392. The monument is very damaged, but shows the remains of a standing human figure with a captive lying behind his feet. The text may name a ruler of Río Azul, Zak Balam (Fig. 3–32, glyph B8: "White Jaguar"; Fahsen 1988), and possibly the contemporary Uaxactun (Tikal?) ruler, Smoking Frog (Fig. 3–32, glyph B12). However, no decipherable conquest statement can be read in the text. Another monument, Stela 3, although very badly destroyed, belongs to this period as well, according to Proskouriakoff's style-dating method and the nature of the remaining glyphs (1950). It, too, has the remains of a standing human figure with a subsidiary captive figure at its feet. The fragmentary and destroyed text has not yielded any further information.

At the end of the Late Preclassic, Str. G-103 temple to the south was razed from its substructure, which was covered with a huge amount of specially quarried debris to form a symmetrical and flat-topped platform. The locality was abandoned and not occupied again except for casual residence five hundred years later. No Early Classic pottery was found in the excavation at G-103.

Briefly, we see these events as connected. The termination of use of the most important temple on the river, the commemoration of the execution of persons of importance, the commemoration of a conquest, and the building of two new temples in a new location all indicate a change in the political control of the area. The mention of a possible Tikal-Uaxactun ruler, Smoking Frog, points to that zone as the possible source of change. Further, the tomb paintings from a period of about seventy-five years indicate even more firmly a connection between the rulers of Río Azul and Tikal.

We interpret this evidence to mean that Río Azul was conquered by Tikal about A.D. 385. The specifics of the conquest—open warfare, intrigue, conspiracy, betrayal, or other features—are not available to us at this time. Perhaps texts yet to be discovered or deciphered will shed light on the means used by Tikal. The executed captives, possibly the independent rulers of the Río Azul zone, and the captive figures on Stelae 1 and 3 at Río Azul would indicate that there had been some resistance to the takeover and that therefore the monuments also had an admonitory role in addition to being victory monuments. Conquered populations have to be reminded of the consequences of resistance.

The area between C-67 and G-103 complexes was chosen by the victors for urban development, and it is at this time that Río Azul came into being as a city. The entire ridge of about 1 km in length was leveled and paved. This enormous platform was divided into large plazas and small courtyards, all of them surrounded by formal architecture.

Although we do not have definite confirmation of military fortifications at Río Azul, there is no doubt that it was defensible. The site map shows that the west and north sides of the site are protected by the river and by the extensive swamps to the west of it (Fig. 3–3). The eastern boundaries of the center are defined and probably protected by long, linear structures that close off access. Reservoirs, dry moats, and linked quarries effectively channel the approaches to the city. The rising terrain also adds to defensibility. Partial confirmation that this was not an accidental circumstance lies in the fact that the majority of population in the Río Azul region seems to have lived inside the city. Rural population dropped drastically, perhaps by two-thirds, at the beginning of the Early Classic. Late Preclassic communities such as that at Kinal, 12 km distant, were abandoned.

Reasons for the defensive features and population nucleation are to be found in the shape of the Tikal Regional State, which was expanding at this time (Fig. 1–2). The Río Azul region was part of its natural frontier, given the northeastern and eastern trend of the river's course. The stream also provided access to the Bay of Chetumal and thereby to the Caribbean Sea and the extensive trade via canoe known to have existed there. At this point, then, Río Azul can be convincingly explained only by reference to the larger political, military, and economic context within which it existed.

An enormous amount of building took place at Río Azul between A.D. 390 and 530, the apogee of the city's history. Probably 95 percent, or 692 or more of the 729 buildings in the city were erected during this time (Orrego 1987:45). Acres of pavement were laid down or redone. Large and small complexes of stone buildings were created, all having a similar pattern. There were usually one or more mortuary structures, or temples, at or near the centers of clusters of residences. Cooking facilities were included in the complexes, and cisterns or small reservoirs may have been present as well.

These complexes appear to have been the residences of extended families or lineages, together with housing for servants. An example of a medium-sized complex of this sort is B-56 Complex (Ellis 1991). The mortuary building was continually enlarged for an ever increasing number of tombs. Some of the tombs were associated with adjacent sanctuary rooms, within which were wall niches in which incense was burned. Bed-benches built into the sanctuary rooms indicate that people may have meditated there for lengthy periods.

The elaborate nature of these housing facilities, together with the sumptuous artifacts, painted tombs, and other indicators of superior social status, strongly suggest that the residential complexes were occupied by aristocratic families. Patterns of ancestor worship and of ritual references to divine powers confirm this interpretation. The association of subordinate families of lower social status who seem to have provided service indicates patron-client relationships between families of distinct ranking.

There is a definite hierarchy in Early Classic housing, with at least four classes. There is little doubt that these differential residence patterns reflect social and therefore economic and political differences among the inhabitants. Very large palace complexes are physically linked with the largest temples; specifically, B-8 Palace Complex is tied to the A-3 Temple Complex 300 meters away. We assume that these most elaborate and grandiose buildings were occupied and used by the ruling families. The smaller palace and mortuary complexes were probably the homes of secondary aristocracy. Smaller and less elaborate clusters of houses attached to or near the first two classes of housing probably represent commoner housing for the dependent families of servants. A fourth level of housing is rural, distant by at least 2 km from the city. These remains consist of very low platforms with relatively few artifacts either in quantity or diversity. We believe that these represent the lowest socioeconomic class, perhaps equivalent to serfs. Río Azul social structure is discussed more thoroughly in a separate section, but it should be mentioned here that we have used a generalized feudal model of society based on data from the Maya lowlands (Adams and Smith 1981). Vertical patron-client relationships among social classes and horizontal relationships emphasizing kinship linkages are important features of the model.

Ranking the site according to its construction mass and paved area leads to an estimated figure of about thirty courtyards of major architecture. Even compared to Tikal, which was about double this size in the Early Classic, Río Azul seems impressively large. However, based on covered space calculations (Karbula 1989), the estimated population is much less than that at Tikal, probably no more than 5,500. Tikal is estimated to have had about 25,000 inhabitants at this time (Culbert et al. 1990:Tables 5.2, 5.3).

Clearly, Río Azul was a different type of city, with a heavy proportion of aristocratic families and immediate retainers. It seems to have lacked the rural population support that Tikal and Uaxactun possessed. This presents a problem of explaining how the immense construction projects at Río Azul were carried out, given the lack of commoner labor in the immediate vicinity. One solution available to a large political system is to shift labor from one zone to another. Tikal may have temporarily moved a labor pool to the Río Azul zone in order to create a planned fortress city on its northwestern frontier. The existence of a powerful neighboring regional state with its capital at Calakmul might have motivated this development (Fig. 1–2; Adams and Jones 1981:Fig. 1); Río Azul is on the edge of a "buffer zone" at least 80 km long and 20 km wide between these states. This "no-man's land" contains only small farmstead and housemound ruins as far as we know, and was probably in existence by A.D. 350.

A series of Early Classic rulers who were subordinate to Tikal began with Zak Balam, if not earlier, and continued with several other rulers, whose names remain unknown. These rulers appear to have governed a district or zone around Río Azul, for which it was the administrative center. Those names of rulers that have survived are associated with a distinctive emblem glyph (Stuart 1986:120), which is the ancient name of Río Azul or its ruling family. The meaning and translation of the glyph is disputed, and therefore we will simply use the modern designation. Rulers and their relatives were buried in tombs of a distinctive nature that include murals with hieroglyphic and artistic notations. Most of these tombs date from the fifth century A.D.

The most elaborate and informative of these interments is that of a ruler we call Governor X, who was buried in Tomb 1, over which temple Str. C-1 was built. Unfortunately, Tomb 1 was looted and most of the artifacts were scattered, destroyed, or sold into the antiquities market. However, the impressive murals are intact (Fig. 3–1, Plates 2, 3) and include a hieroglyphic text, which is read as a statement of the birthdate of Governor X, A.D. 417. Large motifs flanking the hieroglyphic text appear to be "coats of arms" of the governor's parents, Stormy Sky and Bird Claw, and his grandfather, Curl Nose. Curl-Nose and Stormy Sky are known to have been rulers of Tikal. The sun god appears in the mural as the ultimate ancestor of all of these family members, confirming the hypothesized institution of divine kingship among the Classic Maya. We estimate that Governor X died about A.D. 460 and that the tombs of his advisors are slightly later, but no later than A.D. 480.

Tombs 19 and 23 are physically associated with Tomb 1, and appear to have been the burials of two advisors of Governor X. Luckily, we found these tombs intact. One of the advisors was probably a foreigner from Teotihuacan, while the other may have been Mayan. Both burials had very little in the way of Maya pottery in them, instead emphasizing Teotihuacan-style ceramics and other stylistic elements similar to those from the central Mexican city. This is especially interesting because Governor X's father, Stormy Sky, is known from Tikal Stela 31 to have had military assistance from Teotihuacan. Curl-Nose, Governor X's grandfather, appears to have been a usurper of the Tikal throne and to have made the original alliance with Teotihuacan. The Teotihuacan presence at Río Azul has also been demonstrated in other ways. Governor X's palace (C-46 Complex) has been found and partially excavated, revealing pottery probably imported from Teotihuacan and a Teotihuacan-style cremation burial (Eaton and Farrior 1989). A piece of green obsidian, probably imported from central Mexico, was found in Tomb 25 (Ponciano 1989:184).

Other tombs at Río Azul dating from the same century indicate family or dynastic ties through their frequent use of the storm god as a motif in murals. Many of these tombs are clustered under the five temples of A-3 Complex, which grew to be an enormous structure over 34 meters in height. These are presumed to be the burials of rulers and their immediate relatives. The grandiose mortuary temples carried memorializing hieroglyphic texts; a partial text still remains on the south side of Temple A-2 (Frontispiece). Not until the eighth century A.D. did Tikal's temples surpass the height of A-3 Complex. Other tombs are located in the smaller mortuary temples among the residences of the secondary aristocracy.

As we have seen, rituals of various kinds are indicated by inventories of tomb furnishings and their placement, periodic caches of various materials in special pottery vessels, and burning and ceremonial destruction. Based on these details, we can attempt to reconstruct the motivations for such ritual. Funerary ceremonies were elaborate at both the upper and lower levels of aristocracy, but were especially so for rulers and their families. Provision of elaborate textiles, food and chocolate drinks, jewelry, carved wooden bowls, painted stucco gourds, and carved bone and shell objects was an important part of these ceremonies. Wrapping of the dead, mural decoration of the tomb, incense burning, and possibly blood-letting are other common features. Later the dead were memorialized through the construction of temples above the tombs and ceremonies held in those temples. In some cases, small sanctuary rooms next to the tombs provided means for communication with and memorialization of the deceased. Modification of the mortuary structures was accompanied by offerings of special items before and after renovation projects. Smashing of especially

elaborate and decorated pottery was also a part of these construction ceremonies.

All of these elements were as ideologically determined as were the
much more obvious ritually dedicated materials. While some of this
material and behavior is presaged in the Río Azul Preclassic, most of
it is not. It is clear that much of this liturgical activity was an importation from the Tikal-Uaxactun zone, where evidence for it occurs in
the Preclassic. It is noteworthy that all of the architecture at Río
Azul, except for perhaps six buildings, falls well within the style of
structures at Tikal and Uaxactun. This contrasts strongly with the
contemporary styles of building to the north in the Río Bec region
(Potter 1977).

Nearby cacao production and/or transhipment through Río Azul
is indirectly indicated by rural evidence from later periods, and from
the direct detection of cacao powder residues in covered pottery jars
from Tomb 19 (Hall et al. 1990). Río Azul's connection with the
canoe trade routes around the Yucatan peninsula is documented by
the presence of many marine shells from parts of the Caribbean and
the lower Gulf of Mexico. The presence of stingray spines and other
marine objects reinforces this implication.

For approximately one hundred forty years, or seven generations,
Río Azul fulfilled the geopolitical, commercial, military, and other
functions assigned to it by Tikal and its rulers. Its fate from A.D. 385
onward, therefore, was determined not by the internal dynamics of
cultural evolution, as in the Preclassic periods, but by the dynamics
of a much larger system of which it was now a part. For an explanation of the end of the Early Classic at Río Azul we must recall the
episode called The Hiatus in Maya archaeology.

This period of attempted resurgence by older ruling families at
Tikal and elsewhere may have triggered a series of civil wars that
devastated Maya civilization (Coggins 1979). But Willey (1974) has
suggested that The Hiatus was a collapse from which there was a
recovery and, from the point of view of the Río Azul data, this seems
a fair characterization.

About A.D. 530 Río Azul appears to have been destroyed by
human agency. Palaces were burned, and the debris we found
filling the rooms included fragments of human bones. Several
tombs were looted, and Early Classic Stelae 1 and 3 were mutilated
and burned. Afterward, the city was abandoned for about 130

years (over six generations), during which time buildings fell into dilapidation and disrepair, their vaults collapsing and walls cracking. The temples were also allowed to fall into desuetude. This implies that the ruling families and their dependent aristocracy no longer occupied the city and no longer commemorated their ancestors buried in and under the temples. As noted in chapter 1, the older, displaced ruling Maya families had probably been opposed to the Teotihuacan connection. During the destruction of Río Azul, it appears that a deliberate effort was made to destroy all the symbols of the linkage with Teotihuacan, including the ubiquitous cylinder-shaped black pottery jars with lids. These jars were not only destroyed but often the sherds were broken into very small bits and included in construction fill.

Ultimately, the descendants of the Teotihuacan-linked rulers seem to have won out. Ah Cacau (Ruler A) of Tikal came to power at Tikal about A.D. 681 and claimed descent from the earlier kings of Tikal (Jones 1977). The great revival and rebuilding of Tikal took place afterwards.

The Late Classic: Reoccupation and
Rural Recovery; A.D. 600–850

Most of the Late Classic construction at Río Azul involved the rehabilitation of older structures. In the worst cases, buildings were filled in and used as platforms for new construction. A-11 Palace Complex is an example of such a drastic renovation. Even some of the smaller palace complexes show a desire to reuse older buildings in some manner. New construction did occur, including a ball court and a very large temple complex (B-11/13) that was built toward the end of the eighth century. Stela 2 in front of the temple, erected in A.D. 690, names a ruler and his parents and gives him the title of Bacab, which means "ruler of a place" (Fig. 3–43). While this title may be associated with a paramount ruler, it also names an office that was occupied by people on the second level of administration. Stela 2 seems also to commemorate a conquest, showing the usual standing principal figure with a recumbent captive figure at its feet. No direct evidence of linkage with Tikal is available, but Río Azul may have been part of a larger polity and not independent. As noted before, there is some indication of an alliance with La Milpa. Another alternative is suggested in the final chapter.

At this time a very large building program was carried out at nearby Kinal, where a defensible citadel was constructed. The whole city has the appearance that Río Azul had during the Early Classic, that of a planned, geopolitically important center. Kinal appears to have assumed the administrative functions for the zone during the last part of the Late Classic. It may have been that evil memories and military vulnerability rendered Río Azul unsuitable for this role.

The zone of BA-20 was reoccupied during this period, and rural population appears to have reached an all time high with perhaps as many as 205,000 people in the 177 sq km region. There is excavated evidence of localized raised fields in the swamps of BA-20 (Culbert, Levi, and Cruz 1989; Fig. 3–4). Radar survey has indicated the possible existence of extensive systems of raised fields in the larger swamps near Río Azul and Kinal (Adams, Brown, and Culbert 1981; Adams 1993). Likely evidence of intensive agriculture at BA-20 comes in the form of huge dumps of stone tool manufacturing debris or *debitage*, resulting from the large-scale production of standardized stone cultivation tools. The association between these debitage dumps and raised-field agriculture has also been shown by work in Belize (Shafer and Hester 1983; Turner and Harrison 1983). It is clear that these systems developed in response to population growth (Turner 1974; Boserup 1965; Logan and Sanders 1976).

The general standard of living during this period seems to have been high. BA-20 commoner housing consisted of Preclassic platforms reused as house foundations, partial stone walls, and, probably, thatched roofs. As in the Preclassic, the use of stone in house walls may be an indicator of forest depletion. The eighth-century houses also had amenities in the form of associated cisterns for household water supplies and *chultuns*, underground storage chambers for foodstuffs (Black and Suhler 1986; Ellis 1991). Within Río Azul itself, commoner housing included cut stone and considerable numbers of artifacts (Eaton 1987b). At both of the Class 3, "middle-class" locations, there was a considerable number of imported granite metates and some obsidian from the El Chayal quarries near present-day Guatemala City. Housing of an impoverished variety was also present in BA-20. The inhabitants were at the bottom of the social and economic scales, judging by the very low house platforms and the scarcity and low quality of household pottery and artifacts (Ellis 1991).

The Terminal Classic: Military Disaster, Partial Recovery and Final Collapse, A.D. 850–900

Imported pottery provides evidence of contact with other Maya regional states by A.D. 840. Several ceramic types from the Slate Ware tradition of northern Yucatan appeared at Río Azul. Most of the pottery is of jar form and probably represents the importation of a product from that region—perhaps honey or the prehistoric fermented drink made from it, *balche*. Other types of imported ceramics include Fine Orange ware from the Gulf Coast of Tabasco and a few pieces of Plumbate, which originated on the south coast of Guatemala. The large amounts of Slate Ware indicates the presence of Yucatec Maya long-distance merchants, who often acted as intelligence agents. This trading episode preceded another military disaster at Río Azul. Once more, buildings were burned, temples desecrated, and the fine service ceramics of aristocratic households destroyed in wholesale lots.

The military raid that produced this destruction came from the north and was probably mounted by Maya of the Puuc region, with its large cities such as Uxmal, Labna, and Kabah, where Slate Ware pottery was a long-standing tradition. Further, the newcomers stayed at Río Azul long enough to build a small four-stairwayed platform (Str. B-63) in the middle of a plaza. This small structure has northern Yucatec traits, such as balustraded staircases with tenoned serpent heads set at their tops. Stela 4 is further proof of the origin of the new regime. It is a crudely carved monument that uses a very different symbolism in its depiction. The human figure is a warrior, clad in a serpent skirt, bearing a round shield in one hand and grasping a bundle of darts with the other. These northern Yucatec stylistic elements are reinforced by two Yucatec-style glyphs, which might name a place in northern Yucatan (Fig. 3–47).

Río Azul is only one of five southern cities where we now have evidence of Terminal Classic military intrusion. However, as will be more fully discussed in the next chapter, the militarism of the period was not the primary cause of the southern Classic collapse, but a symptom and an accelerator. Evidently, the northern Maya did not stay on at Río Azul, and it was reoccupied by southern Maya once more. This time, the occupation was a temporary military encampment, perhaps the last effort of Tikal to secure its northern frontier.

The administrative center of Kinal was better placed to resist the intrusion and appears to have held out during those desperate days. No evidence of deliberate destruction by military action appeared in our two years of work at Kinal.

As we will see, the Maya of the late ninth century faced problems of overpopulation, ecological crises of water loss and drought, a consequent upsurge of malnutrition and disease, as well as military competition over diminishing resources. It is suggested that the northern Maya were not only after the obvious accumulated resources of the southern cities, but also wanted a basic economic resource, their human populations. The carrying off into captivity of remnant southern populations would explain the sudden rise in populations of the Puuc region at this time.

At any rate, after this final disaster the region was depopulated, the cities were rapidly abandoned, and the elite class culture disappeared forever. Within fifty years, the vaults of buildings were crashing down and the jungle had overgrown the plazas and courtyards of the great cities. Occasional visits about A.D. 1000 are evidenced by incense burners left in the ancient and deteriorating temples. After that, the only visitors for which we have evidence are those of the Maya hunters and gatherers of the nineteenth century, who left their distinctive incense burners in the now fallen temples. Twentieth-century *chicleros* scratched their initials on the walls of Temple A-2, but that was the only notice taken of Río Azul until it was reported to John Gatling by Trinidad Pech in 1962.

CHAPTER 6

THE RÍO AZUL REGION
IN LARGER PERSPECTIVE

Introduction

THE CITY WE CALL RÍO AZUL was a medium to large administrative center and also fulfilled other urban functions. In this chapter I will make use of the data from regions surrounding Río Azul and from the central and southern Maya lowlands in general in order to place the Río Azul region and site into a context of general evolutionary trends and culture-historical development. This will also give a view of the southern lowland Maya civilization from the perspective of Río Azul and its region.

In archaeology, evolutionary schemes are usually defined as the theoretically designated interactions among cultural and natural systems—human population growth and its effect on the development of communities, for example. Culture history on the other hand, while being partly the stuff of evolutionary theory, is highly detailed and may deal with very specific events such as the conquest of the Río Azul region by Tikal or the burial of Governor X. While both views may shift in response to new research, theoretical formulations are the more ephemeral because they are necessarily based on a limited sample of data. The problems of small samples are always with us in the Maya lowlands and in any complex culture area. Digging at a Maya city for five seasons may yield only as little as a 1–3 percent sample of the total theoretical deposits. Of the thirty-eight major cities now known, only sixteen have been dug even to this limited extent. This ignores the hundreds and thousands of smaller and earlier sites. There are 4,000 registered sites in the state of Yucatan alone. Still, carefully derived samples can be judiciously used to create culture history from chronology and content, and, further, to create explanation from culture history.

The explicit theoretical framework used here is derived from an earlier formulation that I have published elsewhere (1984, 1986a). This scheme is now badly out of date in that only the data from the first season (1983) were used and so, in that case, imperfect data skewed the derived theory. This is a good example of the ephemeral nature of explanation. I hope that the present formulation will be longer lasting. The theoretical structure is an attempt to take into account the various important dynamic elements at distinct stages in the career of Maya Lowland culture. The structure owes much to my colleagues in the Maya Collapse Conference (Culbert 1973), the Maya Origins Conference (Adams 1977), and the Lowland Settlement Patterns Conference (Ashmore 1981), and to the theoretical models that we all contributed to in those seminars.

One of the constant themes in research on Maya culture is the interaction between human cultural systems and natural systems, more often termed cultural ecology. Human population growth is the most obvious and primary of these interactions. Another consistent theme is the role of ideology and its effect on the forms that a culture may assume. The differing effects may be seen by comparison, say, of a religion that emphasizes ancestor worship and one that is essentially animistic and focuses on impersonal but powerful elements of nature. Competition among human societies and segments of those societies is another common theme. This competition may assume the extreme manifestation of warfare, but more often appears in the forms of politics and economics. Cooperation, either voluntary or forced, is the other side of the coin (Sanders and Price 1968). Thus economic competition may ultimately give rise to the cooperation inherent in long-distance trade and far-flung transportation networks. These enterprises may link previously independent and competitive zones with distinct commodities and tie them into a reciprocally beneficial system.

The Earliest Communities:
The Middle Preclassic 1; 900–500 B.C.

The development of the basic agricultural food complex mainly took place elsewhere than in the Maya Lowlands. Although undoubtedly tropical foods were added to the basic inventory, beans, maize, and squash are all highland in origin. The first known Maya Lowland farming village societies are dated about 1200 B.C. at Cuello, Belize

(Andrews and Hammond 1990), 900 B.C. on the Pasión River, and at 700 B.C. in the north at Dzibilchaltun. The earliest material we have in the Río Azul zone dates to 900 B.C. at earliest. The earliest pioneer farmers in northern Belize settled in small communities along the rivers and swamps of that zone (Hammond 1977), and in the southern Petén farmers settled along the large rivers; both were similarly attractive with their adjacent deep alluvial soils (Willey 1977). Thus, Río Azul's early development is somewhat surprising given that this zone is not well-favored in terms of soils.

Andrew Sherratt (1980) has argued that the earliest forms of agriculture were intensive gardening in naturally moist areas—edges of marshes, around springs, and along watercourses. This fits the patterns of distribution derived from the earliest village material yet found in the Maya Lowlands. Clusters and linear communities along rivers would have been the forms of settlement resulting from this type of agricultural preference. Although no early village or housing remains have yet been found in the Río Azul zone, according to this theory they should be located in the areas of best soils along the river. This is indeed where the few fragments of pottery have been found that date to this time, the only evidence thus far of human occupation for this period. Apparently, clusters of early villages were isolated one from another in several parts of the Maya Lowlands; the northern Yucatec plain, northern Belize, the Pasión River, and the Tikal zones were all occupied early. Around them were vast zones of unoccupied and heavily forested lands. For the next five hundred years the major dynamics were population growth, multiplication of villages, and the destruction of the tropical forest. Some confirmation of this comes from an unpublished computer simulation by Seymore H. Koenig (personal communication 1978) that yielded an essentially even distribution of villages over all arable land. This arable land–driven simulation convincingly matches the distribution data that we have for the Middle Preclassic, in which by 500 B.C. villages occupy most of the available arable land.

Therefore, because of its limited arable soils, it makes good sense that the Río Azul zone should be occupied late, but no later than 500 B.C., when the first population maximum appears to have been reached in the lowlands. Sherratt's theory indicates that as the conditions of optimum soil moisture were exhausted, an extensive land use pattern developed. This means a slash-and-burn type of cultivation system, which is the kind of system in use today in the lowlands where there are vast unoccupied zones and thin populations. In the present-day system, a piece of land is used for a few years until soil exhaustion sets in, then abandoned for as much as twenty years until soil nutrients have been replenished by forest processes. With this kind of cultivation system, as populations expand in numbers, they also expand through space. Assuming that the same dynamic was in operation in earliest agricultural times, this describes the mechanism for the eventual Middle Preclassic occupation of all easily cultivated lands.

As nearly as can be detected, at this early time Maya Lowland society was largely egalitarian, with an emphasis on achieved social prestige. In most regions no special structures or other material indicators of complex ritual life have been found. The extraordinary exceptions to this general picture are those at Nakbe and Río Azul. At Nakbe very large terraced platforms and buildings were constructed about 620 B.C. (Hansen 1990, 1991). The Middle Preclassic temple platform discovered by Valdez at Río Azul, G103 sub 2, dates to about 300 B.C. or earlier. The temple decoration has already been discussed, but is noteworthy here for its connections to the Izapan art style.

The explanation for these exceptions is best given by the excavators, but I will tentatively advance one here, based on the circumscription theory of Robert Carneiro (1970). Carneiro argues that growing populations tend to concentrate around limited resources or within well known ecological zones. Increasing densities lead to new sets of problems and new solutions (Netting 1977). In the case of construction at Nakbe, it appears that the resource was the shallow lake and marsh environment near the center, which would have fulfilled the conditions for early agriculture as outlined by Sherratt. The very large marshes would have allowed an unusually large population and a greater number of closely spaced villages. This formulation explains the available manpower, but not the motivation for investment of labor into structures of unprecedented size. For the latter, we must turn to ideological and political motivations.

Social-structural explanations alone are inadequate to explain the origins of complex society, given the lack of evidence for any prior social stratification and hereditary or otherwise established leadership. Ideological factors include religion, and indeed, the Nakbe structures appear to have the forms of later temple buildings. However, these temples were probably not used like the later ancestral memorials. Their rituals may have had more to do with the placation and manipulation of natural forces, the kind of animistic practices that seem to characterize certain agricultural societies today in the Pacific (Oliver 1951).

Here we have a refutation of the extreme cultural-materialist point of view, which holds that ideology generally and religion in particular are epiphenomenal (Sanders 1981). The argument advanced by the culture materialists is complex, but can be distilled to the statement that economics, population growth, and social forms are all determinant of ideology. Given this premise, religion conforms to the overwhelming influence of the political system, for example. However, in the case of the Maya, the earliest large structures are not administrative, but religious in function. In other words, the argument can be made that religion did indeed affect the formal qualities of Maya civilization as it emerged. We must not go so far as to argue that religion was a determinant of the culture. I prefer to take the stance that cultural institutions are interactive and that they can vary in determinative influence at various developmental stages. In our second case, the presumed Middle Preclassic Río Azul villages were the agricultural support for the surprisingly early Río Azul temple G103 sub 2, with its modeled-incised stucco decoration. We assume that the villages were concentrated in the strip along the Río Azul and that therefore the circumscription theory would also pertain to them. However, none of this is very satisfactory because the data are so new, and we are still in the process of exploiting the finds.

Regional Centers: The Middle Preclassic 2; 500–250 B.C.

Throughout the Maya Lowlands the gradual population increase of the previous four hundred years appears to have accelerated after 500 B.C. Villages became thicker on the ground. There was a proliferation of regional centers, which at first were of religious importance but later assumed commercial and administrative functions as well. Therefore religion appears to have begun a chain of development that ultimately led to the appearance of cities. These early centers varied in size, serving the rural populations of anywhere from several hundred square kilometers to as little as a few dozen.

In these centers an interesting and crucial pattern was established early: periodic occupation, florescence, collapse, and abandonment.

This pattern is first evident in the flowering of Nakbe and its abandonment after several hundred years at about 250 B.C. (Hansen
1990). Before its demise, however, a causeway had been built across
marshy ground linking Nakbe with the Late Preclassic site of El
Mirador, 17 km to the north. This was then a zone of shallow lakes
and marshes, which are now only present in the remnant forms of
bajos, or periodic swamps. A basic geographic and geological tenet is
that lakes and ponds are ephemeral features. Perhaps the specific local
circumstances of abandonment and reoccupation were due to the
drying up of formerly abundant surface water. When El Mirador
began to bloom, some of the largest buildings ever erected by the
Maya were built on the edges of large and as yet uncultivated swamps
(Matheny 1980; Hansen 1990).

Presumably, the Río Azul zone underwent the same population
growth patterns as elsewhere, but in a more muted form due to the
less favorable soil and forest conditions. Little direct evidence is available to us from the zone itself. However, given patterns of Preclassic
land use in surrounding regions, we may assume that most of the
forest was cut down, the land converted to agricultural use, and the
jungle that remained heavily selected for economically valuable
species.

Early Cultural Climax: The Late Preclassic; 250 B.C.– A.D. 250

Through nearly all of the 97,000 square miles of the Maya lowlands a remarkable similarity in material culture characterizes the Late
Preclassic. Lustrous red, black, and cream ceramics were used in
households for food service. Food preparation was aided by rougher,
unslipped pottery, which held water, soaking grain, soups, porridges,
and stews for cooking. Not only the same pottery but many of the
same stone tools were in use throughout the region, including axes,
knives, adzes, hoes, and other forms. Stone tools, along with bone
and wooden implements, were devoted to numberless daily tasks,
such as cutting trees, working wood, weeding and cultivating gardens,
quarrying stone, and digging storage pits. This basic technology and
the skills to use it were now fully developed, changing little through
the next seventeen centuries. Formal and stylistic qualities did change,
as I noted in the discussion of chronology.

Regional centers became ever more common, and large platforms
were built at many sites to support various kinds of public and private

buildings. The largest such structures known are from El Mirador, where the Danta building complex reached a volume of over two million cubic meters (Matheny 1980). In fact, with several such building complexes, El Mirador is the largest Late Preclassic site known at present, with perhaps the largest structures ever erected by the Maya. However, there are other impressive contemporary sites nearby; Calakmul to the north (Folan et al. 1995), Tikal to the south (Culbert 1977), and Lamanai to the east (Pendergast 1981) were all constructing very large temple platforms. Smaller but also important Preclassic centers are Becan in the Río Bec region and Cuello, Cerros, and Colha in northern Belize (Fig. 1–2). A distinct hierarchy of communities developed in the Late Preclassic with the largest sites in each region at the top (Adams 1982).

At some point in the five hundred-year span of the Late Preclassic, population growth made slash-and-burn agriculture unsustainable, and farmers shifted to various forms of intensive agriculture. The importance of this shift cannot be overemphasized, because it established the economic basis for Classic Maya civilization. This economic transformation was based on the application of the basic stone-tool technology to the problems of wetland gardening. At Pulltrouser Swamp in northern Belize, a network of drainage canals was dug in the swamp to create a system that had both irrigation and drainage functions (Turner and Harrison 1983). The first major increase in production of stone tools for use in this labor-intensive gardening appears about 30 km to the south of Pulltrouser, at Colha, where high-quality chert suitable for mass production was found. A system for manufacturing standardized tools of a few types was developed, and several thousand such tools were manufactured and exported each year to places like Pulltrouser (Shafer and Hester 1983; Shafer 1983). Huge dumps of manufacturing waste material called debitage were piled up at Colha.

This well-documented system of production, export, distribution, and usage is one of the best examples we have of the development of Late Preclassic trade patterns. Such trade both integrated and stimulated cultural development in several fields (Webb 1973). Trade was vastly important in many areas, among them Cerros, a Late Preclassic port on the sheltered waters of the Bay of Chetumal (Freidel 1986). Presumably several commodities were shipped out of and through this center. The Maya Lowlands produced both salt and honey—

crucial items in the ancient Mesoamerican world. Medicinal herbs, tropical woods, cacao, kapok, tropical bird feathers, textiles, and many other products and commodities were traded from the low-lands, being exchanged for obsidian, jade, and other items as early as the Middle Preclassic. Trade moved overland by means of porters and via water routes with probably thousands of canoes, as in the sixteenth century.

Several other mechanisms of social, economic, political, and ideo-logical integration were simultaneously developed during the period. Occupational specialization appeared in many fields beside the artisan craft of tool production. Ritual leadership was already in being and these leaders resided in the regional centers. By analogy with ethno-graphic cultures, we assume that these leaders were originally heads of both kinship units and villages. The offices of traditional village leadership are usually based on some specific genealogical principle, but the functions are generalized. Such kin-group and village leaders also usually operate by consensus and with a council. By some means, usually considered to have been economic as well as ideological, these leaders managed to make their superior positions hereditary. At this point, probably imperceptible in the archaeological record, consen-sual leadership groups became hereditary elites. An important ideo-logical shift was also made by the new aristocrats to protect their status. They encouraged the trend in Maya religion away from the early emphasis on animistic worship of natural powers (sun, wind, rain, etc.) and toward veneration of ancestors, to whom appeal might be made for intervention with the natural powers.

Given the establishment of permanent leadership, it was natural that these groups would begin to accumulate additional functions. Anyone with experience of modern governmental bureaucracies can fill in the details for themselves at this stage. In the cases of the Maya, the new elites apparently took control of the long-distance and internal trade networks, as well as the food production systems and public works projects. This suggested scenario of transformation is not necessarily correct or the only one possible. However, it does have the virtue of fitting the data now available.

Accepting this scenario of origination makes it easier to under-stand how an elite group, once established, might entrench itself and endow itself with continuity. There are many modern and historical analogies for this process. There are also more data from the Maya lowlands for the Late Preclassic period than for earlier times (Willey 1977). Trends from this period include continued population growth and the proliferation of regional centers, as noted. Interaction among the centers through the period increased and intensified. The mechanisms for interaction were not only trade, but also religious pilgrimages to famous shrines, political alliances, and intermarriage, as well as competition, among the elite groups. Warfare became endemic toward the end of the period, as certain elites attempted to incorporate other zones into their spheres of political control. This in turn created a forcing atmosphere in which those regions and zones that had not developed centralized political and economic systems did so in self-defense. More major military fortifications date from the end of the Late Preclassic than from any other period (Webster 1976; Adams 1977). Another important and new element is that the Maya lowlands finally lost their relative isolation from the rest of Mesoamerica. While not unaware of or sealed off from major events elsewhere in the Early and Middle Preclassic periods, the Maya nonetheless had been able or forced to go their own way up to about 250 B.C. Thereafter they were increasingly integrated into the larger culture sphere of Mesoamerica.

Finally, it should be mentioned that the development of complex art forms had originated in the Middle Preclassic and matured through the Late Preclassic. Hieroglyphic writing, apparently derived from art, also appeared in the Late Preclassic. At first, both art and writing appear to have been devoted to ideological matters—depictions of the deities and recording of creation stories and the like. The leadership groups developed and used writing and art as means of self-glorification, in addition to the already extant forms of ritual. In other words, the media became the tools of elite class propaganda, its expression multiplying into sculpture, modeled stucco, mural painting, lapidary work, and, eventually, polychrome pottery—all of which appeared at the end of the Preclassic.

The Río Azul Region

On a smaller scale, some of the same processes were happening in the Río Azul region, which now became much more integrated into the cultural evolutionary events of the Maya Lowlands in general. Population growth became more rapid and approximately doubled its size from the previous period. Along the Río Azul and in the 177 sq km of arable land to the east of it, a maximum of 17,500 people lived in small villages. At least four major platforms were built, located about a kilometer apart on the east bank of the river (Fig. 3–2). A possible regional center of about four courtyards in size was built east of the river at BA-22. It is also possible that the supporting villages were more thickly clustered along the river. Village leadership had now evolved to the point where it could persuade great numbers of people to labor for considerable periods building large constructions.

By the end of the Late Preclassic period, ca. A.D. 250, there were at least four classes of housing, which seem to reflect the various social statuses of the inhabitants. The top level of residential structures, Class 1, occupy literally the highest elevations and have the advantage of the breezes, which both cooled and blew away clouds of insects. A very large platform, 17,000 cubic meters in volume, supported elaborate housing (C-69 complex) at what later became Río Azul. Similar or larger platforms are located at Arroyo Negro, about 3 km north, and at G-103, 1 km south. These buildings may represent the ruling elite. Elite class residences (Class 2) are also located at the heads of monumental staircases cut from hillsides—as at BA-20, locality 210—or on large platforms—such as in the 209 locality (Hendon 1989; map). BA-22 buildings may also represent a Class 2 site. It is difficult to know whether these residences represent a distinct social class, or are simply the country homes of the same people living in Class 1 residences. Class 3 housing is substantially built, but is less elaborate and lacks monumental platforms. However, considerable landscape modification was done in preparing home sites for these people of presumed lesser status. Much humbler housing (Class 4), found in the 211 zone, represents the lowest social level (Ellis 1987). These houses were made entirely of perishable materials and are either on the ground or on very low platforms.

G-103 sub 1 is a crucial structure whose function is not clearly understood. It appears to have been a combination residential and ritual structure (Valdez 1993). That is, it seems to have the characteristics of both later palaces and temples. With its use of terraced, stone masonry walls in highly patterned forms, it is a much more formal structure than the contemporary elite residential zones of 210 locality. This building seems to overlap the transition between Late Preclassic and Early Classic.

The river's value as a water and communication resource clearly had become crucial for the further development of human communities in the region. Surface water in the Río Azul region virtually disappears each March after about six weeks of dry weather. The river ceases to flow and dries up into segmented lagoons, but these hold millions of gallons of potable water which can sustain large numbers of people until the beginning of the rains in mid-May. It is possible that some of the lagoons are also spring fed through the dry season. The control of such a limited but vital resource would be a lever for social control used by the new elites. In Carneiro's terms (1970), they could take advantage of a special form of resource circumscription to consolidate their power. The later development of additional water supplies in the form of artificial reservoirs would only enhance their use of this social instrument (Scarborough and Gallopin 1991; Scarborough et al.; Adams 1991).

In summary, the principal early driver for cultural evolution would seem to have been population growth, with all of its consequent demands for reorganization as higher densities were achieved. In the Middle Preclassic, the existing ideology oriented the use of social surpluses like labor and time. These resources were put to use in building temples elevated on high platforms. The collaboration of hundreds of people needed for such endeavors served also as an integrative factor, as did the temple centers once they were built. This pattern of temple centers supported by villages proliferated in the Late Preclassic and some of the centers apparently became towns, with permanent populations. Regional systems of temple center support came into being, and these same systems were adapted to the trade of desirable objects and commodities. Control of the villages was at first lodged in councils, but passed into the hands of specific kinship units, probably lineages. Lineage heads possibly became the temple center managers.

An ideological transformation that occurred was probably a deliberate strategy designed by the leadership to ensure their own continuity in power. Religious emphasis shifted from the worship of impersonal deities to the veneration of ancestors and the conception that they were interceding members of the supernatural. This change produced an hereditary leadership based on genealogy—in a word, an aristocracy. Further, the communicative devices of art and writing were co-opted by the new elite for their own purposes. Thereafter the accumulation of functions and power was an assured process accelerated by competitive situations, including warfare. Local, zonal, and regional political systems were created and were the bases for the next cultural florescence. Río Azul was not a major player in this game, but had developed a local and regional elite who continued to rule from their small temple centers. As it turned out, both rulers and centers were very vulnerable to the larger and more predatory regional states that had developed around them.

Second Florescence and Localized Apogees:
Early Classic 1; A.D. 250–360

In some zones and regions there was an easy transition between the Preclassic and Early Classic. Nohmul (Fig. 1–2), 92 km to the northeast, appears to have made the shift successfully. In other parts of the lowlands, changes appear to have been traumatic, perhaps even terminating development at sites such as Seibal. The gigantic center of El Mirador, the lesser centers of Nakbe, and the port of Cerros were entirely abandoned with only insignificant reoccupation in much later times. There are probably as many explanations for these interruptions as there are sites. At Becan in the Río Bec region, the fortified late Preclassic fortress was apparently attacked, but survived. Tikal, already a small city at the end of the Preclassic, was safe behind its extensive defenses and continued its development. In the cases of El Mirador and Nakbe, there is the likelihood of ecological disaster. The shallow lakes and marshes that surrounded these sites may have dried up at this time, and it is possible that Late Preclassic intensive use of these wetlands in the Late Preclassic hastened the process (Gill 1999). It is also possible that other Preclassic sites were subdued in the military competition of the transitional period.

The advance of hereditary principles among the controlling families of the regional centers led to the development of two concepts—divine kingship and the hierarchical levels of administration. The seeds of these concepts had been sown in the preceding periods, but their full potential was developed in the Early Classic 1 phase. Increasing rivalry for prestige, trade, and food production among the regions drove them to increasingly integrated systems of all kinds. We see evidence of this in the Río Azul region, although the details are not well understood at present. Eventually, these rivalries forced the appearance of regional states. Warfare continued to be present as an element of competition and as an accelerator of change. This appears to have been especially the case in the southern and central lowlands. Here development focused increasingly around dominant primate sites such as Tikal, Calakmul, and Becan–Río Bec as they became the capitals of regional states. The appearance of buffer zones between these regional polities was simply another aspect of the process of consolidation. Both rural food production zones and hierarchically sorted communities were organized into integrated systems.

Settlement patterns of the period show several levels of complexity. Dispersed single- or extended-family farmsteads were present in some but not all regions. Considerations of personal security may have kept the populations of certain zones nucleated. The simplest communities were agricultural villages descendant from those of the Preclassic, and lacked any significant formal architecture. Regional and local centers came into existence, with formal construction consisting of masonry, vaulted buildings, modeled stucco, paved plazas and courtyards, and functionally differentiated zones. We have defined the probable boundaries and political heads of regions by using various analytical techniques developed by geographers (Fig. 1–2; Appendix 2; Adams and Jones 1981:Fig. 1).

Such settlement pattern analysis indicates a hierarchical pattern wherein Tikal, Calakmul, and Becan or Río Bec were probably primate cities as early as the Early Classic and dominated their immediate regions. At the lower levels of the hierarchy, there appear to have been no centers between one and four courtyards in size in the Early Classic. Centers above five courtyards of architecture carried out the basic functions of preindustrial cities (Childe 1950; Steward 1956; Adams 1981). Sites having between five and ten courtyards may have operated as local and regional administrative centers, while cities with ten to forty courtyards were more likely to be political and economic capitals. Permanent nonelite populations with craft specializations serviced both the surrounding countryside and the resident elites. Aristocratic residences (palaces), large religious structures (temples), administrative headquarters (palaces), market zones, fortifications and other functionally designated zones made up the cities. The number of functions increased as size increased, and primate cities performed more functions than other cities. Such settlement hierarchies can be compared to those derived from hieroglyphic hierarchies developed by Martin and Grube (1994).

Río Azul in Early Classic 1.

Perturbations are apparent at this point in the Río Azul sequence. Some regions experienced a gradual development of Early Classic culture, while other regional centers appear to have been abandoned. BA-22 and the Arroyo Negro centers were vacated and not reoccupied until several hundred years later. The ultimate explanations for such local terminations are still vague. One possibility is that there was an ecological crisis that led to a voluntary consolidation of elite centers and elite groups. If this were the case, however, it is difficult to see why Arroyo Negro, with its large lagoon, would have been abandoned. Another explanation suggested by the competitive atmosphere elsewhere is that the BA-22 and Arroyo Negro elites were driven out of existence, literally or figuratively, and their territories incorporated into larger local and zonal political units. Or one can combine these elements into a third explanation. A competitive political situation combined with a series of crop disasters brought about by a prolonged drought led to either forcible or voluntary consolidation. In any case, the original five Preclassic regional centers appear to have been reduced to two.

G-103 and C-47 platforms appear to form a unit. They face one another across a large paved zone of nearly a kilometer in extent. A small Preclassic platform occupied the position later taken by A-3 complex. BA-20, with its formal architecture, may represent a country residential zone for the Río Azul elite. An extensive renovation of the locality 205 temple was carried out during Early Classic 1.

There are some indications of further development of separate elite-class residences at B-56 complex in Río Azul. In this case, small stone buildings arranged around a courtyard anticipate the larger complexes of a century later. A low platform in the center of the courtyard was evidently a center for ritual activity. When the courtyard underwent drastic modification, a remarkable jar decorated in polychrome colors was broken over the platform in a termination ceremony. J. J. Adams has analyzed the jar and concludes that it allows a view of very early Classic religion (1990). The vessel (Fig. 3–33) shows a scene in which the four gods of the principal directions are opposed to one another in their positions on the vase. Large and small birds of identifiable species cling to the deities' masks. A feline figure with lolling tongue rests atop one deity mask, and at least two monkeys view part of the scene with alarm. According to Adams, this scene summarizes the most important religious elements of the Early Classic and perhaps the Terminal Preclassic. Gods of the directions are associated with divine animals, which represent other elements of the universe. These figures are so arranged as to provide a kind of cosmic diagram. It is interesting to note that no humans appear in the scene. It is possible that the monkeys represent humanity or that the scene may represent a period before the appearance of people. At any rate, there is a striking difference between this art and that of Early Classic 2, which emphasizes human or abstract geometric elements.

The overlap between the older Preclassic pottery and the newly developed polychrome ceramics occurs during the last years of the Preclassic and Early Classic 1. At first polychrome design motifs emphasize the natural subject matter of the Cosmogram Jar, whose figures include jaguars, parrots, and other birds. Along the eastern rim of the Petén region, at sites such as Nohmul and Holmul (Fig. 1–2, nos. 101 and 18), this was an easy transition, which indicates that polychrome pottery developed as a response to a taste for status symbols as well as for additional means of ideological and artistic expression. Meanwhile, it appears that the mass of population living in the countryside continued to use the traditional and older monochromes of the Preclassic.

We might speculate that the regional elite along the Río Azul identified themselves with the powers of creation through their service to the gods. While it did not produce a formal theocracy, religious sanction was probably a great source of the superior status that the leadership enjoyed. This fairly archaic aristocracy has both ethnographic and historical parallels, such as in the more highly developed sacred kings of Southeast Asia (Heine-Geldern 1956) or many sixteenth-century Mesoamerican elite groups (Adams 1991). It may also be that this kind of society was vulnerable to others, such as those around Tikal and Uaxactun, that had become more secular and power oriented.

The settlement pattern in the Río Azul region is very loosely integrated and linear. It is oriented to the river, with what might be termed "nodes" at intervals of about 2 km. There is no single large center or nucleation that would reflect centralization of political authority. This appears to be different from the Tikal-Uaxactun zone, where nucleation appears to have taken place earlier, and possibly reflects an earlier trend to political centralization as well (cf. W. R.

Coe 1990; Laporte and Fialko 1990). In any event, beginning about
A.D. 360, Tikal experienced a series of remarkable changes that rapidly
transformed both that city and, eventually, the Río Azul region.

Transformations and Crises: Early Classic 2–3; A.D. 360-530.

One indicator of the nature of the transformations of the fourth
century A.D. is that in at least three major regions of the southern
lowlands, there was relatively little rural population (Appendix 2;
Adams 1977; A. L. Smith 1971), indicating that people preferred to
live in concentrated communities with strength and security in numbers. This urbanization appears to have happened at a time of increasing elite class demands for labor to build, maintain, and service palace
societies. The appearance of more extensive and more formal fortifications around the larger cities of Tikal, Becan, and Calakmul indicates that the motivating factor was probably warfare and other forms
of unrest. All through the area of 1,200 sq km sampled by our
projects, evidence confirms that there was very light rural population
during this period, and even some vacant zones.

By giving priority to the elements of population growth, especially
growth of the elite sector, as the driving force in cultural evolution,
we can consider other elements as secondary effects. This is not to say
that these elements, such as warfare and ideological competition, were
not important. The point is that the forms and intensity of competition were somewhat defined by a context of increasing scarcity,
caused by the appropriation of finite resources by the upper classes.

Into this roiled context came an outside element, which now
appears to have been more potent than most scholars have been
willing to credit. This is the influence of Teotihuacan in the southern
lowlands, and possibly throughout the whole vast Maya area. It is
clear to most of us who have worked in the Río Azul region that this
appearance was more intrusive, more intense, and more defining than
had been thought. Based on our own work and that or our colleagues
and predecessors, we are now in a position to suggest the nature of
the interchange.

In order to understand the importance of this transformational set
of events, we must first consider the nature of Teotihuacan itself at
the time of Maya contact. For this we turn to syntheses of material
published by Millon (1973, 1988) and Cowgill (1997). The great
city of Teotihuacan appeared around 100 B.C. and reached an apogee

of development about A.D. 300. The city eventually consisted of about 2,000 large apartment compounds which housed as many as 120,000 people. These were the farmers, merchants, artisans, and members of other occupational classes. Their standard of living was very high, perhaps higher than that of the average peasant in the area today. A favored elite class lived and worked in large, sprawling palace complexes.

The city was rigorously laid out according to a plan that emphasized two major avenues, approximately oriented to the cardinal directions. Most of the major palaces and ritual complexes were located in the northern arm of the north-south avenue, the "Street of the Dead," and at its intersection with the east-west avenue. The gigantic temples of the Sun and Moon, with complexes of smaller ritual buildings, were in this northern sector. The administrative and ritual headquarters appear to have been inside a fortified enclosure today called The Citadel. Recent work inside this enclosure has revealed more than two hundred sacrificial victims associated with the most elaborate temple of the city and with war ritual (Sugiyama 1989). One of the city's largest palaces is also inside the enclosure and was probably the ruler's residence. The population of the Basin of Mexico appears to have been largely concentrated in this great city. The rest of the basin was thinly populated as the rural, food-raising zone for the new society formed at Teotihuacan.

Teotihuacan was pretty clearly a militaristic-commercial state; it expanded at the expense of its neighbors and attempted to control most of the major commodity areas of Mesoamerica. There is irrefutable evidence for the presence of foreigners in the city in the special residential quarters for lowland Maya, Zapotecs from Oaxaca, and people from other parts of the civilized world. Reciprocally, it has also been demonstrated that the Teotihuacanos established diplomatic relations with Monte Alban in Oaxaca and went as far as the Maya highlands in their search for new sources of goods. The large center of Kaminaljuyu in the Maya highlands was taken over and drastically modified by the Teotihuacanos sometime in the fourth century A.D. For the Teotihuacanos, the options appear to have been commercial ties, diplomatic linkages, collaborative foreign rulers, and total takeover of zones of special interest with inserted colonies of Teotihuacanos. There was also a sequence of takeover activity which seems to have started with commercial exchange or elite-class status item exchanges. These initial ventures then seem to have led to more intense and controlling relationships if they were judged to be worthwhile. It might be noted that this is the same suggested sequential process practiced later by the imperialistic Aztecs. In any case, the interests of Teotihuacan in the Maya Lowlands appear to have begun with commercial contacts, which we presume were initiated through contacts with the Maya elite.

The earliest appearance of Teotihuacan in the lowlands seems to be at Altun Ha in the form of numerous obsidian artifacts, which may date to the Protoclassic and certainly date to Early Classic 1 (Pendergast 1971; Pring 1977; Cowgill 1993). The artifacts take various forms with ritual significance and belong together as a deposited group. They represent elite contacts between a twelve-courtyard Maya center and a huge metropolis of central Mexico. This is clearly a case of interaction between unequal partners, unless one considers that this may be the tentative initiation of trade with the Maya Lowlands. Altun Ha is much closer to the sea than is Tikal, which later became a focus of interaction between the cultures.

The Maya Lowlands were the great repository of a number of valuable commodities, including salt, honey, medicinal herbs, tropical woods, tropical bird feathers, beeswax, incense, jade, chocolate (cacao), and various manufactured goods, such as bright polychrome pottery, fine textiles, carved jades, and wooden carvings, among other things. It should be noted that, excepting raw jade and incense, these artifacts and commodities are mainly labor intensive goods. Thus, to exploit such commodities and assure continual supplies it would be most desirable to make a linkage with the most highly organized and largest of the Maya centers; in this case, Tikal.

As nearly as we can now reconstruct, Tikal was the home of some of the most aggressive aristocrats in the lowlands. They had already created a very large center and aggregated a large number of people in and around it. The repeated mentions of the date A.D. 378 in texts at Tikal seem to be associated with a link between Teotihuacan and the Tikal ruling dynasty (Culbert 1991:132). Teotihuacan iconography and other influences were apparently present at Tikal a few years prior to 378, but the date is crucial in that it seems to commemorate the displacement of the Maya ruler Jaguar Paw (II or III) by a foreigner called Curl Nose (Coggins 1979). Christopher Jones sees this as leading to "new 'Classic Maya' sites, trade routes and alliances expanding Tikal's sphere of influence" (1991:112).

More to the point, Clemency Coggins posits that Curl Nose, although a Maya aristocrat, was both from outside of the Tikal region and a collaborator with Teotihuacan. His monuments at Tikal show him dressed in Teotihuacan regalia, and, as Robichaux has recently shown (1993), even Tikal's emblem glyph seems to have been derived from a Teotihuacan symbol, the tassel. A colleague of Curl Nose, known as Smoking Frog, was evidently a military leader who ruled Uaxactun. Smoking Frog is shown on Uaxactun Stela 5 dressed as a Teotihuacan warrior. The son of Curl Nose, Stormy Sky, continued the dynasty and is shown on one of his monuments (Tikal Stela 31) flanked by two Teotihuacan warriors. Thus, it is farily clear that military muscle was involved in the equation, and this was likely part of the payoff for Tikal in their alliance with Teotihuacan. Tikal benefited by gaining military and political advisors, probably military cadres, and the profitable commercial linkage.

Imported pieces and imitations of Teotihuacan pottery are the most common evidence of Teotihuacan presence. Based on our studies at Río Azul and earlier studies at Tikal, Uaxactun, and Altar de Sacrificios, it appears that the use of black colored, cylindrical, tri-pod vessels with lids was a mark of status during this period. Further, the status conferred on the owner of such pottery likely was tied to its association with Teotihuacan. The Balanza Black Ceramic Group constitutes the majority of Teotihuacan-influenced types in the Maya Lowlands. That such pottery was highly prized is indicated by its frequent inclusion in the grave offerings for deceased members of the elite. That is, Teotihuacan-style pottery was included among the most-valued possessions that accompanied a Maya aristocrat to the tomb. While often undecorated, the pottery is also frequently incised with designs, including chocolate and associated symbols. Other symbols on the Río Azul specimens include depictions of the Maya rain god, Chac, and the equivalent of the central Mexican rain deity, which appears to have been so important at Teotihuacan. The motifs, monochromy, preference for incision, and forms all belong much more to the Teotihuacan ceramic tradition than to that of the Maya Lowlands.

Teotihuacan materials at Uaxactun and Tikal during this period nearly all come from elaborate elite tombs. Other sites in the central

and southern lowlands have produced occasional finds of the definitive black tripod pottery, but none so abundantly as at Río Azul.
More typical of the sites farther from Tikal is that of Altar de
Sacrificios, 135 km south, on the Pasión River. At Altar, the one pot
of this category found intact was decorated by a glyph representing
Zotz, the leaf-nosed bat, which is definitely a Maya motif. It is likely
that the item was a Maya imitative production.

Río Azul in Early Classic 2–3 Period

If this was a period of general and drastic change for Tikal, it was
even more so for Río Azul. Indeed, we in the project regard the
period as crucial in the life of the city. To reprise, the evidence indicates that Río Azul was founded as an urban center ca. A.D. 380, that
it was established as a fortified city, and that it belonged to a regional
political state headed by Tikal. Moreover, the data indicates that the
region was acquired by military force and with the help of Teotihuacan advisors, if not an actual cadre of Teotihuacan warriors. Río
Azul Stela 1 retrospectively refers to this conquest and to Smoking
Frog. The provincial elite of Río Azul were probably executed as
commemorated by depictions on the column altars in front of a small
temple.

The city was fortified in order to protect the frontier of the Tikal
Regional State, which was located just to the west of the Río Azul
(the river) itself. It also seems likely that this conquest was intended
to assure the access of Tikal to the Caribbean Sea via the Río
Azul–Río Hondo–Bay of Chetumal trade route. Tikal's only alternative route to the Caribbean was eastward through the Belize Valley.
However, the large city of Naranjo dominated the headwaters of the
Belize River and was only an intermittent and inconstant ally of
Tikal. Work directed by Hammond and Tourtellot (1992–1997) at
the large site of La Milpa, situated near the Río Azul–Río Hondo
junction, will probably produce more information on this latter
aspect. In any case, the geopolitical analysis of the new Tikal rulers
appears to have been sound. The boundary with the Calakmul
Regional State to the northwest and with the more fragmented
political units to the north remained stable for centuries.

Perhaps the greatest contribution of the Río Azul project to our
understanding of the Teotihuacan connection in the Maya Lowlands
is that it was military, pervasive, and long lasting. About fifty-five

years after its conquest the governor of Río Azul was Governor X, a son of the Tikal ruler Stormy Sky. This reveals at least one administrative option for the maintenance of political coherence in these early states. It also appears to have been one which was used continuously into the sixteenth century in Yucatan.

The one intact elite woman's burial from Río Azul, Tomb 25, contained a mix of imitative Teotihucan pottery and Maya polychrome bowls. The latter include a motif that suggests that the woman was from Uaxactun, where the motif occurs more commonly on nearly identical bowls. That intermarriage among the elites of the lowlands was practiced as a means of tieing together the different cities and parts of a political system has long been suggested (Molloy and Rathje 1974). There is strong evidence that a female known as Woman of Tikal and noted in the texts of the large city of Naranjo (Coggins 1975:218–19) is commemorated and mentioned on two Tikal monuments (Tikal Stelae 23 and 26; Mathews and Willey 1991:62). Her parents appear to have been rulers of Naranjo, which is located about 32 km to the east. Woman of Tikal is assumed to have married into the ruling dynasty and to have become a key ancestress for later rulers who mentioned her.

Thus, marital alliances, kinship ties, outright conquest, and establishment of new and strategically located cities were all means of extending the boundaries of large Classic states. Río Azul has produced evidence of all four expansionist techniques. It also illustrates a number of the processes outlined by J. Marcus in her study of Mesoamerican political fluctuation (1992).

The operation of subordinate administrative centers such as Río Azul was probably somewhat unique to each city. However, our data indicates some basic and probably common functions for these second- and third-level cities. Because they were part of a larger political system, such centers were established for political control over a segment of territory. Judging by the territory around Río Azul and its boundaries as we can define them, its jurisdiction was as small as 1,500 sq km or as large as 4,219 sq km (Adams and Jones 1981:319). One analytical problem is to distinguish between cities that succeeded one another from those that were contemporary, but dominant over their regions. Archaeological field work over the past ten years has suggested strongly that fluctuation—of occupation, florescence, and political importance—is a characteristic of Classic period history. In the Río Azul region, we now find that Kinal was a very late center and did not exist before about A.D. 740. Therefore, the early urban network around Río Azul was formed only by the adjacent cities of La Honradez, 40 km south, and La Milpa, about the same distance east. Thus, in the Early Classic, there were fewer urban centers on the landscape than in Late Classic. Looked at from the other end of the evolutionary trajectory, however, the Early Classic saw the establishment of true urbanism in the Maya Lowlands. We have no excavated data from La Honradez and very little from La Milpa as yet, but both sites possess significant numbers of Early Classic stelae. These monuments indicate early political importance as well as occupation.

In its early history, Río Azul underwent a continual and active building program, which included military defenses and therefore suggests another important function. It has already been noted that the Early Classic boundary defined for the Tikal Regional State lies along the watercourse of the Río Azul itself (Fig. 1–2; Adams and Jones 1981:Fig. 1). Military functions would be logical if the region had been acquired by conquest in the first place, as has been suggested. Tikal has extensive Early Classic earthworks, perhaps as long as 40 km (Puleston and Callendar 1967). Calakmul to the north is also defensible and has large walls, although it is not known to what date these belong (Fletcher et al. 1987; Folan et al. 1995). In general, the Early Classic is a period of the construction of extensive and formal fortifications, such as have been noted at Becan, 72 km north of Río Azul (Webster 1976; Adams 1981). That trade connections were an important consideration is indicated by the location analysis done for Río Azul, along with the confirming evidence of imported seashells, jade, obsidian, Teotihuacan or Gulf Coast pottery, and other materials.

Administration and collection of surplus food production is another basic function indicated by the Río Azul data. Considering the reconstructions made of Maya economics and subsistence patterns, it is clear that this function is of prime importance. Support of the elite, the urban dwellers, and the political and military specialists was all done by the commoners in the countryside who were both protected and exploited by the cities.

Thus, administration, trade, military defense, and securing of the basic commodities of life rested largely in the hands of the elite who resided in and worked from these subordinate centers. This pattern was firmly established and extended in this period and is perhaps the most characteristic general trait for Maya Lowland culture from this time until the collapse, five hundred years later. This type of political and social arrangement appears traditional and conservative for the Maya as viewed from the Late Classic. However, viewed from the Late Preclassic perspective, it was truly a new order of society. For Mesoamerica as a whole, interaction between different cultural traditions was an important dynamic for change. The relations between the lowland Maya and the highland Teotihuacanos is clearly an instance of such interaction. As I have said elsewhere, it seems that we cannot fully understand Lowland Maya civilization without understanding Teotihuacan and vice versa.

The relatively drastic and rapid nature of the change apparently created perturbations, as revolutionary or major cultural changes often, perhaps always, do. The Maya suffered a cultural setback beginning about A.D. 530, which seems to be partly a social and political reaction, but also was triggered by a climatic shift. About one hundred fifty years after the foundation of Río Azul, a disaster befell it which was part of a general period of troubles for the Maya.

The Hiatus: A.D. 530–593

The factor of long-term weather change has been too little noticed by most scholars dealing with the Maya Lowlands, with certain notable exceptions (Folan et al. 1983; Gill 1999). If it is included in the explanatory equations, however, climatic change not only helps to explain the origins, forms, and events of the Early Classic, but also the eventual crisis that we call The Hiatus.

The work of Richardson Gill (1999) shows convincingly that certain perturbations in Maya culture history were triggered by drastic climatic changes. Further, he describes how the intermittent prehistoric eruptions of the volcano El Chichón, in southern Chiapas near Palenque, caused worldwide shifts in general circulation patterns that were a possible source of recurrent environmental disasters for the Maya. Radiocarbon dates indicate a possible eruption of El Chichón at the onset of The Hiatus, coincident with the onset of a period of severe global cold. In Europe this period lasted from A.D. 536 to 590. Gill's meteorological model ties episodes of severe European cold to periods of severe drought in the Maya Lowlands. The correlation of the two events suggests that The Hiatus was indeed something that Willey has called "a rehearsal for the collapse" (1974). The later collapse, as we shall see, was initiated by a period of drought, leading to food, health, and social problems. The principal difference between the two periods of extreme stress is that there was a recovery from the earlier catastrophe.

And catastrophe it appears to have been, at least in the central lowlands, which includes the area of Tikal and Río Azul. In fact, R. J. Sharer thinks that The Hiatus was as prolonged at Tikal as it was at Río Azul, perhaps lasting until A.D. 692 (Morley, Brainerd, and Sharer 1983:115). At this same time, the great city of Teotihuacan began to turn inward, breaking off far-flung connections. Coggins has suggested that the older line of rulers at Tikal attempted a comeback when Teotihuacan linkages were severed (Coggins 1979). The usurping rulers of Tikal had been sponsored by the central Mexican power, but now found themselves adrift. A Tikal ruler named Jaguar Paw Skull, married to Woman of Tikal, was fourth in the line of descent from Curl Nose, the usurper (Jones and Satterthwaite 1982:Table 6). However, intermarriage into older ruling lines was apparently not enough to legitimize the Curl Nose Dynasty, and Coggins suggests that civil war resulted (1979).

This makes sense out of the destruction and abandonment that we have noted at Río Azul for the period of The Hiatus. Further, it also should be noted that nearly all imitative or imported Teotihuacan pottery at Río Azul, Altar de Sacrificios, and Seibal that was found in trash heaps was smashed into pieces much smaller than normal (measurements by the author). The only surviving whole pieces were found in elite tombs, which even in times of civil strife appear to have been sacrosanct. We have no data on the preservation of Teotihuacan related pottery at Tikal itself. But based on what we know at the moment, it appears that there was a deliberate effort to extirpate all traces of Teotihuacan symbolism. Because Río Azul was so closely related to the Teotihuacan episode and also because it was on the frontier, it would have been an especially provocative target for those Maya elite attempting to overthrow the descendants of the imposed rulers.

There is also the possibility that the Calakmul Regional State to the north of Río Azul took advantage of or caused the weakness and distraction of Tikal in its internal power struggles and was responsible for the destruction of Río Azul. William Folan's work has indicated that Calakmul was occupied early in the Preclassic, with a florescence in the Late Preclassic. After that, there is relatively little indication of political activity until the Late Classic, when the site evidently burgeoned into one of the largest of all Maya cities, rivaling Tikal (Marcus 1976, 1987; Folan et al. 1995; Adams and Jones 1981:Fig. 3).

For the period of The Hiatus, we have relatively thin populations in the countryside, indicating once more that the event was far-reaching and not just a political perturbation among the elite classes. Climatic shift and widespread warfare would create conditions affecting the total social structure. For one thing, Río Azul was nucleated, and rural population was relatively thin anyway. The fall of the city and its destruction may have driven refugees from the zone south into safer spots.

A general population decline also appears to have been a part of The Hiatus. It is not until the end of the seventh century that Río Azul shows signs of revival, and not for another fifty years after that did the rural population begin to recover. We have very little skeletal material from the period and therefore relatively thin evidence for malnutrition or other health problems that might be caused by short rations or famines. Frank P. Saul's career-long work with Maya materials will undoubtedly yield further insights into Early Classic health statuses (Saul 1972; Saul and Saul 1989). Applying the model of the Late Classic collapse to The Hiatus is risky, but doing so indicates that health problems may have been a major component of the earlier disaster. We can only look for new data to confirm or refute this surmise.

Late Classic 1; A.D. 550–692

The general recovery from the rigors of The Hiatus began perhaps as early as A.D. 550 in certain favored zones, but may have been as late as A.D. 650 in regions such as Río Azul. As noted, Sharer would extend The Hiatus at Tikal to 692. This date is the traditional end of Late Classic 1, based on ceramics. The date of accession to power of Ah Cacau, the first great ruler of Late Classic Tikal, is A.D. 682. Two of his ancestors had ruled during The Hiatus (Morley, Brainerd, and Sharer 1983:118).

Ah Cacau, also known as Ruler A, revitalized Tikal, beginning a major building program and reasserting political control over the southern territory of the Pasión River. This suggests that the Tikal Regional State had disintegrated during The Hiatus and that Tikal had lost control of regions such as Río Azul.

Río Azul during Late Classic 1; A.D. 550–692

There was relatively little new major construction at Río Azul during this period, but a great deal of refurbishment of older structures was carried out. Stela 2 dates from this period (A.D. 690) and mentions a ruler and his ancestry (Figs. 3–45, 3–46). His title is given as the Bacab of Río Azul, or "Governor of a place." We call him Governor Z. Fifty years later, Bird Jaguar II of Yaxchilan used the same title, and it is clear that he was an independent ruler (Adams 1971:Fig. 94). Therefore, it appears that Governor Z of Río Azul perhaps was an independent ruler who was linked to local elites of the northeastern Petén, but probably not to the Tikal ruling family. The clause on Río Azul Stela 2 that refers to a visit to Río Azul by the ruler of La Milpa (Robichaux 1997) might indicate that La Milpa's ruler was Governor Z's overlord. The one important building dating to this period is Str. B-11/13 Complex, probably the funerary temple dedicated to Governor Z.

The renewal of urban life in Río Azul was a part of the general phenomenon of renewal among the battered and bruised cities of the Classic Lowlands. Very thin populations are indicated in the countryside, and therefore the population base and labor supplies were probably shaky. This preceded a period of exponential population growth and rapid expansion of intensive farming.

Late Classic 2; A.D. 692–840

With the reestablishment of a strong rulership at Tikal in A.D. 682 and an apparently favorable weather cycle of balanced wet and dry years, Maya civilization underwent an explosive development. There were not only changes in size, but also structural changes, which led to a fundamentally different society after one hundred sixty years. The already noted thin populations of Late Classic 1 were presumably a result of the ecological-political stresses of The Hiatus. However, there appears to have been a recovery of both organizational and demographic character in Late Classic 1. By about A.D. 692, lowland populations had reached a takeoff point.

Cowgill (1975) has commented that motivations and imperatives for human population growth in any given case are subtle, multiple, and sometimes problematic. We can, however, refer to the attractive (and sound) correlation drawn by Demitri Shimkin, who observes that village-oriented societies tend to be population conservative while state-level societies tend to be population encouraging. The former have experience with periodic disaster—crop failures, for example—and know that they can depend only on themselves for their own survival. They know that their survival depends in part on keeping populations in check. State-level societies, especially those with hereditary elites, may encourage population growth for reasons having nothing to do with physical survival. The elites, hereditary or managerial, have their own agendas.

The Maya fit the bill as a state-level society, especially in the middle of the Late Classic. There were probably other factors involved, some of them unknowable, but whatever the explanation, it is certain that populations began to grow at what were probably exponential rates from depressed Hiatus levels. Tikal grew to over 60,000 in the city, with a minimum of an additional 30,000 directly tied to the city. Even if one accepts the minimalist political model of the epigraphers, Tikal's estimated minimum population, city and countryside, was more than 425,000 (Culbert, Kosakowsky, Fry, and Haviland 1990: 117). If we opt for the Regional State model, then it is possible that the elite at Tikal controlled several million people. (It should be pointed out that Culbert and his colleagues [1990] do not make any allowance for a short-term but drastic depression in Maya population during The Hiatus. That construal is my own.)

Whatever the eventual consensus on the number of people involved in a social and political unit at Tikal, and how fast the numbers grew, it is clear that high population density and totals were a part of the dynamic in Late Classic development. All of these people, with their minimum needs for water, food, firewood, housing, clothing, and the like, put an immense stress on the Maya landscape. Along other lines, a sanitary engineer visiting the project commented that an adult human produces about one pound of solid wastes per day. Thus, a theoretical population of only 10,000 produces up to 10,000 pounds of problems daily, and 300,000 pounds in a month. This total does not include other waste matter, such as garbage and the like.

Elite marriages in the Late Classic clearly took place across political lines, as the case of a middle-aged woman ruler (?) at Altar de Sacrificios illustrates. The woman's funeral was attended by the ruler of Yaxchilan, a member of the ruling family at Tikal, and a ruler from the Maya highlands. Tikal and Yaxchilan are agreed to have been politically independent, whether they were city-state or regional state capitals. Family ties, therefore, overrode political divisions, although trade and political alliances were also important in forming and reforming linkages.

The very large number of huge buildings from the Late Classic are the product of dense, well-organized populations laboring over a relatively short period of time. The size of the elite segment of society expanded to four times that of the Early Classic. This alone meant an unprecedented demand for goods and services. The superior quality of housing, food, clothing, comfort items, and other luxuries required by the upper classes put a great strain on the rest of society. It will be recalled in this regard that Juvenal said, "luxury [is] more ruthless than war." Stress is not the same as vulnerability, but the one may lead to the other. It appears to have done so in the Maya case. The secondary effects of overpopulation and ecological and social stresses can be seen to increase throughout the period of A.D. 692–840.

Maya agriculture became increasingly intensive as population rose, and the scale of the subsistence economy was much larger than we previously realized. Both terrace and raised field systems in some parts of the lowlands covered territories of great size. The support systems of the largest sites probably involved transportation of large volumes of foodstuffs from substantial distances (50 to 100 km). I believe that large-scale intensification occurred late, probably as a response to population growth. In the short term the system was successful enough to maintain dense populations for a century or two before the collapse. Culbert has written perhaps the most succinct and definitive statement on the relationship between Late Classic population growth and agricultural intensification (1990). He makes the point that some form of developmental overshoot is apparent in many cases of ecological disaster (1988:100). In the case of the Maya, he argues, increases in agricultural potential beyond a certain point were inherently unstable. This was because of water and soil losses through leakage and erosion, as well as the increasingly severe problems with insects, plant diseases, and declining soil fertility.

Another viewpoint is that of J. W. G. Lowe, who emphasizes the problems of management faced by the Maya and essentially argues that the failure to solve these problems were crucial to the ultimate collapse (Lowe 1985). This is a valid and interesting contention that is really complementary to Culbert's interpretation. The main difference is that Culbert looks at population growth and the consequences of agricultural intensification as being the main events, with other problems such as those of management being spin-offs. I agree with Culbert in this regard.

Taking this stance enables one to view Maya civilization and its decline in a coherent manner. Population growth, whether caused by political decisions or not, led to agricultural intensification. The large-scale use of intensive food production systems then led to a number of other consequences, of which problems of management, military competition, gradual ecological degradation, and increasing social stress were the most apparent.

Maya leadership was hereditary, which means that talent was not necessarily concentrated at the top. There is no indication of any adaptive shift in management style in response to the increasing problems of the Late Classic. Military predation was one solution to problems at home. Seizing the assets of other polities is a way of delaying the effects of overstressed economic and political systems. In the case of the Maya this predation took the form of raids from the northern regional states, probably from the Uxmal zone. The raids were probably designed to gain food, labor, and control of superior agricultural systems in the south. The unintended effects were to disturb the delicately structured and balanced wetland garden systems of the south and to close down parts of them through damage or the removal of people needed to maintain them.

Meanwhile, gradual ecological degradation was probably taking place through loss of ponded water in the perched swamps of the south. The cracked seals of such swamps probably leaked water down to inaccessibly deep water tables. Further, the terracing of upland zones took place over thousands of square kilometers of land in the central Yucatan zone, but also led to severe deforestation. The drastically increased need for firewood and wood for all purposes would have led to denudation of the landscape during Late Classic 2. This in turn would lead to the erosion of soils from the hillsides in spite of terracing, and, in some cases, the infilling of the raised field zones.

The Maya would have also been afflicted with short-term agricultural problems still with us today, including locust and other insect outbreaks, as well as plant diseases encouraged by excessive reliance on single crops, such as corn. Health problems would have been exacerbated by the increasingly polluted water standing in the irrigation and drainage ditches. In a tropical environment, these zones of standing water would form a perfect medium for the development and transmission of viruses.

The social stress factors are more easily seen in this context of food production and its problems. The apparent Late Classic political decentralization of the previously more integrated Early Classic regional states would make management yet more difficult. It was every noble family for themselves in some senses, and the feudal structure and dispersed manor-house land tenure system apparently was a reaction to that situation. Thus, at about A.D. 840 Maya society was in a state of extreme vulnerability when a series of increasingly severe drought years triggered an unprecedented collapse of all social, economic, and political systems.

Río Azul in Late Classic 2; A.D. 692–840

Río Azul appears to have been suppressed as an independent political unit during this period, and may have been reincorporated into the Tikal Regional State. Population estimates are high for the city, perhaps as many as 7,500 based on covered space studies (Karbula 1989). However, Río Azul seems to have lost its role as the district administrative center. Beginning in this period, a new and fortified administrative city was built at Kinal, about 12 km distant. No elite-class monuments have been found at Kinal, in spite of two years of intensive work at the site. It therefore appears that the ruling group at Kinal was secondary in importance although of enough consequence to build elaborately fortified palace and temple structures within a period of seventy-five years or less. The major city of La Milpa is about 25 km distant from Kinal and has a number of monuments that date from the Late Classic. It is possible that new political alignments appeared in the southern lowlands during this period and that these were more fragmented and smaller in dimensions. Therefore, we might speculate that La Milpa headed a smaller regional state to which Kinal belonged. Río Azul would have been still farther down the hierarchy in this arrangement.

Very large amounts of Late Classic 2 pottery and other debris at Río Azul indicate that the site was heavily occupied at this time. It had not completely lost its importance, notwithstanding the withdrawal of many of the elite to the Kinal fortress. Numerous imported types of pottery show a lively and intense commercial contact with other parts of the Maya world, especially the north. It is evident that great quantities of liquid or semi-liquid commodities were imported to Río Azul, judging by the great number of sherds from Trickle Ware jars that have been found. We think that the main commodity involved in this trade was honey and/or the fermented honey drink, balche. Large but ephemeral palace structures were built of pole and thatch materials at A-11 Complex. The five great temples of A-3 Complex still survived and were used, but apparently were in decrepit condition. Small and unimpressive tombs with relatively small groups of pottery were placed in A-54 Complex. Aside from B-11/13, no major temple-tomb structure was built in Late Classic 2. Unfortunately, B-11/13 was so badly looted and tunneled that it posed an absolute threat to life and limb for the project members working around it. Although we salvaged much information from it, no really new excavations were possible, and therefore we are uncertain as to whether or not the tomb and temple belong to the earlier part of Late Classic 2. The only clue is the date of associated Stela 2, which was dedicated in A.D. 690. This would indicate that the structure and stela both are very early in the period and that the likely date of the A-11 Complex wooden palaces is later, perhaps around A.D. 750. The overall impression of Río Azul by the end of the period is one of weakness, disorganization, and certainly less economic and political power than during the fifth century A.D.

Terminal Classic (Late Classic 3/Early Postclassic 1):
A.D. 840–900.

The collapse of Maya civilization and the attendant demographic disaster were the major events of the period. The previous analysis of the stresses and vulnerabilities of Maya Late Classic society has laid the groundwork for our explanation of the catastrophe.

The major features of the collapse have long been known (Culbert 1973). The event was relatively rapid, seventy-five to one hundred years in length, and involved all sectors of society. The catastrophe was demographic as well as social and political, and there was no recovery. The disaster resulted in the abandonment of nearly all cities of the central and southern lowlands by A.D. 900, the abandonment of the countryside, and the cessation of all cultural activity. The ever fascinating question is what set of conditions and factors produced such an astoundingly complete disaster from which there were so few survivors?

By 1970 it was apparent that the answer was available in the large amounts of new data that had been produced in the preceding twenty years. A conference in that year considered all the new information and produced a model of the collapse that has stood the test of time (Culbert 1973). I have essentially outlined the model in my treatment of the data on Late Classic 2. Maya civilization fell because of internal and external stresses, which produced a condition of extreme vulnerability. The resultant fragile and immensely complex cultural structure was beset with ecological changes over which it had no control and to which it could not adapt.

To state matters more concretely, over a period of one hundred fifty years, Maya populations grew exponentially. These masses of people required ever more foodstuffs, which were produced by ever more intensive forms of cultivation. However, terracing, wetland gardens, and short fallow systems also led to long-term problems. The direct problems were soil exhaustion, soil erosion, and loss of surface water. Indirect problems included a decline in the nutritional quality of diet, and therefore, a decline in health status. This led to increased vulnerability to diseases endemic to the area—malaria, syphilis, yellow fever, Chagas' disease, and other maladies. The rising elite population increased the burden on the economically productive commoners. Maya states took an increasing fraction of energy and investment out of the food production sector. The state of vulnerability reached critical proportions about A.D. 840. At that time a triggering crisis began in the form of a series of severe drought years. Military predation increased and became more destructive. Raids from the northern zones into the central and southern areas pushed crises past the thresholds of manageability. Feedback problems, such as increasingly poor nutrition leading to a need for more food production by an increasingly debilitated population accelerated the disintegration of all cultural systems. Management by the elite was unable to adapt to the continual and accelerating problems. Famines, plagues, and other disasters such as class warfare and military raids from the Gulf Coast of Mexico and perhaps the highlands produced a demographic decline in which perhaps eight of every ten Maya perished. It is estimated that only a 15 percent remnant population was left by A.D. 900.

The lack of recovery was probably due to both the demographic and ecological dimensions of the disaster. There were not enough people left to reconstruct Classic social structure. The economic basis for civilized life was largely destroyed with the extensive loss of ground water, exhausted soils, and the rapid capture of productive land by secondary growth. The latter would quickly cover the landscape with thorny, dense vegetation even more difficult to deal with than primary forest. (The above statement and summary are based on work of my colleagues in Maya archaeology and in other fields [Culbert 1973, 1974, 1988; Willey and Shimkin 1973; Yoffee and Cowgill 1988] as well my own work.)

Late Classic 3 at Río Azul: A.D. 830–900.

Late Classic 3, or Terminal Classic as it is also known, was one of radical change and termination at Río Azul. There is evidence of trade with northern Maya merchants in the preceding period. Mesoamerican cultures habitually used their long-distance merchants also as intelligence agents. This certainly was the case in the sixteenth century among the Aztecs and probably also with the Teotihuacaños in the fourth and fifth centuries. Northern Maya presence at Río Azul early in the period makes possible a scenario of commercial contact and increasing foreign presence followed by a military incursion based on the intelligence gained by the merchants. In A.D. 830, Río Azul was still important but seemed to be increasingly seedy; the buildings were deteriorating and many of them had been closed or filled in and used as foundations for perishable structures. It is possible that B-5 Complex is mainly Late Classic 2 and 3 in its construction phase, although we excavated only one test pit there. Certainly this enclosed and defensible zone was in use during the period.

The evidence suggests that about A.D. 840 a military raid on Río Azul took place, which resulted in its final destruction. Buildings were burned during this episode, burials were looted, and large amounts of polychrome pottery was broken. The raiders were apparently tempted to stay and make themselves the new elite rulers of the district, as happened at Seibal. A special monument, Stela 4, with stylistic affinities to Chichen Itza sculpture, shows a person who is apparently assuming power. A small four-sided platform with tenoned serpent heads at the top of balustraded stairways was built in the middle of the largest paved plaza at the site. These two pieces of evidence indicate that the raiders were probably from a Puuc city, or Chichen Itza in its earlier phase. If, as seems likely, their intention was to impose a new dynasty of rulers, the attempt failed. Their stay might have been aborted because of the nearby and unconquered fortress of Kinal, from which the southern Maya elite might have made sorties against the intruders. It might also have been because the invaders found the land deteriorated and the population decimated. Río Azul was already showing specific instances of the general stresses mentioned above. At any rate, the episode was short, perhaps a matter of months or a year or two.

After the departure of the intruders, there is evidence of continued internal collapse at Kinal. Although the people inside the fortress may have survived the disasters, the countryside appears to have been largely abandoned, with the exceptions of a few small houses built in remote zones. These may have been the refuges of remnant populations hiding from raiders or from the generalized violence that accompanies large-scale social breakdown. In the palaces and temples of Río Azul and Kinal there is evidence of a few survivors, perhaps of the elite. Houses were built in the previously sacrosanct and exclusive palace courtyard at Kinal (Hageman 1992). A well-made elite burial under the floor of a palace room dating from ca. A.D. 900 argues that some elite groups kept a few retainers with them. Graffiti in the palaces include sketches of ceremonies and glyphs and probably were the work of surviving elite. However, we estimate that the vaults of the stone buildings began to collapse within twenty-five or thirty years after the raid on Río Azul, which means about A.D. 870. The buildings would have become increasingly dilapidated and dangerous with time and were eventually abandoned. The remnant populations of the district probably moved south to amalgamate with other groups around the central Petén lakes. Small cities were built on these lakes after A.D. 1000, including the sites of Topoxté, Macanché, and Tayasal. It was here that the Spaniards found the remnants of Classic Maya civilization in the sixteenth and eighteenth centuries.

Meanwhile, the long abandoned cities of Río Azul and Kinal were occasionally visited by people who burned incense in special pottery vessels and apparently paid reverence to the damaged stelae and in the collapsed temples. Outside and inside the dead cities, the jungle had reclaimed the land, and it has remained so until the present day.

Culbert has analyzed an appallingly similar model for the collapse of the *modern* world, developed independently by the Club of Rome (Meadows, Meadows, Randers, and Behrens 1972). The model of the modern collapse is nearly exactly the same in its dynamics as the model of the Maya collapse, except for the element of industrialization in the modern case. In other particulars—exponential growth of population, pollution, use of non-renewable resources, and food production—the models parallel one another. The difference is that the Maya case is retrodictive and the other is predictive. Further, there is at least one major historical parallel to the Maya collapse, that is, the set of disasters that were associated with the Black Death in Europe (Adams and Smith 1981). Beginning in 1348 there was a series of plagues that, some historians argue, destroyed the fabric of European medieval society and prepared the way for the eventual rise of the Renaissance. But European civilization reformulated itself and made a recovery; the Maya did not.

We shall have to await the outcome of our present trends to see how the Club of Rome predictions fit with reality. So far, in the twenty years since the publication of the model, they seem to be unnervingly on target. None of the various types of leadership that humanity has developed—managerial, elected, or hereditary elites— seem able to deal with intense and radical long-term crisis. It will be of immense interest to observe how (or if) the underlying ecological, demographic, and managerial crises of our times are resolved. So far, the results of attempts to resolve the Somalia crisis of 1992 and the problems of Bosnia in 1998 are not encouraging.

OUTLINE OF CULTURE HISTORY AT RÍO AZUL AND KINAL

ca. 900 B.C. Pioneer farmers settle along Río Azul.

ca. 500 B.C. Early temple structure built (G-103 sub 2); regional center forms around it.

ca. 300 B.C.–A.D. 350 Population growth and platform building along the Río Azul. Rebuilding of G-103 Temple (sub 1) into larger and higher structure. Development of small political units headed by aristocratic families. Possible amalgamation of these political units by A.D. 350 into one or two small states.

A.D. 378 Tikal ruler, Jaguar Paw 2, displaced by usurper Curl Nose with aid of Teotihuacan through military and political advisors.

ca. A.D. 385 Tikal expands to Río Azul zone with aid of Teotihuacan military and political advisors. Río Azul rulers executed. Río Azul urban center established. Construction labor imported from elsewhere in the Tikal Regional State. Fortified zones established within the city and settling of several military aristocratic families at Río Azul. The river has become the northern frontier against a disorganized region or the Calakmul Regional State.

A.D. 392 Stela 1 erected with Zak Balam appointed to rule the region. Possible mention of Smoking Frog in Stela 1 text. Temple A-3 Complex begun by this time. Stela 3 erected ca. A.D. 400.

A.D. 417 Governor X (Plant Leaf?) born to Stormy Sky and Bird Claw, rulers of Tikal.

ca. A.D. 440 Governor X is appointed ruler of the region by his father (?), Tikal ruler Stormy Sky. Teotihuacan military and political advisors accompany Governor X to Río Azul.

ca. A.D. 460 Governor X dies and is buried in painted Tomb 1; Temple C-1 is built over his tomb as a memorial.

ca. A.D. 480 By this time "Advisors A and B" have been buried next to Governor X in adjacent Tombs 19 and 23.

ca. A.D. 450–530 Painted tombs of Río Azul proliferate as Tikal-related aristocrats die and are memorialized by temples above their tombs (Tombs 5, 6, 7, 8, 9, 12, 13, 17, 25). By A.D. 500 Temple A-3 Complex assumes final form with five temples on a unified substructure.

A.D. 530–660 Río Azul burned, abandoned in civil (?) wars of the sixth century.

A.D. 690 Stela 2; Río Azul revitalized and a possibly independent ruler (Governor Z) erects this stela.

ca. A.D. 696 Governor Z dies and is buried and memorialized by Temple Str. B-11.

A.D. 661–800 Gradual remodeling, refurbishment of Río Azul. Contact with Yucatec traders toward end of the period. Population explosion with consequent development of intensive agriculture and large-scale stone tool production. Establishment of "manor houses" in the surrounding countryside. Decentralized political authority. Feudal society develops.

A.D. 720 Kinal fortress built over the next ten (?) years. This citadel becomes the administrative center for the district.

A.D. 850 Río Azul raided and burned by Yucatec Maya possibly from Puuc Hills area. Short lived occupation. Stela 4 commemorates the beginning of the "new order." Kinal fortress survives.

A.D. 860 Río Azul deserted; countryside abandoned. Surviving elite are in Kinal fortress, but in straitened circumstances due to loss of most of their supporting population.

A.D. 1000 By this date Kinal is abandoned.

Nineteenth century A.D. Visits to Río Azul A-3 temples by Maya hunters; incense burners left.

TABLE 1.
Summary of Ceramic Sequence and Culture History at Río Azul

Christian Chronology	Maya Chronology (Gmt Corr.)	Río Azul Ceramic Sequence		Stratigraphic Evidence	Culture History and Processual Events
	Stela 4				
830	10.0.0.0.0	3		Ops. 5U, 7A1–2	City destroyed in military raid
					Resident northern Maya traders
800		T			
		E			
		P	Late Facet	Ops. 202D, E, F	Trade with Yucatan, Chontal
		E		203, 684–6	regions; ca. 4,500 inhabitants
		U			
					Intensive gardening, large-
		2	Early Facet	Ops. 1 M, N. O,	scale tool making, BA-20
				P	Craft specialization ceramics,
700					lithics
692	9.13.0.0.0				
685??	*Stela 2 ded. date?*	T			BA-20 farming zone redeveloped
		E		Ops. 202C	Gov. Z allies with La Milpa?
661	*Stela 2: 9.11.9.5.2*	P		5C	Gov. Z born
		E		6F2	New palaces built; old buildings
600		U			refurbished
593	9.8.0.0.0	1			Río Azul reoccupied

TABLE 1. *continued*

Christian Chronology	Maya Chronology (Gmt Corr.)	Río Azul Ceramic Sequence	Stratigraphic Evidence	Culture History and Processual Events
530			(ca. 530–650)	Civil Wars (?)
		H I A T U S		Río Azul abandoned
500	*Stela 3*		Tomb 23	Gov. X. Counselor B. dies
			Tomb 19	Gov. X Counselor A dies
		T	Tomb 1	Governor X dies, Temple C-1 built
455	9.1.0.0.0	Z		
		A		
		K		Governor X takes power at Río Azul
		O		
416	8.19.1.9.13	L		
		2 - 3		
				Governor X born (at Tikal?)
393	*Stela 1: 8.17.16.12.10*		Op. 4B1	Urban center of Río Azul built
357	8.16.0.0.0			Military expansion of Tikal
				to Río Azul (?)
300		T		
		Z		
		A		
278	8.12.0.0.0	K	A-3 sub 7 built	
		O		
		L		
250		1		

TABLE 1. *continued*

Christian Chronology	Maya Chronology (Gmt Corr.)	Río Azul Ceramic Sequence	Stratigraphic Evidence	Culture History and Processual Events
		C		
200		H	Arroyo Negro Mound (7 km ne of Río Azul) G-103 sub 1 built	
		I		
100		C		
A.D. / B.C.		A		
100		N		
		E		
250		L		
300		M	Str. G-103 sub 2	First major temple?
		A	OP. 4A17–18	
400		M		
500		O		
600 700		M		Pioneer farmers?

SETTLEMENT PATTERNS IN THE THREE RIVERS REGION

I. Residence classes, covered space, and social distinctions
    A. Assumptions
        1. Previous research is correct in:
            a. designating housemounds as common residences;
            b. designating rooms in formal buildings with built-in benches as residential;
            c. outlining patterns of hierarchical relationships in which the most elaborate housing is least frequent, and the simplest is most frequent.
        2. Research is correct in demonstrating the presence of auxiliary buildings in physical association with residential structures (e.g., cooking zones with palaces).
        3. Research is correct in demonstrating the presence of both elaborate and simple housing in many residential groups.
        4. The relative elaborateness of housing corresponds to the social level of the ancient inhabitants.
        5. The conclusion in 4 is demonstrated by the differential distribution of artifacts in the hierarchical levels of housing, most sensitively, by the presence of polychrome pottery and the presence or absence of status materials in associated burials or caches: jade, pyrite mirrors, stingray spines, exotic shells, mother-of-pearl objects, etc.
    B. The following methodology is based on assumptions in A and further postulates that:
        1. Measurement of area of structures and paved interior courtyards is adequate to provide the basis for rank ordering.
        2. At least four detectable classes of housing are present in and around Río Azul and Kinal.

    3. The four classes are:

        a. Class I: Elaborate palace (formal range structures) com-
plexes that include auxiliary structures (perishable or
formal) and in which elite residences individually
measure more than 150 sq meters. Mortuary structures
are usually present.

        b. Class II: Minor palace complexes with all or nearly all
the auxiliary structures of Class I residences, but in
which individual elite residences measure less than 150
sq meters. Service zones were both servant residences
and work areas.

        c. Class III: Perishable houses built on substantial mounds
faced with stone and provided with associated amenities
such as cisterns, auxiliary buildings, courtyards paved
with plaster, compound walls, and "half-walls" of stone
in the superstructures.

        d. Class IV: Perishable houses built upon low earthen or
rubble mounds with few or no amenities in the form of
auxiliary buildings, cisterns, or location. In fact, at Río
Azul houses of this class are located in the least
desireable places (i.e., lowest, nearest to the swamps,
nearest to the river flood plain, etc.).

    4. The ratio of space per person increases in progressively
more elaborate housing, and this is detectable in each of
the four classes from excavated units.

II.   Ratios of people to space

    The following ratios of space to people are derived from previous
studies (Adams 1974, 1981; Eaton, 1975, 1978) and from mapping
and excavated evidence at Río Azul (Eaton 1986, 1987a, 1987b;
Orrego 1987).

Class I (most elaborate)

Structure Type	Space per capita, in square meters
elite/residence	20
service/residence	10
covered space	14
paved/covsp	20.6

Derived from A-11 Grp excavations (Eaton 1987a). Comparative material from Adams 1974, 1981.

Class II (minor palaces)

Structure Type	Space per capita, in square meters
elite/residence	8.2
service/residence	5
covered space	6
paved/covsp	20.6

Derived from B-56 Grp excavations (Ellis 1991)

Class III (perishable A)

Structure Type	Space per capita, in square meters
residence	7.5
crtyd-res	10

Derived from C-63 Grp excavations (Eaton 1987b). Comparative material from Eaton 1975, 1982; also from excavations in Op. 202 structure (BA-20).

Class IV (perishable B)

Structure Type	Space per capita, in square meters
residence	7.5
crtyd-res	10

Derived from Op. 211 excavations (Ellis 1987). Comparative material from Colha (Gibson 1982, personal communication 1981).

III. Rank-order and rank-size analyses of the Combined Río Bravo and Río Azul Sectors (Three Rivers Region)
    A. Comments on method
        1. The general effect of my reassessment of the Río Bravo sites is to bring them more in line with my rank-ordering

TABLE 2.

Rank-Ordered Three Rivers Regional Sites with
Occupation Periods Known as of February 1997.

Site Numbers and Names	Maximum Courtyard Counts	MPC	LPC	EC1	EC2-3	LC 1	LC 2	LC 3
1 Río Azul	39	A	A	A	A	B	A	B
2. La Milpa	25		A	A	A	B	A	B
3. Kinal	20		B				A	B
4. Xultun; monument-based period estimate	20			A	B	B	A	A
5. La Honradez; monument-based period estimate	20						A	B
6. La Frontera*	15						A?	
7. Chan Chich	14		B	A	B?	B	A	
8. Dos Hombres	12		A				A	B
9. Blue Creek	12			A	A		A	B?
10. RB-44	12?						A?	
11. RB-43; Gran Cacao	11		A?	A?	A?		A	B?
12. Punta de Cacao	11						A	
13. Chochkitam; monument-based period estimate	8						A	
14. BA-22 a,b,c,d	8		B			C	A	C
15. RB-45; Ma'ax Na	8					B?	A	B?
16. San Jose	7	B	A	B	B	B	A	A
17. Quam Hill	5		B	A?	A?			
18. El Infierno	5+							
19. Wari Camp	5						A?	
20. Say Ka	4			A?	B?			
21. BA-20, Pedernal	4		A	A	B		B	B

TABLE 2. *continued*

Site Numbers and Names	Maximum Courtyard Counts	MPC	LPC	EC1	EC2-3	LC 1	LC 2	LC 3
22. Gallon Jug	4		B	B		B?	A?	B
23. Laguna Seca	3							
24. E'kenha	3							
25. Osh Lut	3						A	
26. Las Abejas	3				B		A	B?
27. Thompson's Group	3						A	
28. RB-11	2				A	B?	A	B
29. Mula'an	2				B	B	B	B
30. Gongora Ruin	2							
31. Tzi'kal	2							
32. Rosita	2		B				B?	
33. Polvitz	2?							
34. 28/195-3	2?							
35. 28/196-2	2?							
36. 29/.196-1 Betson Bank?	2+							
37. BA-24	2							
38. BA-30	2							
39. BA-33	2						A	B
40. BA-34	2	B	A	C?	B		A	B
41. Arroyo Negro	2	C?	A					
42. Mile 5 Ruin	1							
43. X'noha	1							
44. Tzi'kal Cab	1					B	A	B
45. 29/197-7	1							
46. Hunal	1							
47. 29/197-10	1							

TABLE 2. *continued*

Site Numbers and Names	Maximum Courtyard Counts	MPC	LPC	EC1	EC2-3	LC 1	LC 2	LC 3
48. 28/197-5	1							
49. Laguna Verde	1							
50. 28/195-4	0							
51-75. (Small BA sites)**	0-1						A?	

Major formal construction = A; Occupation = B; Activity trace = C. Periods of maximum construction activity are boldfaced.

* La Frontera is a major site northwest of Río Azul split by the modern frontier of Guatemala and Mexico. It was discovered by Miguel Orrego C. in 1985 and briefly explored by Orrego and Richard Bronson in that year. Given its hilly location, the site is both remote and difficult to explore. The site name was changed in 1994 to Aguada Cancuen.

** The small BA sites were located by John Gatling and the Sun Oil Company seismic and exploration crews. The Río Azul and Ixcanrio projects were unable to visit most of them, but many, if not all, appear to be one courtyard in size. Some may be groups of relatively large housemounds. The extrapolated dating is based on the dating of similar groups explored in the Río Azul–Kinal zone or in the adjacent Programme for Belize region.

of Petén and Río Bec sites. This is possibly as much a function of a single scholar's consistency in dealing with the whole data mass as a correct elicitation of patterns from the data. From whatever source it derives, there is a consistency.

2. Guderjan has modified the original rank-ordering system (Adams and Jones 1981) in an interesting manner by adding qualitative elements to the numerical values of sites that possess stelae and ballcourts (Guderjan 1991a). His other modifications may make it possible to refine the system and to more clearly define ancient political and economic relationships among the sites. I have chosen to only rank order according to the amount of architecture present at each site. This will allow the addition of other weighting factors from excavations in research phases 2 and 3. Such factors might include sensitive indicators of social status such as the amount of sumptuary ceramics in principal residences of a site.

B. Comments on analytical patterns

    1. The attached rank-size analysis of the Three Rivers Region sites is preliminary in three ways. First, the sample region is somewhat arbitrary in its southern boundary. Second, the nearest neighbor analysis has been done only on the largest sites—those above twelve courtyards in size. Third, sorting of sites was done according to occupation dates, but these can only be estimated in most cases. This will mean that eventually several charts will be produced to reflect ancient political, economic, and demographic evolution in the region. However, this level of analysis is better reserved for technical publication.

    2. Taking the above defects into consideration the following tentative implications can be drawn from the rank-size chart (Chart 4).

        a. The sample of sites at the lowest levels (smallest sites) is quite distorted and there should be perhaps as many as thirty-five more one-courtyard sites in the sampled zones. Robichaux's settlement pattern analysis of the eastern zone indicates that it probably contains two or more major sites, that is, above twelve courtyards in size (Robichaux 1995, personal communication 1997).

        b. Rank-Size Rule analysis can be done with rank-ordered sites that also are discriminated by nearest-neighbor analysis (Adams and Jones 1981). Notwithstanding the probable distortion due to sampling errors and procedural limitations, in terms of the Rank-Size Rule, it seems that La Milpa was a primate site in the eastern zone in the Late Classic period and possibly in the Early Classic period. The known major amounts of construction in both periods overshadow all other known sites of the region by a factor of two; that is, they are in a logarithmic relationship with La Milpa, which is twice as large as the next largest sites. Thus Chan Chich, the next ranking site, is half as big as La Milpa in the Late Classic. This implies that Chan Chich was a site subordinate to La Milpa. The primate pattern is reflected on the chart by the concave line under the log-normal line. According to modern geographic rank-size analytical theory (Adams and Jones 1981), this reflects the overwhelming dominance of a community in its region. Modern parallels to this are Buenos Aires in Argentina, which far overshadows cities like Mendoza. In the western zone, Río Azul was a primate site in Early Classic 2–3 and possibly in Late Classic 2. Kinal was built ca. A.D. 760 and probably took over the administrative functions from Río Azul.

c. It would appear that the northwestern Belize sequence of settlement development was characterized by what Jones has called a "chrysalis" development (Adams and Jones). This means that from the Late Preclassic when La Milpa first appears as a major center, it retained its primacy in the region. It also means that the nature of regional evolution was largely a matter of scale rather than of qualitative change. The latter kind of change appears to have taken place to the west in the central Petén around the city of Tikal. That is, Tikal's political and economic structure changed in qualitative (metamorphic) ways, whereas the more provincial center of La Milpa grew mainly in size (Adams and Jones 1981:318).

IV. Population histories, urbanization, and periodicity of center occupations within the Three Rivers Region

TABLE 3.

Estimated Late Classic II Period Urban Populations in the Three Rivers Region
(Río Azul and Río Bravo Sectors) Based on the Robichaux West Oil Transect Survey

Courtyard Counts from 3 Rivers sites of 5 or more	Est. size of sustaining zones[1] (in square kilometers)	Est. size of habitable zones[2] (totals) (in square kilometers)		Estimated population density[3] (people per square kilometer)	Est. urban populations of communities this size	Number of communities this size	Est. total pop. for communities this size
25	70	49	(49)	900	44,100	1	44,100
20	28.2	19.7	(49)	900	17,730	3	53,190
14–15	20.4	14.3	(29)	900	12,870	2	25,740
11–12	14.1	9.9	(50)	900	8,910	5	44,550
7–8	10.6	7.4	(30)	800	5,920	4	23,680
5	7.0	4.9	(15)	500	2,450	3	7,350

Total: 198,610[4]

1. This calculation uses Tikal data as a benchmark for all but La Milpa and Dos Hombres site vicinities. For other sites, actual survey data was used from the sustaining areas around them. Summarily, the Tikal figures are: a 85-courtyard rank order (Adams and Jones 1981:Table 1) with a 120 sq km sustaining area (Culbert et al. 1990: 117).

2. The area in the preceding column has been reduced by 30 percent due to the presence of uninhabitable swamp (bajo) zones.

3. A population density of 900 persons per sq km has been used for communities having a courtyard count of eleven or greater based upon the survey data from La Milpa and Dos Hombres. Other population densities are adjusted estimates based on the field work judgments of the authors.

4. The total habitable urban zone is 242 sq km. The total remaining habitable land (1396 less 242) is 1154 sq km. Using Robichaux's average rural density figure of 177.5/km, we can conclude that Late Classic 2 rural population for the Three Rivers region totals 204,835. Adding the rural population estimate to the figure of 198,610 for urban population gives a grand total of 403,445 people for the Three Rivers region in Late Classic 2 (A.D. 680–840).

TABLE 4.

Reconstructed Population Figures for the Three Rivers Region Showing Both Rural and Urban Fractions.

Periods	Approximate Dates	Possible Res/km²	Possible Pop/km²	Net Pop/ 1,158 km²	Total Pop 2,000 km²
Early Postclassic 2	A.D. 1000– 1250	11 (10%)	urb: unknown rur: 18	1/2 rural area urb: 500 est rur: 907	1,407
Late Classic 3/ Postclassic 1	A.D. 840– 1000	96 (94%)	urb: 772 rur: 167	1/2 rural area urb: 93,412 rur: 96,693	190,105
Late Classic 2	A.D. 680– 840	102 (100%)	urb: 821 rur: 177.5	urb: 198,610 rur: 205,545	404,155
Late Classic 1	A.D. 550– 680	RA sector, urban only 22 (22%)	urb: 181 rur: 39	1/2 rural area urb: 11,041 rur: 22,581	33,622
Early Classic 2–3	A.D. 400– 550	62 (61%)	urb: 501 rur: 108	1/4 rural area urb: 60,621 rur: 62,532	123,153
Early Classic 1	A.D. 250– 400	5 (5%)	urb: 41 rur: 9	1/2 rural area urb: 496 rur: 5,211	5,707
Late Preclassic	250 B.C.– A.D. 250	34 (33%)	urb: 0 rur: 60	1/4 rural area urb: 0 rur: 17,502	17,502
Mid. Preclassic	600– 250 B.C.	8 (8%)	urb: 0 rur: 14	1/4 rural area urb: 0 rur: 4,060	4.060

*X-factor = uninhabitable land; includes scrub swamp, riparian, transitional, marsh, and mangrove areas. Possible residences per sq km was derived from Robichaux's Table 11 (1995:181). Terminal Classic is Late Classic 3 and Protoclassic is referred to as Early Classic 1. The number 18, the largest ceramic count from the Late Classic 2, is set equivalent to 100%. Therefore: 17/18=94%, 4/18=22% (Adams counted 4 from the Subops. for Late Classic 1), 11/18=61%, 1/18=6%, 6/18=33%, and 1.44/18=8% (the number 8 is also derived from Adams). Culbert's 21.5% (Culbert et al 1990:115) residence reduction formula is used. Using these percentages and 102 [derived from Robichaux's Table 12 (1996:186)] as 100%, the mathematical process is then 102x.94=96, etc. Five people are assumed per household. Total urbanized area is maximized at 242 sq km in Late Classic 2 period and urban populations are calculated from that figure and courtyard count ratios.

Population histories are graphically shown in Charts 1 and 2.

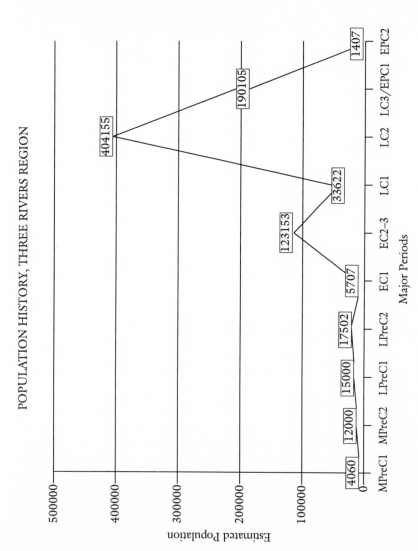

Chart 1. Graphic display of data in Table 4. Total population history of the Three Rivers Region. A calculated net residential area of 1158 km² (2000km² - 30% residentially unusuable land) with an extrapolated population history derived from the West Oil Transect settlement pattern survey by H. R. Robichaux, adjusted with data from the Río Azul subregion.

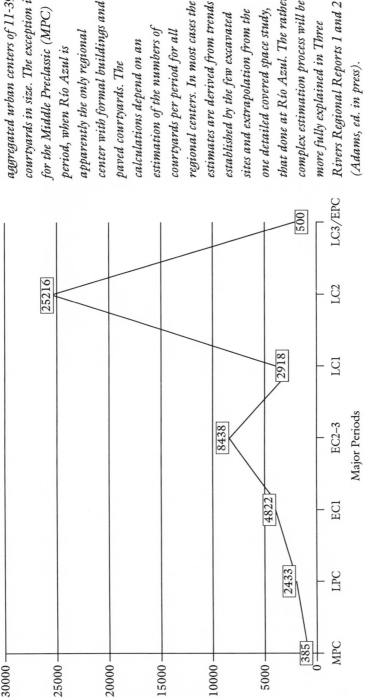

Chart 2. *Graphic display of estimated populations in aggregated urban centers of 11-39 courtyards in size. The exception is for the Middle Preclassic (MPC) period, when Río Azul is apparently the only regional center with formal buildings and paved courtyards. The calculations depend on an estimation of the numbers of courtyards per period for all regional centers. In most cases the estimates are derived from trends established by the few excavated sites and extrapolation from the one detailed covered space study, that done at Río Azul. The rather complex estimation process will be more fully explained in* Three Rivers Regional Reports 1 and 2 *(Adams, ed. in press).*

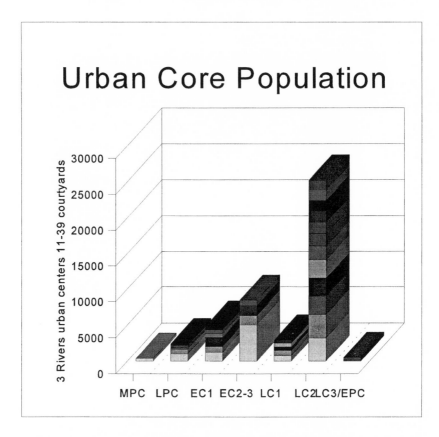

Chart 3. Graphic display of data in Tables 3 and 4 and Chart 2. The notable aspect indicated in this chart is the generally increasing aggregate sizes of urban populations in increasing numbers of centers. Each period is represented by a stack of shaded blocks. Each shade represents a different urban center. For the Three Rivers Region, therefore, the twelve different cities in LC2 period represent not only the maximum urban population but also the maximum period of urbanization. Río Azul is the bottom block in each stack except for the last.

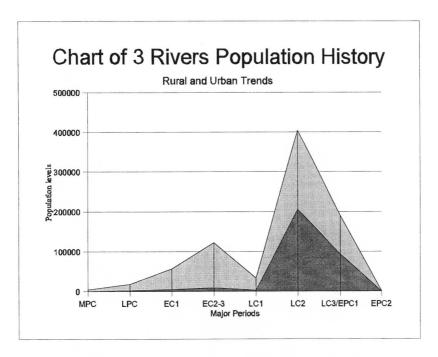

Chart 4. Graphic display of material in Table 3 and Chart 2. Light shading denotes rural population and dark shading designates urbanized populations within to 4.5 km of centers of 5 to 39 courtyards in size. Note that time is compressed on the left side of the chart. If all periods were temporally adjusted, Preclassic population buildup would be perhaps three times as long as is indicated here.

V.   Summary and commentary

As is always the case with archaeological reconstructions, the data is uneven in reliability—sparse in some parts, and altogether lacking for other segments of culture history— in spite of fifteen years of site-specific and intensive rural countryside work in the region. We have taken our best data from parts of the region and extrapolated and adjusted it. The work continuing in The Programme for Belize Archaeological Project under the direction of Dr. Fred Valdez, Jr., will undoubtedly improve the quality of the data and allow more sophisticated analyses.

Patterns of rural population growth show a long buildup in the Preclassic to about 4 percent of the maximum eventually reached. This growth takes about 850 years to accomplish and is likely the result of natural increase. An apparent drop of about 67 percent takes place at the end of the Late Preclassic but a strong recovery follows in Early Classic 2–3, building to a new high of about 123,000 people. This is the first population surge in the region and represents about a 95 percent increase in a period of about one hundred fifty years. A combination of immigration into the region and natural increase are suggested as the cause of this first surge. A second population drop takes place at the end of the Early Classic during The Hiatus, a diminution of about 73 percent in a period of about 100 years. Thereafter comes the second and greatest population surge, which builds to a maximum of about 404,000 within 125 years, a rise of 91 percent. This is almost certainly largely the result of immigration from outside the region, but what fraction is to be allocated to that factor and how much to natural increase can only be estimated with present data. A decline in the Terminal or Late Classic 3 period is on the order of 53 percent for about 100 years, continuing thereafter without recovery to the less than 1 percent (.003) level by A.D. 1200.

Based on comparisons with artifact, iconographic, and epigraphic material, we reach the following tentative conclusions about urbanization in the region. The small and large centers along the Río Azul are the earliest known in the region, and Río Azul is only exceeded or matched in age and size in the southern lowlands by Nakbe, which dates ca. 620 B.C. Small religious and administrative centers proliferate during the Late Preclassic and form a generally pluralistic pattern, likely reflecting a diffused pattern of political authority. This pattern apparently continues through the Early Classic 1 period with a mosaic of small principalities building up around the many centers. This pattern changes drastically during Early Classic 2–3 period with the establishment and construction of the city of Río Azul. I have interpreted this as being a result of the conquest and political integration of the Río Azul zone by the Tikal Regional State (Adams 1990). Perhaps the lognormal relationship between La Milpa and Río Azul at this time reflects a subordinate position for the former. Tikal almost certainly has a primate relationship with most of its subordinate cities at this time, with an estimated size of fifty courtyards.

The Hiatus and the putative civil wars of that period are reflected in abandonment, destruction of centers, monument breakage, and other evidence. Rural population appears to have dropped drastically in our region, but how this relates to other regional population histories is unclear.

Late Classic 1 is a period of recovery and political decentralization. Río Azul's ruler of A.D. 690 puts up a monument in front of a major temple structure, but this is the only one from the Late Classic at the site. La Milpa shows a stronger recovery and apparent political independence in its monument series and building program, both now and later in the Late Classic. The Late Classic is a period of maximum construction, except at Río Azul. The Kinal fortress is built from scratch, perhaps motivated by the military disaster that had overtaken Río Azul at the end of the Early Classic. La Honradez, La Milpa, and all the other smaller centers of the region flourish in their context of vast supporting populations. However, all of this apparent prosperity leads to disaster and collapse.

Looking at urban population histories (summarized in Table 3, Charts 2 and 3) it is clear that those residents of the courtyard complexes and paved zones of the centers were always a small fraction of total regional population. We have distinguished these people from those judged to be interactive with a center but living outside of it. The limits to the interactive rural residential areas have been defined as those zones within which population density is several orders of magnitude greater than beyond their boundaries. In the Three Rivers Region, sites larger than twelve courtyards in size have an average population density around them of about 820 person per sq km, a density which extends outward for about 6 km in diameter. Smaller centers of the five to eleven courtyard size were surrounded by high-density populations for about 4.5 km in diameter. Beyond these boundaries, population densities dropped to an average of 177.5 per sq km in Late Classic 2. The average core urban population is 7 percent of the total regional population for the entire Classic period (A.D. 250 to 840), but is only a 6 percent fraction in Late Classic 2. However, the interactive population total in Early Classic 2–3 period is an astounding 49 percent.

This is the period of the establishment of Río Azul and may represent a relatively brief episode of political and military instability in the region. The consequence would have been concentration within the western urban zones for security reasons. The persuasiveness of this explanation depends on how much credence one gives to the interpretation advanced by Adams, that Río Azul became a part of the Tikal Regional State at this time. After the long interval of The Hiatus and its population drop, the Late Classic 2 demographic maximum again produces a 49 percent fraction of the total population as interactive with centers. Another notable pattern in the data and the analyzed estimates is that of increasing numbers of urban zones through the Classic, culminating in Late Classic 2 with twelve urban centers of medium to large size compared with only five of those sizes in Early Classic 2–3.

In terms of evolutionary perspective, the rank-order and rank-size patterns combined with construction and population histories seem to show several interesting features. First, the regional urban centers show chrysalis growth patterns rather than transformational change. That is, growth patterns do not produce much qualitative change in the nature of the centers before they reach a threshold of twenty-five courtyards or more. As suggested by my geographer colleague, Richard Jones, this threshold excludes those sites that were not either capitals of regional states, or administrative capitals of districts. Río Azul shows a transformational growth, but it was also an extraordinarily rapid growth. La Milpa shows a periodic growth pattern, one enlargement in the Early Classic and one in Late Classic 2, when it reached its threshold size. La Milpa may have become a regional capital in Late Classic 2, according to the above analysis. Indeed, Robichaux has recently deciphered a clause on Río Azul Stela 2 that alludes to a visit to Río Azul from an important personage from La Milpa. Río Azul at this time is long past its prime; it is being reconstructed somewhat, but adds only the equivalent of four courtyards of architecture during the Late Classic.

Secondly, the feudal model or analogy proposed by Adams and Smith (1981) best fits the Late Classic 2 period. Criticism of the model has partly been on the basis of its lack of fit to the processual circumstances of the Late Roman Empire, which produced Europe's feudal societies. The latter were partly the result of political and economic decentralization; disintegration is probably a more accurate term. Now our proposed feudal model now is not only structurally similar to Late Classic 2 society, but also has processual similarities. Its utility in explaining earlier patterns, however, is problematic.

Finally, in the Three Rivers version of Late Classic 2, ontogeny possibly recapitulates phylogeny. This processual analogy to palaeontology means that the embryonic development of the individual summarily recapitulates the evolutionary history of its species. The great number of new centers that are established in the Three Rivers region in Late Classic 2 may recapitulate some of the Late Preclassic developmental history. If this is so, then a similar case of recapitulation might be embodied in the Río Bec regional settlement patterns as well.

RÍO AZUL
CERAMIC SEQUENCE SUMMARY

THIS APPENDIX GIVES A SUMMARY view of the ceramic sequence as developed at Río Azul, Petén, during the period 1983–1987. Some information is included from the work of the later regional project, 1990–1994.

The samples for the Río Azul sequence come from within the site and are derived from several kinds of operations. Because of the extensive looting at Río Azul before the arrival of the archaeological project, it was necessary to salvage as much information as possible from the 125 trenches and tunnels and the 28 tombs and burials opened by the vandals. Salvage material consisted largely of material that was discarded as unsaleable by the looters because it was being broken, too plain in decoration, or consisted of sherd material encountered during their search for tombs. Our own excavations produced massive quantities of sherds, an estimated 350,000 of which were analyzed. Several dozen whole or nearly whole vessels were also studied. Most of the latter came from the eight tombs and sixteen caches found by the project. A few vessels, approximately fifteen, were reconstructed from sherd material by the project or by the Conservation Department of the Guatemalan Institute of Anthropology and History.

The following lists of type-variety: mode characteristics of the Río Azul ceramic complexes assume a basic familiarity with the analytical system that has become the standard way of dealing with lowland Maya ceramics. Although the system has been criticized by various competent scholars (e.g., Forsyth 1989:1–12; Hammond 1975: 294–95), it is my contention that at times they have neglected some of the advantages of the system, have misunderstood it, or are attempting analytical operations that were not intended to be covered by the system. Indeed, Gifford, in his later writings, insisted that modal analysis be a separate although parallel operation. In the end, however, nearly all who have used type-variety have agreed that it achieves one of its basic aims, which is to produce comparable analytical units in spite of different samples, different sites, and different analysts.

Possible Xe-Bolay Complex

Chicago Orange: variety unspecified
Consejo Red: variety unspecified
Modes: Tecomate forms
Relative brightness of monochrome colors, especially reds and oranges

Mamom Sphere Complex

Achiotes Unslipped: variety unspecified
Modes: Tecomate forms
Sapote Striated: Sapote Variety
Joventud Red: Joventud Variety
Pital Cream: Pital Variety
Chunhinta Black: Chunhinta Variety
Deprecio Incised: variety unspecified
Guitara Incised: Guitara Variety
Additional: Handmodeled human figurines

Chicanel Sphere Complex

Sapote Striated: Sapote Variety
Modes: Grooved Rim
Sierra Red: Sierra Variety
Hongo Red: Hongo Variety
Flor Cream: Flor Variety
Polvero Black: Polvero Variety
Lechugal Incised: variety unspecified
Laguna Verde Incised: variety unspecified
San Diego Zoned Punctated: San Diego Variety
Usulutan Group (rare; four sherds only)
Late Facet type: Ixcanrio Orange Polychrome
Modes: Late Facet
San Antonio Golden Brown slip
Sierra Red in basal-flange, ring-base bowls

Sierra Red in Z-Angle, ring-base bowls
Imitation Usulutan (positive wipe) decorations on Usulutan forms.
Mammiform footed vessels
Early polychrome

Early Classic 1 Sphere

Triunfo Striated: Triunfo Variety
Triunfo Striated: Diamond Crossection Rim Variety
Aguila Orange: Aguila Variety
Caribal Red: Caribal Variety
Dos Arroyos Orange Polychrome Group
Pucte Brown: Pucte Variety
Paradero Fluted: Paradero Variety
Modes:
Especially heavy (basal flanges exaggerated)
Overlap in modes between Aguila Orange and Sierra Red

Early Classic 2–3

Triunfo Striated: Triunfo Striated
Triunfo Striated: Square Rim Cross-section Variety
Triunfo Striated: Grooved Rim Cross-section Variety
Aguila Orange: Aguila Variety
Modes: Giantism in plates and bowls
Heavy Red (Provisional type):
Balanza Black: Balanza Variety
Lucha Incised: Lucha Variety
Urita Gouged-Incised: Urita Variety
San Roman Plano-Relief: San Roman Variety
Buj Incised: Buj Variety
San Clemente Gouged-Incised: variety unspecified
San Blas Red on Orange: variety unspecified
Dos Arroyos Orange Polychrome Group
Mucu Orange Polychrome: Mucu Variety (this study)
Caldero Buff Polychrome: Caldero Variety
Caal Red Polychrome: Caal Variety
Modes: Motifs No. 1 and No. 2.
Specials: Trickle Ware (Yucatec; Río Bec??)
Modes: Basal flange, ring-based bowls
Cylinder tripods with slab or nubbin feet

Pot lids (Balanza Black); some with anthropomorphic handles
Napkin ring earspools
Flaring sided, ring-based bowls
Mortuary subcomplex:
Flaring-sided, ring-based bowls, Aguila Orange
Cylinder tripods with lids and human head handles; some rounded handles with slits
Special flange top–lidded vessel with stirrup handle, painted stucco decoration, stucco medallions with glyphic motifs.

Late Classic 1

Encanto Striated: Encanto Variety
Tinaja Red: Tinaja Variety
Achote Black: Achote Variety
Subin Red: Huicoy Variety
Saxche Orange Polychrome Group

Late Classic 2

General:
Encanto Striated: Folded Rim Variety
Encanto Striated: Applique Variety
Tinaja Red: Tinaja Variety
Achote Black: Achote Variety
Infierno Black: Infierno Variety
Glossy Rippled Black: (also at Kinal)
Subin Red Group:
   Subin Red: Subin Variety
   Maquina Brown: Maquina Variety
Palmar Orange Polychrome Group
Mataculebra Cream Polychrome: Mataculebra Variety
Zacatel Cream Polychrome: Zacatel Variety
Saptam Impressed: Saptam Variety
Maculis Modeled: Maculis Variety
Early Facet Diagnostics:
   Encanto Striated: Everted Rim Variety
   Subin Red: Huicoy Variety
   Tinaja Red: Tinaja Variety
   Saxche Orange Polychrome: Saxche Variety
   Uacho Black on Orange: Uacho Variety (rare)

Petexbatun Orange Polychrome: Petexbatun Variety
Chacrio Red Polychrome: Chacrio Variety (Red bar poly)
Black on cream plus yellow and red poly (unnamed)
Late Facet Diagnostics:
  Encanto Striated: Rolled Rim Variety
  Encanto Striated: Giant Variety
  Encanto Striated: Piecrust Rim Variety
  Altar Orange: Altar Variety
Imitation Fine Orange (Provisional type):
Tres Naciones Fine Gray: Tres Naciónes Variety
Puuc Slate Ware
Yucatec brown-on-cream Trickle Ware
Tumba Black on Orange: Tumba Variety (jars and bowls)
Holmul V; red on cream dichrome
Río Azul Pink Polychrome: Río Azul Variety
Juleki Cream Polychrome: Juleki Variety
Yucatec polychromes
Pabellon Molded-Carved: Pabellon Variety
Imitation Pabellon
Miseria Applique: Hollow Handle Variety
Modes: Molded human figurines
Comal forms in Encanto
Kilroy motif in Encanto Striated: Applique Variety
Ladle incensario form

Late Classic 3 (Terminal Classic)

Encanto Striated: Everted Rim Variety
Encanto Striated: Rolled Rim Variety
Achote Black: Achote Variety
Tinaja Red: Tinaja Variety
Subin Red: Brown Variety
Subin Red: Applique Variety
Puuc Slate Wares
Plumbate (group unknown; statistically rare)
Palmar Orange Polychrome: Raptorial Bird Variety
Modes: Flaring sided, tripod rattle-footed, black, interior-slipped
plates (Zopilote?)
Monochrome emphasis
Basins with red mono-chrome interior slipping

Exterior applique bands about 2 cm below basin rims
Nubbin or globular feet on open plate forms
Matte finish on red bar polychrome and resist circles on dress-shirt designs
Hemispherical bowls in polychrome types
Raptorial bird and sun motifs in polchrome types
Increase in carved decoration
Pyriform shapes in highly decorated types

Postclassic

Early: Hourglass-shaped, applique-decorated incense burners (see Adams and Trik 1961)

Comment: This is an incomplete complex; only incense burners as far as we know. Apparently set on the temple floor of Structure A-3.

Implications: Sporadic ritual visits after abandonment of Río Azul as in the case of Tikal Temple 5D-1 (Adams and Trik 1961). Visits must have been within 50–75 years after abandonment based on fact that burner was on the floor and not in the debris of the fallen vault. The vault seems to have been still intact at the time of deposit.

Late: Lacandon-style, effigy incense pots; smudged, unslipped but with human faces appliqued at rim.

Implications: Sporadic ritual visits long after abandonment. At least seventy-five years after abandonment and perhaps several hundred years later, given that the Lacandon are known to have made this style of incense burner into the nineteenth century. The burner was found in the debris of the vault collapse of Str. A-3 and therefore after the collapse of the temple roof. It is calculated that most of the vaults in classic structures were falling within one hundred years after the Classic collapse (ca. A.D. 900) and, more likely, within fifty to seventy-five years.

NONCERAMIC ARTIFACTS

ALL NONCERAMIC ARTIFACTS ARE categorized by the raw materials used to make them.

Lithics

Although stone tools are not as sensitive to change through time, their study has yielded not only chronological data, but a technological sequence as well. Not much is known of lithics in the Middle Preclassic period, except that blades were made at C-67 locality. These long, thin, specialized flakes were probably all-purpose knives. The Late Preclassic stone tool inventory continued to be made and used in the Early Classic as well. Some specialized tools, such as adzes, were added to the blades and ax-hoes, mainly for woodworking purposes. No proliferation in types or numbers occurred here, as it did at Colha, Belize in the Late Preclassic (Shafer and Hester 1983:Fig. 4). Both Preclassic and Early Classic complexes of tools seem only adequate for jungle clearance, cutting of timber for housing, cultivation, and woodworking. These tasks, as well as stone quarrying and cutting, plastering, paving, and mixing mortar, must have been partly taken care of by now missing wooden tools. Excavation of the Early Classic tombs (Tomb 19 for example) was apparently done by a pick-like tool whose marks were left on the soft marl walls under the bedrock (Hall 1987).

After the lapse of The Hiatus, a truly impressive change in stone technology took place in Late Classic 2 period. Thousands of high-quality and standardized stone tools were produced at BA-20 for use in building and in cultivation of drained field systems. Adzes, axes, hoes, and other tools were made at the edges of the fields, leaving immense dumps of manufacturing debris, or debitage. Each cubic meter of debris contains between five and seven million pieces of chert, indicating the intensity of tool manufacturing activity (Thomas R. Hester and Irwin Rovner, personal communication 1985). The dumps have very little dirt in them, and one discard heap measures 314 cubic meters and includes an estimated 1.5 billion flakes! Such intensive tool production and usage has been found and studied at two other sites—Colha, Belize (Hester et al. 1981) and Pulltrouser Swamp (Shafer 1983). A connection between mass production of stone tools and intensive wetland agriculture has been demonstrated by this work. The remnants of the very tools being produced at Colha were identified in the raised fields at Pulltrouser Swamp.

Terminal Classic tool production fell drastically and many of the late lithic items appear to be more suitable for hunting activities or war. Small and large chert points become common, probably reflecting the more frequent use of arrows and spears. The intensive production of tools ceased as the wetland gardens were abandoned. Stone technology returned to the simplified needs that had characterized the early farmers of the Late Preclassic.

Various Artifact Classes

Most archaeological materials are made either from pottery or stone, but there is a multitude of other productions that are rarely found in quantity. This may be either because of problems of preservation, as in the case of wood, or because they were genuinely rare productions, only one or a few being made. At Río Azul we were lucky enough to find a series of tombs that were, in effect, hermetically sealed, and in which items usually missing from the inventory were present at least in trace amounts or forms.

Wood

Two fragments of wooden bowls were found. One was recovered by Rafael Morales and Ian Graham from the looters' camp, where it had been dropped in their hasty flight. Fragment A is carved into the form of a round-sided bowl, with an extremely complex design partially preserved on it (Figure 3–35). The design matches a part of the tomb mural of Tomb 1, and therefore it seems likely that the bowl fragment came from that burial. The other piece of wooden bowl, Fragment B, is from Tomb 7, and was recovered by the archaeological project during salvage work. The bowl was also round sided, but the fragment is smaller. The design is of a glyph placed as if it were a fruit or nut on a branch (Figure 3–18). Tomb 7 Mural is entirely glyphic, and therefore we could not have associated this fragment with it had it not been found *in situ*. Fragment A, in particular shows us how much has been lost in the disintegration of wooden artifacts. It is an extraordinary bit of woodcarving art by any standard.

Other wooden artifacts included the litter constructed of poles and lashed together with cordage found in Tomb 19. Wooden planks were found in both Tombs 19 and 23. What appeared to be a badly warped wooden armature for a headdress was found in Tomb 23.

Bone

Bone items were found in Tombs 19 and 23 and were largely decorative and clearly nonutilitarian. The peccary jaws carved into human profiles from Tomb 23 are examples of this sort of artifact.

More humble and common forms are exemplified by the so-called spatulas common at Maya sites. Jane J. Adams has demonstrated that these artifacts were likely weaving picks, based on their similarity in form to those still in use among the highland Maya today (J. J. Adams, personal communication, 1990; Hendon 1991:902).

Jade

Jade is not very common in the legal collections from Río Azul, but reportedly was very common in the looted graves. The most famous object is the "near-jade" Sun God mask now in a private collection (cover, *National Geographic Magazine*, April 1986). The mask is a composite piece with shell inlays and insets, and its basic material is fuschite, a rich green stone. This piece appears to have been the death mask of a ruler, so unique and well-done is the piece and so valuable was such "near-jade" among the Maya. No other piece known from Río Azul comes near it in size and workmanship. The incised text on the rear of the mask indicates that it belonged to a ruler from Río Azul (Mayer 1987). Given that the Sun God is mentioned in Governor X's tomb as an ultimate ancestor, it is possible that the mask came from Tomb 1 and therefore is Early Classic 2 in date. This date is confirmed by the style of the mask and the fact that the Stela 1 ruler, Zak Balam, who was alive in A.D. 392, is mentioned in the text. The mask is rumored to be presently in a private collection in Germany, having passed through Zurich, Switzerland in transit.

The concept of "cultural" jade was one of considerable importance among the Maya. The best gemstone-quality material was either very rare or was made rare by tight controls over the nearest source, which appears to have been the Motagua Valley. However, the symbolism of the sacred green color was replicated in other stones, as well as in "costume jewelry" such as the hollow, stucco, green-painted beads found in Tomb 128 at Altar de Sacrificios (A. L. Smith 1972:267).

Two other jade objects from Río Azul have appeared in Brussels in a private collection (Mayer 1987). Two matching jade earspools carry texts which are Early Classic in style and include the Río Azul emblem glyph. Thin slices of jade, incised with crocodile designs, were found in Caches 3 and 6 from Early Classic Structure B-56 (Figs. 3–21, 3–22).

It has been impossible to petrographically source jade from Río Azul, but it seems likely that it came from the source most commonly used by the southern lowland Maya, the Motagua Valley.

Obsidian

Volcanic glass is not common at Río Azul and only occurs as a rare item among the stone tools in Preclassic or Classic contexts. Six pieces from various periods at Río Azul were sourced, and all were found to be from the obsidian quarry of El Chayal near Guatemala City (Hester and Dreiss 1989). The only exception to this is the green obsidian blade from Tomb 25, which appears to be from the highlands of central Mexico. Obsidian appears to have been imported into Río Azul in the form of blades.

Composite Artifacts

These are items made of several materials and at times are of very high quality in their conception and execution.

Mirrors

Remains of mirrors were found only in tomb burials (burial types 1, 2, 3, and 4). Maya mirrors are variants of Mesoamerican mirrors made of pyrites (iron ore crystals), polished to a reflective surface and then attached with an (unknown) adhesive to a stone, pottery, or wooden backing in a mosaic to produce a larger surface. Often such mirrors are only found in the form of a puffy pile of yellow sulfuric oxide material, the decomposed remains of the pyrites. Occasionally a few polished pyrites remain. Two pyrites found at Río Azul were incised with hieroglyphs. All such remains were Early Classic in date. Pyrites were imports, probably from the Guatemalan highlands where they occur in mines in northern Quiché in the Cotzal Valley zone. Given the difficulties of manufacture and assembly, it seems likely that these mirrors were imported as finished pieces.

Mosaic masks

Unfortunately, mosaic masks were found only in fragments. These were not found intact and *in situ* by the project but were encountered by the antiquity hunters who evidently did not recognize them for what they were. We managed to salvage parts of the masks, but they had been badly disassembled and scattered by the looters' clumsy work. All were from Early Classic burials. The masks were made of dozens of carefully cut and polished pieces of jade, mother-of-pearl, and shell. They were probably death masks of the principal human occupants of tombs, of the same type as the later death mask of Pacal at Palenque. Certain features, such as the nose, might be carved from a single piece of jade, but most of the features were made up of composite assemblies of materials. The mosaics were laid over wooden backings and attached with an adhesive. Such a technique was used for various items from Tikal (Morley et al. 1983:Fig. 13.51).

Textiles

Textiles are an extremely important craft among the present-day Maya of the Guatemalan and Chiapas highlands. In their traditional forms, Maya textiles are brightly colored, highly varied, and entirely produced on backstrap looms. Motifs and designs indicate the status, community of origin, and even special role of the wearer (Petterson 1976). Although remnants of ancient textiles are rare today, the ancient Maya demonstrated their interest in textiles by depicting many varieties in murals, sculpture, and on polychrome pottery. Weaving is directly indicated by artifacts, such as bone picks, spindle whorls, weft weights, and other technical aids to the craft. Such items, made of stone but also of pottery, were found at Río Azul.

Small fragments of textiles were found in tombs opened by the archaeological project. Because such remains require special and immediate treatment in recovery and stabilization, it is also likely that other remains were found in the looted tombs, but that these were destroyed through the incompetence of the antiquity hunters. All Río Azul textile fragments and impressions are Early Classic in date. Like stone tool making, weaving was probably fully-developed technology by the time of the Classic period and underwent very little change thereafter.

Textile specialist Robert Carlsen, aided by a number of colleagues, analyzed the remains of fabric from Río Azul Tombs 19 and 23 (1986, 1987). He concluded that cotton and hemp were used to make the six different pieces of cloth represented. All of the ancient textiles were produced on backstrap looms. The cotton piece from Tomb 19 possibly was brocaded and is a fine gauze weave of the sort still manufactured in the northern Guatemalan highlands. Some of the cloth in the tombs was covered with cinnabar to give it a dark red color. Other pieces show evidence of dyeing, but not enough to identify the colors or materials used.

Impressions of loose-weave, burlap-like material were found on the remains of a pyrite mirror. This was perhaps a cloth made of hemp (sisal), as was the case with several of the textiles from Tombs 19 and 23 (Carlsen 1986, 1987). An impression of an open-work, gauze-weave material was left in damp clay in Tomb 12. This was perhaps the same type as the cotton cloth found in Tomb 19. The forms into which cloth was made included burial shrouds, found in Tombs 19 and 23, as well as belts or bags, as found in Tomb 23. A possible *huipil* or sleeveless blouse was found in Tomb 19. There was also a mattress in Tomb 19, and its cover was likely made of the sisal or hemp textiles.

Although Río Azul has produced more direct evidence of ancient Maya weaving than any other site, the remnants of what was once an economically and socially important manufacture are relatively slight. Undoubtedly, we are missing a great amount of clothing and other items for which textiles were used. As Carlsen notes (1987:152), we can only lament that the looters destroyed so much of the evidence about the background of the extraordinarily rich tradition of Maya weaving.

Basketry, and Matting

Important utilitarian techniques were used for making mats and baskets during the Classic period. Once again, the only evidence, direct or indirect, is from the Early Classic, but the basic technology appears to have been fully developed by the beginning of that period.

Impressions of mats were found in Tomb 12, where they were apparently used to cover the burial while the vault was built. The mats are the standard type shown in Classic Maya sculpture. Mats had more than a practical significance, in that they could symbolize leadership and legitimate political power.

Tombs 19 and 23 produced evidence of decomposed basketry (Hall 1986, 1987). There is also indirect evidence for basketry in the designs used on some Balanza Black pottery in the Early Classic. Presumably these useful items were made for gathering and holding agricultural and forest products of various kinds.

Kapok

The cotton-like kapok fibers of the ceiba tree were used as stuffing for the mattresses in Tombs 19 and 23 (Hall 1986:92, 1987:123).

Leather and Fur

Two garments of leather and/or fur were found in Tomb 23. Possibly these are the remnants of animal skins or of a cape laid over the body. (Hall 1987:123–30).

Cordage

Well-preserved remnants of cordage were found in both Tombs 19 and 23. Again, the Maya must have developed this manufacture in the Preclassic. In addition to vines, rope and cords were basic fastening and wrapping materials for the ancient Maya.

REFERENCES

Acronyms

CIW   Carnegie Institution of Washington, Washington, D.C.

HMAI *Handbook of Middle American Indians.* 13 vols. Ed. Robert Wauchope. Austin: University of Texas Press, 1964–1974.

ICA   International Congress of Americanists (meets every three years and alternates between New and Old Worlds).

IDAEH   Instituto de Antropología e Historia de Guatemala, Guatemala City.

INAH   Institutio de Antropología e Historia de Mexico, Mexico City.

MARI   Middle American Research Instutite, Tulane University, New Orleans.

NWAF   New World Archaeological Foundation, Provo, Utah.

PMP   Papers of the Peabody Museum, Harvard University, Cambridge, Massachusetts.

Adams, Jane Jackson
  1991   An Early Classic Polychrome Jar from B-56 Complex, Río Azul, Guatemala. In R. E. W. Adams, 1991.

Adams, R. E. W.
  1970   Suggested Classic Period Occupational Specialization in the Southern Maya Lowlands. In *Monographs and Papers in Maya Archaeology,* 487–502. Ed. William R. Bullard, Jr., PMP, vol. 61.

  1971   *The Ceramics of Altar de Sacrificios.* PMP, vol. 63, no. 1.

  1974   A Trial Estimation of Classic Maya Palace Populations at Uaxactun, Guatemala. In *New Approaches to Mesoamerican Archaeology,* 285–96. Ed. N. Hammond. Austin: University of Texas Press.

  1977   Río Bec Archaeology and the Rise of Maya Civilization. In *The Origins of Maya Civilization,* 77–99. Ed. R. E. W. Adams. Albuquerque: University of New Mexico Press.

  1978   Routes of Communication in Mesoamerica: The North Highlands of Guatemala and the Southern Maya Lowlands. In Lee and Navarrete, 1978: 27–35.

  1981   Settlement Patterns of the Central Yucatan and Southern Campeche Regions. In Ashmore, 1981: 211–57.

1982   Rank Size Analysis of Northern Belize Maya Sites. In Hester, Shafer, and Eaton, 1982: 60–64.

1984   (ed.) *Río Azul Reports, No. 1: The 1983 Final Report*. San Antonio: Center for Archaeological Research, University of Texas.

1986a   (ed.) *Río Azul Reports, No. 2: The 1984 Season*. San Antonio: Center for Archaeological Research, University of Texas.

1986b   The Maya City of Rio Azul. *National Geographic Magazine* 169, no. 4 (April):420–51.

1987a   (ed.) *Río Azul Reports, No. 3: The 1985 Season*. San Antonio: Center for Archaeological Research, University of Texas.

1987b   The Río Azul Archaeological Project, 1985 Summary. In R. E. W. Adams, 1987*a*:1–27.

1989   (ed.) *Río Azul Reports, No. 4: The 1986 Season*. San Antonio: Center for Archaeological Research, University of Texas.

1990a   Archaeological Research at the Lowland Maya City of Río Azul. *Latin American Antiquity* 1:23–41.

1990b   Salvaging the Past at Río Azul, Guatemala. *Terra, Bulletin of the Natural History Museum of Los Angeles County*. Los Angeles.

1991   *Prehistoric Mesoamerica*. Revised edition. Norman: University of Oklahoma Press.

1995   Maya Early Classic Civilization; A View from Río Azul. In *The Emergence of Lowland Maya Civilization: A Conference at Hildesheim, Germany*, 35–48. Ed. N. Grube. *Acta Mesoamericana* No. 8. Bonn, Germany: Verlag Anton Saurwein.

Adams, R. E. W., and Jane Jackson Adams
1991   The Ceramics of Río Azul and Kinal. Manuscript.

Adams, R. E. W., W. E. Brown, Jr., and T. P. Culbert
1981   Radar Mapping, Archeology, and Ancient Maya Land Use. *Science* 213:1457–63.

1993   Analysis of 1990 NASA-JPL Synthetic Aperture Radar Imagery of the Río Azul–La Milpa Regions, Central America. Manuscript.

Adams, R. E. W., T. P. Culbert, W. E. Brown, Jr., P. D. Harrison, and L. J. Levi
1990   Rebuttal to Pope and Dahlin. *Journal of Field Archaeology* 17:241–44.

Adams, R. E. W., and J. L. Gatling
1964   Noreste del Petén: Un Nuevo Sitio y un Mapa Arqueologico Regional. *Estudios de cultura Maya* 4:99–118. (Republished in the Boletín del IDAEH, 1965. Republished in English in Adams, 1986a).

Adams, R. E. W., and R. C. Jones
1981   Spatial Patterns and Regional Growth Among Classic Maya Cities. *American Antiquity* 46:301–22.

Adams, R. E. W., and H. R. Robichaux
1992   Tombs of Río Azul, Guatemala. National *Geographic Research and Exploration* 8 (4):412–27.

Adams, R. E. W., and W. D. Smith
1981   Feudal Models for Classic Maya Civilization. In Ashmore, 1981: 335–49.

Adams, R. E. W., and A. S. Trik

1961 Temple I (Str. 5D-1): Post-Constructional Activities. *Tikal Report No. 7.* Philadelphia: University Museum, University of Pennsylvania.

Andrews, E. W., V, and N. Hammond

1990 Redefinition of the Swasey Phase at Cuello, Belize. American Antiquity 55:570–84.

Ashmore, W.

1981 (ed.) *Lowland Maya Settlement Patterns.* Albuquerque: University of New Mexico Press.

Ball, J. W.

1977 *The Archaeological Ceramics of Becan, Campeche, Mexico.* MARI Publication No. 43.

Black, S. L.

1987 Settlement Pattern Survey and Testing, 1985. In R. E. W. Adams, 1987a:183–221.

Black, S. L., and C. K. Suhler

1986 The 1984 Río Azul Settlement Survey. In R. E. W. Adams, 1986:163–92.

Boserup, Ester

1965 *The Conditions of Agricultural Growth: The Economics of Agrarian Change Under Population Pressure.* Chicago: Aldine.

Bricker, V. R.

1988 A Phonetic Glyph for Zenith: Reply to Closs. *American Antiquity* 53 (2):394–400.

Cannell, Barbara

1984 Drawings of Tomb Murals from Río Azul, Guatemala. In R. E. W. Adams, 1984: various figures.

Carlsen, Robert

1986 Analysis of the Early Classic Period Textile Remains—Tomb 19, Río Azul, Guatemala. In R. E. W. Adams, 1986a:122–55.

1987 Analysis of the Early Classic Period Textile Remains from Tomb 23, Río Azul, Guatemala. In R. E. W. Adams, 1987a:152–60.

Carneiro, R.

1970 A Theory of the Origin of the State. *Science* 169:733–38.

Childe, V. G.

1950 The Urban Revolution. *Town Planning Review* 21:3–17.

Closs, Michael

1988a A Phonetic Version of the Maya Glyph for North. *American Antiquity* 53 (2):386–93.

1988b Response to Coggins and Bricker. *American Antiquity* 53 (2):402–10.

Coe, W. R.

1967 *Tikal: A Handbook of the Ancient Maya Ruins.* Philadelphia: University of Pennsylvania Press.

1982 Introduction to the Archaeology of Tikal, Guatemala. *Tikal Report No. 12.* Philadelphia: University Museum, University of Pennsylvania.

1990   Excavations in the Great Plaza, North Terrace and North Acropolis of Tikal. *Tikal Report No. 14* (six volumes), University Museum Monograph No. 61. Philadelphia: University Museum, University of Pennsylvania.

Coggins, Clemency C.

1975   Painting and Drawing Styles at Tikal: An Historical and Iconographic Reconstruction. Ph.D. diss., Harvard University.

1979   A New Order and the Role of the Calendar: Some Characteristics of the Middle Classic Period at Tikal. In *Maya Archaeology and Ethnohistory*, 38–50. Ed. N. Hammond and G. R. Willey. Austin: University of Texas Press.

1988   Reply to Closs: A Phonetic Version of the Maya Glyph for North. *American Antiquity* 53 (2):401.

Colby, B. N., and P. L. van den Berghe

1969   *Ixil Country*. Berkeley and Los Angeles: University of California Press.

Coulborn, R. (ed.)

1956   *Feudalism in History*. Princeton: Princeton University Press.

Cowgill, George L.

1975   On Causes and Consequences of Ancient and Modern Population Changes. *American Anthropologist* 77:505–25.

1997   State and Society at Teotihuacan, Mexico. *Annual Review of Anthropology* 26:129–61.

Culbert, T. P.

1965   *The Ceramic History of the Central Highlands of Chiapas, Mexico*. NWAF Paper No. 19.

1973   (ed.) *The Classic Maya Collapse*. Albuquerque: University of New Mexico Press.

1974   *The Lost Civilization: The Story of the Classic Maya*. New York: Harper and Row.

1977   Early Maya Development at Tikal, Guatemala. In R. E. W. Adams, 1977:27–43.

1988   The Collapse of Classic Maya Civilization. In Yoffee and Cowgill, 1988: 69–101.

1991a   (ed.) *Classic Maya Political History*. Cambridge, England: Cambridge University Press.

1991b   Polities in the Northeast Petén, Guatemala. In T. P. Culbert, 1991a: 128–46.

Culbert, T. P., L. J. Kosakowsky, R. E. Fry, and W. A. Haviland

1990   The Population of Tikal, Guatemala. In *Precolumbian Population History in the Maya Lowlands*, 103–21. Ed. T. P. Culbert and D. S. Rice. Albuquerque: University of New Mexico Press.

Culbert, T. P., Laura J. Levi, and Luis Cruz

1989   The Río Azul Agronomy Program, 1986 Season. In R. E. W. Adams, 1989:189–214.

Eaton, J. D.
  1975   Ancient Agricultural Farmsteads in the Río Bec Region of Yucatan.
          Contributions, University of California Archaeological Research Facility,
          27:56–82. Berkeley.
  1982   Operation 2025: An Elite Residential Group at Colha. In Hester,
          Shafer, and Eaton, 1982: 123–40.
  1986   Operation 6: An Elite Residential Group at Río Azul. In R. E. W.
          Adams, 1986:46–53,
  1987a   Group A-11: An Elite Residential Complex at Río Azul, Guatemala. In
          R. E. W. Adams, 1987a:66–88.
  1987b   The C-63 Group: A Middle Class Residential Complex at Río Azul,
          Guatemala. In R. E. W. Adams, 1987a:93–106.

Eaton, J. D., and J. S. Farrior
  1989   Archaeological Investigations at the C-42 Complex: An Elite Class
          Residential Complex at Río Azul, Guatemala. In R. E. W. Adams, 1989:
          152–74.

Ellis, W. Bruce
  1987   The 1986 El Pedernal (BA-20) Settlement Survey. In R. E. W. Adams,
          1987a:136–51.
  1991   Excavations in the B-56 Complex, Río Azul, Petén, Guatemala: 1985–
          1987. Master's thesis, University of Texas, San Antonio.

Fahsen, Federico
  1998   The Hieroglyphic Texts of Río Azul Stela 1. In R. E. W. Adams, Río
          Azul Reports No. 5. San Antonio: University of Texas.

Flannery, K. V.
  1972   The Cultural Evolution of Civilizations. *Annual Review of Ecology and
          Systematics* 3:399–426.

Fletcher, L. A., J. M. Hau, L. M. Florey Folan, and W. J. Folan
  1987   *Un Analysis Estadistico Preliminar del Patron de Asentamiento de
          Calakmul.* Campeche City, Mexico; Universidad Autónoma del Sudeste,
          Centro de Estudios Históricos y Sociales.

Folan, Wm. J., Joel Gunn, Jack D. Eaton, and Robert W. Patch
  1983   Paleoclimatological Patterning in Southern Mesoamerica. *Journal of
          Field Archaeology* 10:453–68.

Folan, Wm. J., Joyce Marcus, Sophia Pincemin, Maria del Rosario Dominguez
Carrasco, Laraine Ftetcher, and Abel Morales Lopez
  1995   Calakmul: New Data from an Ancient Maya Capital in Campeche,
          Mexico. *Latin American Antiquity* 6 (4)310–34.

Forsyth, D. W.
  1989   *The Ceramics of El Mirador, Petén, Guatemala.* El Mirador Series, Part
          4. NWAF.

Freidel, D. A.
  1986   Introduction. In *Archaeology at Cerros, Belize, Central America.* Ed. D. A.
          Freidel and R. A. Robertson. Dallas: Southern Methodist University Press.

Garcia, Adrian
  1990   Excavations in Site BA-33. (Forthcoming in *Río Azul Regional Project Reports. No. 1.*)

Gibson, Eric C.
  1982   Investigations at Operation 1002, A Late Classic Maya Household Group at Colha, Belize. In Hester, Shafer, and Eaton, 1982:141–51.

Gill, Richardson B.
  1999   *The Great Maya Droughts.* Albuquerque: University of New Mexico Press.

Graham, Ian
  1967   *Archaeological Explorations in El Petén, Guatemala.* MARI Publication No. 33.
  1984   Río Azul Stela 2. In R. E. W. Adams, 1984: Figures 33–36.
  1986   Looters Rob Graves and History. *National Geographic Magazine* 169 (4):453–61.

Guderjan, Thomas H.
  1991a (ed.) *Maya Settlement in Northwestern Belize: The 1988 and 1990 Seasons of the Río Bravo Archaeological Project.* Culver City, Calif.: Maya Research Program and Labyrinthos.
  1991b Aspects of Maya Settlement in the Río Bravo Area. In Guderjan 1991a: 103–13.

Hageman, Jon B.
  1992   The 1991 Test Pit Program at Kinal, Guatemala. M.A. thesis, University of Texas at Austin

Hall, G. D.
  1984   Tombs at Río Azul. In R. E. W. Adams, 1984: 53–61.
  1986   Results of Tomb Investigations at Río Azul, Season of 1984. In R. E. W. Adams 1986b: 69–110.
  1987   The Discovery of Tomb 23 and Results of Other Tomb Investigations at Río Azul, Season of 1985. In R. E. W. Adams, 1987a: 107–51.
  1988   Realm of Death: Royal Mortuary Customs and Polity Interaction in the Classic Maya Lowlands. Ph.D. diss., Harvard University, Cambridge.

Hall, G. D., S. M. Tarka, W. J. Hurst, D. Stuart, and R. E. W. Adams
  1990   Cacao Residues in Ancient Maya Vessels from Río Azul, Guatemala. *American Antiquity* 55:138–43.

Hammond, N.
  1974   The Distribution of Late Classic Maya Major Ceremonial Centers in the Central Area. In *Mesoamerican Archaeology. New Approaches*, 313–34. Ed. N. Hammond. Austin: University of Texas Press.
  1975   *Lubaantun, a Classic Maya Realm.* PMP, Monograph No. 2.
  1977   The Early Formative in the Maya Lowlands. In *Social Process in Maya Prehistory: Studies in Honour of Sir Eric Thompson*, 77–101. Ed. N. Hammond. London: Academic Press.
  1991   (ed.) *Cuello: An Early Maya Community in Belize.* Cambridge, England, and New York: Cambridge University Press.

1996 *Ancient Maya Civilization*. 5th ed. New Brunswick, N.J.: Rutgers University Press.

Hansen, R. D.
1990 *Excavations in the Tigre Complex. El Mirador, Petén, Guatemala*. NWAF Paper No. 62.
1991 The Road to Nakbe. *Natural History* May:8–14. New York: American Museum of Natural History.

Hassig, R.
1988 *Aztec Warfare*. Norman: University of Oklahoma Press.

Haviland, William A.
1968 *Ancient Lowland Maya Social Organization*. MARI PublicationNo. 26:93–107.
1977 Dynastic Genealogies from Tikal, Guatemala: Implications for Descent and Political Organization. *American Antiquity* 42:61–67.

Hendon, J. A.
1989 The 1986 Excavations at BA-20. In R. E. W. Adams, 1989:88–135.
1991 Status and Power in Classic Maya Society: An Archaeological Study. *American Anthropologist* 93 (4):894–918.

Hester, T. R., and M. Dreiss
1989 Trace Element Analysis of Obsidian from Río Azul, Petén, Guatemala. (Forthcoming in R. E. W. Adams, ed., *Río Azul Reports. No. 5*.)

Hester, T. R., H. J. Shafer, and J. D. Eaton (eds.)
1982 *Archaeology at Colha, Belize: The 1981 Interim Report*, Center for Archaeological Research, San Antonio: University of Texas.

Hester, T. R., H. J. Shafer, T. C. Kelly, and G. Ligahue
1981 Observations on the Patination and the Context of Antiquity: A Fluted Point from Belize, Central America. *Lithic Technology* 11 (2):29–34.

Hopkins, N. A.
1988 Classic Maya Kinship and Descent: An Alternative Suggestion. *Estudios de Cultura Maya* 17:87–121.

Houk, Brett A.
1992 Excavations at Nak'nal (BA-22A); Small Site Excavations in North-eastern Peten. Master's thesis, University of Texas at Austin.

Houk, Brett A., and Hubert R. Robichaux
1996 *The 1996 Season of the Chan Chich Archaeological Project: Chan Chich Papers. No. 1*. Center for Maya Studies, San Antonio.

Houston, S. D.
1986 Problematic Emblem Glyphs: Examples from Altar de Sacrificios, El Chorro, Río Azul, and Xultun. *Research Reports on Ancient Maya Writing No. 3*. Center for Maya Research, Washington, D.C.
1989 *Maya Glyphs*. Berkeley and London: University of California Press.

Jones, Christopher
1977 Inauguration Dates of Three Late Classic Rulers at Tikal, Guatemala. *Arnerican Antiquity* 42:28–60.

1987   The Life and Times of Ah-Cacau. In *Primera Conferencia de Epigrafia y Arqueologia Maya*. Guatemala City: Asociación Tikal.

1991   Cycles of Growth at Tikal. In Culbert, 1991 a:102–27.

Jones, Christopher, and Linton Satterthwaite

1982   *The Monuments and Inscriptions of Tikal: The Carved Monuments*. Tikal Reports, No. 33A. Philadelphia: University Museum, University of Pennsylvania.

Karbula, J. W.

1989   Spatial Analysis of Seven Maya Centers in the Northeastern Petén. Master's thesis, University of Texas at San Antonio.

Kelley, David H.

1976   *Deciphering the Maya Script*. Austin: University of Texas Press.

Kerr, Justin

1989   *The Maya Vase Book*. New York: Justin Kerr.

Kidder, A. V., Sr.

1950   Introduction. In A. L. Smith, 1950:1–12.

Kosakowsky, L. J.

1987   *Prehistoric Maya Pottery at Cuello, Belize*. Anthropological Papers 47. Tucson: University of Arizona Press.

LaPorte, J. P., and L. Vega de Zea

1988   Aspectos Dinasticos para el Clasico Temprano de Mundo Perdido, Tikal. In *Epigrafia Maya* 127–40. Ed. Asociación Tikal. Guatemala City.

LaPorte, J. P., and Vilma Fialko C.

1990   New Perspectives on Old Problems: Dynastic References for the Early Classic at Tikal. In *Vision and Revision in Maya Studies*, 33–66. Ed. Flora S. Clancy and Peter D. Harrison. Albuquerque: University of New Mexico Press.

Lee, T. A., Jr., and Carlos Navarrete (eds.)

1978   *Mesoamerican Communication Routes and Cultural Contacts*. NWAF Paper No. 40.

Logan, M. H., and W. T. Sanders

1976   The Model. In *The Valley of Mexico*. Ed. Eric R. Wolf. Albuquerque: University of New Mexico Press.

Lowe, G. W., T. A. Lee, Jr., and Eduardo Martinez E.

1982   *Izapa: An Introduction to the Ruins and Monuments*. NWAF Paper No. 31.

Lowe, J. W. G.

1985   *The Dynamics of Apocalypse: A Systems Simulation of the Classic Maya Collapse*. Albuquerque: University of New Mexico Press.

MacNeish, R. S., S. J. K. Wilkerson, and A. Nelken-Terner

1980   *First Annual Report of the Belize Archaic Archaeological Reconnaissance*. Andover, Mass.: Robert S. Peabody Foundation.

Marcus. J.

1973   Territorial Organization of the Lowland Maya. *Science* 180:911–16.

1976   *Emblem and State in the Classic Maya Lowlands.* Washington, D.C.: Dumbarton Oaks.

1987   *The Inscriptions of Calakmul: Royal Marriage at a Maya City in Campeche, Mexico.* Museum of Anthropology Technical Report No. 21. Ann Arbor: University of Michigan.

1992   *Mesoamerican Writing Systems.* Princeton: Princeton University Press.

Martin, Simon, and Nikolai Grube

1994   Classic Maya Politics within a Mesoamerican Tradition: An Epigraphic Model of "Hegemonic" Political Organization. Paper presented at the Primer Seminario de las Mesas Redondas de Palenque, México.

Matheny, R.

1980   *El Mirador, Petén, Guatemala: An Interim Report.* NWAF Paper No. 45.

1983   *Investigations at Edzna, Campeche, Mexico.* NWAF Paper No. 46.

Mathews, Peter, and Gordon R. Willey

1991   Prehistoric Polities of the Pasion Region: Hieroglyphic Texts and Their Archaeological Settings. In Culbert, 1991a:30–71.

Mayer, Karl Herbert

1987   Drei Frühklassiche Maya Miszellentexte. *Archiv für Völkerkunde* 41: 137–44. Vienna.

Meadows, D. H., D. L. Meadows, J. Randers, and W. W. Behrens, III

1972   *Limits to Growth.* New York: Universe Books.

Miller, Arthur G.

1974   West and East in Maya Thought: Death and Rebirth at Palenque and Tulum. In *Primera Mesa Redonda de Palenque, Part II*, 45–49. Ed. M. G. Robertson. Pebble Beach, Calif.: R. L. Stevenson School.

Millon, Rene

1973   *The Teotihuacan Map. Vol. 1, Part One: Text.* Austin: University of Texas Press.

Millon, Rene, B. Drewitt, and G. Cowgill

1973   *The Teotihuacan Map. Vol. 1, Part Two: Maps.* Austin: University of Texas Press.

1988   The Last Years of Teotihuacan Dominance. In Yoffee and Cowgill, 1988:102–64.

Molloy, J. P., and W. L. Rathje

1974   Sexploitation Among the Late Classic Maya. In Hammond, 1974: 431–34.

Morley, S. G., G. W. Brainerd, and R. J. Sharer

1983   *The Ancient Maya.* 4th ed. Palto Alto, Calif.: Stanford University Press.

Netting, Robert M.

1977   Maya Subsistence: Analogies, Mythologies, Possibilities. In *The Origins of Maya Civilization*, 299–333. Ed. R. E. W. Adams. Albuquerque: University of New Mexico Press.

Oliver, Douglas

1951   *The Pacific Islands.* Cambridge, Mass.: Harvard University Press.

Orrego Corzo, Miguel
    1987   Informe del Mapa, Temporada de 1985. In R. E. W. Adams, 1987a:36–61.
    1988   Excavaciones en Complejo A-3, Río Azul, Petén, Guatemala. (Forthcoming in R. E. W. Adams, *Río Azul Reports, No. 5.*)

Orrego Corzo, Miguel, and Erick Ponciano M.
    1988   El Mapa Conturno de Río Azul. (Forthcoming in R. E. W. Adams, Río Azul Reports, No. 5.)

Pendergast, David
    1971   Evidence of Early Teotihuacan–Maya Lowland Contact at Altun Ha. *American Antiquity* 455–60.
    1981   Lamanai, Belize: Summary of Excavation Results, 1974–1980. *Journal of Field Archaeology* 8:29–53.

Petterson, Carmen L.
    1976   *Maya of Guatemala: Life and Dress.* Braunschweig, Germany: Georg Westermann Verlag. (Distributed in Guatemala through the Ixchel Textile Museum.)

Ponciano, Erick M.
    1989   Informe Final y Lista Global de Artefactos de Tumba 25, Río Azul, Petén, Guatemala. In R. E. W. Adams, 1989:175–88.

Ponciano, Erick M., and Carolina Foncea de Ponciano
    1988   Excavaciones en Complejo A54. (Forthcoming in R. E. W. Adams, Río Azul Reports, No. 5.)

Pope, K. O., and B. H. Dahlin
    1989   Ancient Maya Wetland Agriculture: New Insights from Ecological and Remote Sensing Research. *Journal of Field Archaeology* 16:87–106.

Potter, David F.
    1977   *Maya Architecture of the Central Yucatan Peninsula, Mexico.* MARI Publication No. 44.

Pring, D. C.
    1977   The Dating of Teotihuacan Contact at Altun Ha: The New Evidence. *American Antiquity* 42:62–28.

Proskouriakoff, T.
    1950   *A Study of Classic Maya Sculpture.* CIW Publication No. 593.
    1960   Historical Implications of a Pattern of Dates at Piedras Negras, Guatemala. *American Antiquity* 25:454–75.
    1961   The Lords of the Maya Realm. *Expedition* 4:14–21.
    1963   Historical Data in the Inscriptions of Yaxchilan, I. *Estudios de Cultura Maya* 3:149–67.
    1964a   Historical Data in the Inscriptions of Yaxchilan, II. *Estudios de Cultura Maya* 4:177–201.
    1964b   El Arte Maya y el Modelo Genetico de Cultura. In *Desarrollo Cultural de Los Mayas*, 187–202. Ed. E. Z. Vogt and A. Ruz L. Mexico City: Universidad Nacional Autónoma de México.

Puleston, D. E.
1983   The Settlement Survey of Tikal. *Tikal Reports. No. 13.* Philadelphia: University of Pennsylvania.

Puleston, D. E., and D. W. Callendar, Jr.
1967   Defensive Earthworks at Tikal. *Expedition* 9 (3):40–48.

Quirarte, Jacinto
1973   *El Estilo Artistico de Izapa.* Mexico City: Instituto de Investigaciones Estéticas. Universidad Nacional Autónoma de México.

1976   The Relationship of Izapan-Style Art to Olmec and Maya Art: A Review. In *Origins of Religious Art and Iconography in Preclassic Mesoamerica.* Ed. Henry B. Nicholson. Los Angeles: UCLA Latin American Center Publications and Ethnic Arts Council of Los Angeles.

Rattray, E. C.
1987   The Merchants Barrio, Teotihuacan. Preliminary Report subrnitted to INAH and Instituto de Investigaciones Antropológicas, Universidad Autónoma de México, Mexico City.

Renfrew, Colin, and Paul Bahn
1991   *Archaeology: Theories, Methods, and Practice.* New York: Thames and Hudson.

Robichaux, Hubert R.
1990   The Hieroglyphic Texts of Río Azul, Guatemala. Master's thesis, University of Texas at San Antonio.

1993   A Possible Origin of the Tikal Emblem Glyph. (Manuscript.)

1995   Survey in the Regions of La Milpa and Dos Hombres, Programme for Belize Conservation Area, Belize. Ph.D. diss., University of Texas at Austin.

1997   The Stelae of Río Azul. (Forthcoming in R. E. W. Adams, Río Azul Reports, No. 5.)

Robichaux, Hubert R., and S. C. W. Adams
1993   Excavations on Kinal Structure 61, 62, 63, and the Kinal Causeway Wall. (Forthcoming in R. E. W. Adams, *Río Azul Regional Reports. Nos. 1–2.*)

Robicsek, F., and Donald M. Hales
1981   *The Maya Book of the Dead: The Ceramic Codex.* Norman: University of Oklahoma Press.

Roys, Ralph L.
1972   *The Indian Background of Colonial Yucatan.* 2d ed. Norman: University of Oklahoma Press.

Sanders, W. T.
1973   The Cultural Ecology of the Lowland Maya: A Reevaluation. In T. P. Culbert, 1973:325–65.

1977   Environmental Heterogeneity and the Evolution of Lowland Maya Civilization. In Adams, 1977:287–97.

Sanders, W. T., and B. J. Price
  1968   *Mesoamerica: The Evolution of a Civilization.* New York: Random House.

Saul, Frank P.
  1972   *The Human Skeletal Remains of Altar de Sacrificios: An Osteobiographic Analysis.* PMP, vol. 63, no. 2.

Saul, Frank P., and Julie M. Saul
  1989   A Report to National Geographic Society on Human Skeletal Materials from Río Azul, Guatemala. (Forthcoming in R. E. W. Adams, Río Azul Reports, No. 5.)

Scarborough, Vernon L., Robert P. Connolly, and Steven P. Ross
  1993   The Pre-Hispanic Maya Reservoir System at Kinal, Petén, Guatemala. *Ancient Mesoamerica* 5:97–106.

Scarborough, Vernon L., and Gary G. Gallopin
  1991   A Water Storage Adaptation in the Maya Lowlands. *Science* 251: 658–62.

Seler, Eduard
  1960   *Gesammelte Abhandlungen zur Amerikanischen sprach- und Altertumskunde.* (Five volumes of collected papers.) Graz, Austria: Akademische Druck- u. Verlagsanstalt.

Shafer, H. J.
  1983   The Lithic Artifacts ofthe Pulltrouser Area: Settlements and Fields. In Turner and Harrison, 1983:212–45.

Shafer, H. J., and T. R. Hester
  1983   Ancient Maya Chert Workshops in Northern Belize, Central Arnerica. *American Antiquity* 58:519–43.

Sharer, Robert J.
  1994   *The Ancient Maya.* 5th ed. Palo Alto: Stanford.

Sherratt, Andrew
  1980   Water, Soil and Seasonality in Early Cereal Cultivation. *World Archaeology* 11:313–30.

Shirnkin, D.
  1973   Models for the Downfall: Some Ecological and Culture-Historical Considerations. In Culbert 1973:269–300.

Siemens, A. H., and D. E. Puleston
  1972   Ridged Fields and Associated Features in Southern Campeche: New Perspectives on the Lowland Maya. *American Antiquity* 37:228–39.

Smith, A. L.
  1950   *Uaxactun,Guatemala: Excavations of 1931–1937.* CIW Publication No. 568.

  1972   *Excavations at Altar de Sacrificios: Architecture, Settlement, Burials and Caches.* PMP, vol. 62, no. 2. Cambridge: Harvard University.

Smith, R. E.
  1955   *Ceramic Sequence at Uaxactun.* Guatemala. MARI Publication No. 20.

Steele, D. Gentry
  1986 The Skeletal Remains from Río Azul, 1984 Season. In R. E. W. Adams, 1986a:111–16.
  1990 Skeletal Remains from Río Azul Tomb 23. (Forthcoming in R. E. W. Adams, Río Azul Reports, No. 5.)

Steward, Julian
  1961 Book Review, The Urban Focus. *Science* 134:1354–56.

Stuart, David
  1986 The Hieroglyphs on a Vessel from Tomb 19, Río Azul. In R. E. W. Adams, 1986:117–21.
  1987 The Paintings of Tomb 12, Río Azul. In R. E. W. Adams, 1987: 161–67.

Stuart, David, and Stephen Houston
  1989 The *Way* Glyph: Evidence for "Co-essences" among the Classic Maya. *Research Reports on Ancient Maya Writing*, No. 30. Washington, D.C.: Center for Maya Research.

Sugiyama, Saburo
  1989 Burials Dedicated to the Old Temple of Quetzalcoatl at Teotihuacan, Mexico. *American Antiquity* 54:85–106.

Taube, Karl
  1989 The Maize Tamale in Classic Maya Art. *American Antiquity* 54 (1): 31–51.

Thompson, J. E. S.
  [1950]
  1963 *Maya Hieroglyphic Writing: An Introduction*. CIW Publication No. 589. Reprint, Norman: University of Oklahoma Press.

Turner, B. L., II
  1974 Prehistoric Intensive Agriculture in the Maya Lowlands. *Science* 185: 118–24.

Turner, B. L., II, and P.D. Harrison (eds.)
  1983 *Pulltrouser Swamp: Ancient Maya Habitat, Agriculture, and Settlement in Northern Belize*. Austin: University of Texas Press.

Turner, E. S., N. I. Turner, and R. E. W. Adams
  1981 Volumetric Assessment, Rank Ordering, and Maya Civic Centers. In Ashmore, 1981:71–88.

Valdes, Juan Antonio
  1988 Los Mascarones Preclasicos de Uaxactun: El Caso del Grupo H. *Primer Simposio Mundial sobre Epigrafia Maya*, 165–81. Guatemala City: Asociación Tikal.

Valdez, Fred, Jr.
  1988 The Prehistoric Ceramics of Colha, Northern Belize. Ph.D. diss., Harvard University.
  1990 Excavations at Group I, Río Azul, Guatemala. (Forthcoming in R. E.W. Adams, Río Azul Reports, No. 5.)
  1993 A Middle Preclassic Temple at Río Azul, Guatemala. Manuscript.

Webb, Malcolm
    1973   The Petén Maya Decline Viewed in the Perspective of State Formation. In Culbert, 1973:367–404.

Webster, D.
    1977   Warfare and the Evolution of Maya Civilization. In Adams, 1977:335–72.

Willey, G. R.
    1974   The Classic Maya Hiatus: A "Rehearsal" for the Collapse? In Hammond, 1974:313–34.
    1977   The Rise of Maya Civilization: A Summary View. In Adam, 1977:3 83–423.

Willey, G. R., and D. B. Shimkin
    1973   The Maya Collapse: A Summary View. In Culbert, 1973:457–503.

Wright, H. T., and G. A. Johnson
    1975   Population, Exchange, and Early State Formation in Southwestern Iran. *American Anthropologist* 77:267–89.

Yoffee, N., and G. L. Cowgill (eds.)
    1988   *The Collapse of Ancient States and Civilizations.* Tucson: University of Arizona Press.

INDEX